You Can Always Judg[e]
the Company It

Read What These Top Achievers and Our Clients Are Saying about *The Power of Focus*.

"If you only read one new book this millennium . . . *The Power of Focus* Revised Edition, should be it!"

Harvey Mackay
Author, *Swim with the Sharks*

"*The Power of Focus* is absolutely wonderful and is sure to make an impact on the business world for generations to come."

Ken Blanchard
Coauthor, *The One-Minute Manager*

"The only thing better than focus is even more focus. Make sure you read this terrific revised edition and use the best ideas."

Patricia Fripp, CSP, CPAE
Author, *Get What You Want*
Past president, National Speakers Association

"*The Power of Focus* shows you how to define *your* path and start working *your* plan. It's an amazing compendium; inspiring as well as practical."

Jim Tunney
Former NFL referee

"Your ability to focus is the most important success skill you can ever develop. This revised edition shows you how to develop new skills in every part of your life. Again, outstanding!"

Brian Tracy
International seminar leader,
consultant and bestselling author

"You can be successful at anything in half the usual time by learning how to get focused and remain focused, and this book will show you how. *The Power of Focus* should be a business bible for anyone just starting out, as well as those already established who want to maximize their productivity and income. I own eleven Mexican restaurants. If you want the 'whole enchilada', read this book."

Tom Harken
Author, *The Millionaire's Secret*
Horatio Alger Award recipient

"*The Power of Focus* literally changed my life and my career when the first edition was published. This revised version is even better and for me confirms that the authors' products and programs are now a one-stop resource center that is so complete, you won't need to look elsewhere."

Dan Clark
International speaker,
consultant and bestselling author

"An important book for anyone who wants to succeed in anything! Outlines the master skill for achieving goals and realizing dreams. I not only got a lot out of it but thoroughly enjoyed reading it."

Robert Kriegel
Author, *If it Ain't Broke...Break IT!*

"A powerful, practical book that will inspire you to achieve your dreams."

Barbara De Angelis, Ph.D.
Author, *Real Moments*

"*The Power of Focus* will change your life. It will motivate you to take those small, daily, weekly and monthly actions that will eventually compound your life into a masterpiece. Buy this book immediately—and get started."

Robert G. Allen
Author, *Multiple Streams of Income*

"Without focus, it's hard to build a successful business. This book is an effective road map that will really keep you on track."

Paul Orfalea
Chairperson and founder, Kinko's, Inc.

"I have watched the life of a friend of mine transform and flourish. She has followed these focusing strategies for personal growth and success for four years. This is not theory—this is dynamite—it changed her life, and it will change yours!"

Lance H.K. Secretan
Author, *The Spark, the Flame and the Torch*

It's All About RESULTS!
Here are Some Candid Comments from Our Happy Clients:

"Implementing just one idea from *The Power of Focus* added one million dollars to our bottom line. That's what I call an excellent return on investment!"

Ralph Puertas
President, Zep Manufacturing (Canada)

"Since using *The Power of Focus* strategies, my net worth has tripled, my sales volume reached number two in the country and I was able to build the foundations of a successful team to support me."

Peter Kinch
President, Peter Kinch Mortgage Team

"*The Power of Focus* has turned my life around. I just realized my dream of opening my own recording studio and my debt burden is almost eliminated. On top of that, I have since met and married the most perfect woman I could ever have hoped to meet. Your ideas on building excellent relationships really do work!"

Tony Hunter
President, Freedom Creative Music Centre

"I am realizing profound changes. Due to creating better habits I have regained my health, eliminated prescribed medication, lost 72 pounds in six months and practice regular exercise. I feel terrific!"

Bob Benninghofen
Corporate Secretary, Pathway Society, Inc.

"*The Power of Focus* system made me focus on the financial goals in my life and was a major factor in helping me become debt-free within eighteen months."

Dan Smith
President, Porter Engineering Ltd.

"I adopted the six-week vacation strategy, made significantly more money and had my kids tell me, 'Dad, you are way calmer.' I attribute it all to *The Power of Focus.*"

Reid Schmidt
Partner, Cornerstone Law Group

"*The Power of Focus* has given me the tools to not only take my business to a much higher level but to take all facets of my life to a higher level. The program has given me more than I ever thought possible. It was worth ten times the investment in time and money."

David Udy
President, WealthCo Financial Advisory Services, Inc.

"*The Power of Focus* system has exceeded my expectations. I increased my income and had more time off. My stress level is the lowest it has ever been. I now realize that *I am* in charge of my life. I can make changes and grow. Many thanks."

Jim Wright
Sales Consultant, Wood Windows Specialties Inc.

"Since I started using *The Power of Focus* strategies, I changed my business direction and saw my company flourish beyond my wildest dreams."

Gary Browning
CEO, Browning Design Inc.

"Your contribution has helped me earn a promotion while decreasing my work week from sixty-five plus hours to less than fifty. As a new father, these changes are priceless."

Kurtis Leinweber
Principal, Foundations for the Future

"Due to *The Power of Focus*, my net worth has increased by 75 percent and I've come to appreciate the worth of personal relationships and the effort needed to maintain them."

Robert Stubbs
Partner, Blair Stubbs and Associates

"*The Power of Focus* gave me the insight to deal with a major business crisis that was causing me incredible stress. I now have peace of mind and I understand the difference between choose-to and have-to."

Kathleen Lorist
Owner, Menlo Park Hardware

"*The Power of Focus* has given me tremendous tools and strategies for creating effective change in my life and my business. For example, using just one strategy, I was able to increase sales for my company by 246 percent in one year."

Peter Jarman
Partner, Trimax Inc.

"Thanks to *The Power of Focus*, I am happier, more relaxed and well balanced. My income has increased 80 percent and I have received top performance awards for the second year in a row. I now focus more precisely on my most important tasks and complete them efficiently."

Nigel Grace
Regional Manager, Human Factors International

"When I first started using *The Power of Focus*, my life was definitely controlled by my job. I also had some really bad habits and was the best at procrastinating. Now I am able to separate myself from my business while increasing my net worth by more than 60 percent. Thank you for giving me the tools to self-manage to a higher degree and to learn to get the most out of life in every aspect."

Phil Driedger
President, Hardcore Gym

"My biggest difficulty was balance. *The Power of Focus* challenged me to make changes. Last year I took three months off and our total sales increased by 52 percent."

Phyllis Arnold
President, Arnold Publishing Ltd.

"*The Power of Focus* filled me with practical options for dealing with my business and creating a balance in life that was previously lacking. I am currently enjoying much better relationships at home and business has doubled and even tripled in some instances. My leisure time is also three times what it used to be and I am better able to relax and refocus during family activities."

Harold Line
President, Nam Kee Land and Investment Ltd.

"*The Power of Focus* has taken me out of the passenger seat of my life and put me into the driver's seat."

Betty Anne Tarini
Realtor, CIR Realty

"I can hardly express in words how *The Power of Focus* has impacted our business—everything from defining and prioritizing goals, to building relationships and getting focused. On a personal level, I'm hitting ALL of my goals: business, financial, personal, health, contribution, fun time, learning and relationships. It feels exhilarating to be making such steady progress in every area of my life, not just business."

Drew Betts
Strategic Marketing Coach
Former CEO, Evolve Real Estate Management Inc.

The Power of Focus

Revised 10th Anniversary Edition

How to Hit Your Business,
Personal and Financial Targets with
Confidence and Certainty

Jack Canfield
Mark Victor Hansen
Les Hewitt

Health Communications, Inc.
Deerfield Beach, Florida

www.hcibooks.com

Library of Congress Cataloging-in-Publication Data

Canfield, Jack 1944-
    The Power of focus / Jack Canfield, Mark Victor Hansen, Les Hewitt—10the anniversary ed.
      p. cm.
    ISBN-13: 978-0-7573-1602-9 (pbk.)
    ISBN-10: 0-7573-1602-6 (pbk.)
    ISBN-13: 978-0-7573-1606-7 (e-book)
    ISBN-10: 0-7573-1606-9 (e-book)
    1. Success—Psychological aspects. I. Hansen, Mark Victor. II. Hewitt, Les. III. Title.
    BF637.S8 C2775 2000
    158.1—dc23

                                        2012001034

Publisher: Health Communications, Inc.
           3201 S.W. 15th Street
           Deerfield Beach, FL 33442–8190

Cover design by Utku Lomlu
Contact: utku@utkulomlu.com
Interior formatting by Lawna Patterson Oldfield

Jack

To the teachers who have taught me the most
about *The Power of Focus* principles:

W. Clement Stone, Billy B. Sharp, Lacy Hall, Bob Resnick,
Martha Crampton, Jack Gibb, Ken Blanchard,
Nathaniel Branden, Stewart Emery, Tim Piering, Tracy Goss,
Marshall Thurber, Russell Bishop, Bob Proctor,
Bernhard Dohrmann, Mark Victor Hansen, Les Hewitt,
Pamela Bruner, Lee Pulos, Doug Kruschke, Martin Rutte,
Michael Gerber, John Gray, Armand Bytton, Marti Glenn,
Ron Scolastico, and Lynne Twist

Mark

To Seth and Kira:

The greatest grandkids in the world.

Les

To Fran, Jennifer and Andrew:

You are still the focus of my life.

Contents

ACKNOWLEDGMENTS xix

FOREWORD
The Purpose Of This Book: What's In It For You.............. xxi

FOCUSING STRATEGY #1

Your Habits Will Determine Your Future 1
Successful people have successful habits.

How Habits Really Work.. 6
How to Identify Bad Habits 17
How to Change Bad Habits 21
The Successful Habits Formula.. 26

ACTION STEPS 30
Successful People I Want to Interview
The Successful Habits Formula

FOCUSING STRATEGY #2

It's Not Hocus-Pocus, It's All About Focus 35
Build on your strengths, not your weaknesses.

Focus on Your Natural Talents.. 37
Are You a Starter or a Finisher?.. 44
If You're Feeling Swamped, Get Help! 46
The 4-D Solution.. 51
The Power of No 52

ACTION STEPS 59
The Priority Focus Workshop

FOCUSING STRATEGY #3

Do You See The Big Picture? 62
Designing your crystal-clear future.

Developing Unusual Clarity 64
The Purpose of Goals 66
The Top-10 Goals Checklist 67
Your Master Plan 79

ACTION STEPS 90
The Top-10 Goals Checklist
Know What You Want and Why
Capture Your Best Ideas

FOCUSING STRATEGY #4

Overcoming Setbacks 93
It's not what happens, it's what you do about it!

Cultivate a Champion Mind-set 96
Recession Warning Signs 101
Recession Busters 102
Find Another Way 108
The Problem Solver 108
Be Prepared! 110
Expect the Unexpected 111

ACTION STEPS 116
Ten Best Options
The Problem Solver

FOCUSING STRATEGY #5
Building Excellent Relationships 120
Your entry into the big leagues.

The Double Spiral 123
Say "No" to Toxic People 129
The Three Big Questions 131
Core Clients and the Double Win 133
. . . And Then Some 139
How to Find Great Mentors 143

ACTION STEPS 151
The Double Spiral
Building Your Fortress
Developing Mentor Relationships

FOCUSING STRATEGY #6
The Confidence Factor 155
Eliminating fear and worry.

Resolving Unfinished Business 157
The Twenty-Five-Cent Challenge 162
Forgive and Forget 164
A Winning Attitude 167
Six Confidence-Building Strategies 168
Believe in Your Own Capability 170
What To Do If You Hit a Slump 173

ACTION STEPS 178
Resolving Unfinished Business

FOCUSING STRATEGY #7
Ask For What You Want 182
A seven-point system to help you prosper.

Ask and Receive 185
Seven Ways to Boost Your Business, Simply by Asking 188
How to Ask... 203

ACTION STEPS 209
Asking for What You Want

FOCUSING STRATEGY #8
Consistent Persistence 213
Success is often just around the corner.

The Benefits of Consistency 215
Embrace Your Greatest Power 217
The Double-A Formula 228
The Integrity Factor 233

ACTION STEPS 236
The Integrity Factor

FOCUSING STRATEGY #9
Taking Decisive Action 239
Proven systems for creating wealth.

4 Good Reasons You Procrastinate..................................... 244
Active Decision-Making.. 247
The TA-DA Formula... 252
Let's Talk About Money.. 254

ACTION STEPS 266
Eliminating Procrastination
Financial Certainty

Focusing Strategy #10

Living and Working on Purpose 271

Making your life simple again.

Finding Your Purpose 276
The Marathon of Hope 278
Three Key Points 280
Discovering Your Purpose 282
Statement of Purpose 287

ACTION STEPS 296

Discovering and Living Your Purpose

Focusing Strategy #11

Ideas to Make You Rich 302

Best Success Strategies from Five Wealthy Entrepreneurs.

Sam Beckford: The Small Business Millionaire 304
Karen Stewart: Changing the Divorce Paradigm 309
Phil Carroll: Houseboats to Billion Dollar Deals 315
Debbie Rotkvich: The Jewelry Queen 319
Don R. Campbell: Creating Real Estate Riches 325

FREE AUDIO INTERVIEWS FROM OUR TOP FIVE ACHIEVERS

Gen-Y and Social Entrepreneurism: The Way Forward 331
Gamechanger Companies 334
Great News Ahead! 335

ACTION STEPS 338

Twenty-Five Wealth Building Strategies

FINAL WORDS

It's Your Life…Accept the Challenge!...........................339

The Power of Focus Products and Programs...............341
Keynote Speeches, Workshops, Leadership Training,
One-on-One Executive Coaching
Your Free $500 Success Library

EXCLUSIVE LEADERS RETREAT
WITH AUTHORS JACK, MARK AND LES 342

RESOURCE GUIDE..343

PERMISSIONS...351

ABOUT THE AUTHORS...353

ACKNOWLEDGMENTS

When compiling a book there are always many people "backstage" who support the authors in numerous ways. Our sincere thanks and gratitude are extended to those heroes who often don't get the recognition they deserve.

First, Hildi Squirrell at The Power of Focus Inc. Typing the manuscript from scratch—the scratch being Les's woeful handwriting!—was a task that required concentration, persistence and several rewrites. Excellent job! Also, a big thank you for all the extra hours in the evenings and on weekends.

Next, to Fran Hewitt, my wonderful wife, partner and bestselling author in her own rite. Your stellar support, love, and ability to act as a strong sounding board when the going got hectic, meant more than you may ever know. You are truly a blessing.

To Andrew and Jennifer Hewitt who more than echoed Fran with great ideas, new information and faithful connection. Your prayers, insights and wisdom once again make me a very proud father.

To all of our tremendous *Power of Focus* clients, too numerous to mention, whose stories and dedication to their individual ventures were inspiring and provided a foundation for much of the new material in this book.

A special thank you to everyone who willingly shared their personal stories with us. Your contribution is greatly appreciated. [For details, please see pages 351-352.] Kudos to Wade Webb, Jean Lunt, John Guderyan, Rick Green and Sam Beckford again, for their ongoing support and help in launching the marketing program.

Thanks also to Chris Smith for her mastery in kinesiology,

in testing our early cover designs. And to award-winning book cover designer, Utku Lomlu in Turkey, for creating the final product. Your patience and understanding were very much appreciated as we changed course numerous times.

To Jack Canfield's support team, from his wife Inga, to executive assistant Veronica Romero who was an excellent liaison between our offices and ensured the details were looked after in a timely fashion. Thanks also to Patty Aubery, president of The Canfield Companies, and COO Russ Kamalski, who made sure all of the day-to-day operations and other projects ran smoothly when Jack had to focus on the book.

To Crystal, Mark's wonderful wife, a great anchor and business partner who enabled Mark to work on this project without distraction.

And ten years later, we extend a hearty thank you to the Health Communications team who made sure the book was crafted in the best way possible and printed on time, despite the usual crazy deadlines. A special thank you to publisher Peter Vegso, for the opportunity to deliver *The Power of Focus 10th Anniversary Edition* to many thousands of new readers and businesspeople around the world. Hats off to senior editor Allison Janse, for her steady, calming influence as the book came to the critical stages. And a major cheer for Larissa Henoch and Lawna Oldfield who had the challenging job of creating the new layout from page one right to the end. Thanks for your patience and persistence.

We also acknowledge the input, examples and insights provided directly and indirectly by friends, customers and clients. Due to the scope of this project we may have neglected to mention others who helped in various ways. Know that you are appreciated and accept our apologies for any omissions.

Creating, writing and delivering this special 10th Anniversary Edition has been challenging but extremely rewarding. We discovered once again that a great team blessed with passion, dedication and focus will invariably get the job done.

The Purpose Of This Book: What's In It For You?

> "Trust yourself. Create the kind of self
> that you will be happy to live with all your life.
> Make the most of yourself by fanning the tiny,
> inner sparks of possibility into
> flames of achievement."
>
> —Foster C. McClellan

Dear Reader (or potential reader, if you're still browsing),

Ten years ago we launched our book, *The Power of Focus*, not knowing how it would be received in the marketplace. Since then, we've been gratified and humbled by the tremendous response from hundreds of thousands of people all around the world.

Recently, we realized the demand from our clients was becoming stronger for an updated version. So here it is. A lot has changed in the last decade, with severe economic challenges heading the list. Incredible advances in technology have made our world faster, with much of what we want to know only a few clicks away.

What challenges are you facing today?

We've had our own challenges, too, which we'll share in detail and how we solved them. Time pressure, getting ahead financially, job security, and the struggle to enjoy a healthy balanced lifestyle still remain major challenges for millions of people. Our research shows that a lack of focus is still one of the biggest factors causing these hardships. And yet despite this uncertainty and anxiety, there are many people who are doing exceptionally well. Their businesses are expanding, becoming more profitable and employing more people. You'll meet many of them in this revised edition, and learn how they've done so well—including stories from some amazing teenage entrepreneurs.

If you are one of those people who feel you've been tossed about in an economic storm, or if you're stressed out, burned out, and almost wiped out financially, take heart. There's hope. It's time to refocus, reflect, rethink, and become rejuvenated.

The Power of Focus will help you in many ways, whether you are a CEO, vice president, manager, supervisor, salesperson, entrepreneur, consultant, or the owner of a professional practice or home-based business. And if you're doing well right now, there's always more to learn as you'll find out between these covers, even if it's just one more idea that will leverage your success or help you avoid the subtle onset of complacency.

Here's our GUARANTEE:

If you study and gradually implement the strategies we are about to share, you'll not only hit your business, personal, and financial targets consistently, you'll far exceed the results you are currently experiencing. Specifically, we'll show you how to focus on your strengths, so that you can maximize your income, and at the same time enjoy a healthier, happier lifestyle.

In addition, you'll learn how to build a stronger, sustainable foundation for the future, based on a little-used technique called Unusual Clarity. On top of that, you'll discover how to create financial peace of mind using proven methods from several multimillionaires. There's also a smorgasbord of ideas to help nurture and enrich your most important relationships.

The reason we are so confident that the ideas in this book will work for you is because they have already worked for us and thousands of our clients.

Since the first edition of this book, the three of us have collectively gained thirty years of experience. Our combined business experience since we first began now totals 109 years! This is real-world experience. It's been earned by making lots of mistakes, as well as by focusing on doing some things extremely well. We'll share some of our most important recent breakthroughs with you and tell you the way things are in the real world, instead of giving you vague theories and philosophies. This will help you avoid much of the trial and error in life and save you a lot of time, money, energy, and unnecessary stress.

How to get the most out of this book.

Please note: If you are looking for a magic "quick-fix" formula, you won't find it here. In our experience there's no such thing. It takes a real commitment to create positive transformation. That's why more than 90 percent of people who attend short-term seminars see no improvement in their lives. They don't take the time to implement what they learn and all of their notes usually end up collecting dust.

Our primary goal has been to make this information so compelling that it will galvanize you to take immediate action. **This book is user-friendly—it's really easy to read. You'll even find cartoons and stories along the way that make it fun.**

Every chapter consists of a variety of strategies and techniques enhanced by anecdotes and inspiring stories. The first three chapters lay the foundation. Chapter 4, a new chapter, will show you how to thrive in a turbulent economy and eliminate the word "recession" from your vocabulary. Each subsequent chapter introduces a new set of strategies centered on a specific habit that will help you to focus and perform better. Implementing these habits is vitally important to your future success. Sprinkled through each chapter you'll find lots of our own personal stories and insights: what worked for us and also what didn't. Immediately following each chapter are a series of Action Steps. These are designed to facilitate your progress. It is essential that you follow through and complete these if you want to enjoy a higher level of prosperity. You can initiate them one at a time.

As a final bonus, we have added another significant chapter which features the stories of five entrepreneurs, all self-made millionaires and clients of *The Power of Focus*, who have built successful enterprises using the principles in this book. Each person gives you the five most important reasons they have become so successful. You'll also get a glimpse into exciting "Gamechanger" companies, a new breed of organization setting new standards in employee culture, social consciousness, and profitability. In this revised edition, we have combined the most relevant new information with all of the timeless fundamental strategies from the original edition.

Use this book as a continuous work-in-progress that you can refer to over and over again.

We strongly suggest that you have a highlighter, notepad, or iPad beside you as you read. Use these to immediately capture the ideas that have the greatest impact for you. Remember, it's all about focus. The main reason most people struggle professionally and personally is a lack of focus. They procrastinate or allow themselves to be easily distracted and interrupted. Now you have the opportunity to be different. The only purpose of this book is to inspire you to take action. That's it, pure and simple, even more so than before. So let's get started. Use *The Power of Focus* to guarantee your better future. And may your life be truly enriched in the process.

Sincerely,

Mark Victor Hansen

P.S. If you are the owner of a business and are planning for rapid growth in the next few years, buy a copy of this book for everyone on your team. The momentum created by implementing these focusing strategies together will ensure that you reach your targets much sooner than anticipated.

**Register your book now at
www.thepoweroffocus.com/bonusoffer.asp
and you will receive a free $500 Audio Success Library
from the authors, Jack, Mark, and Les.**

Your Habits Will Determine Your Future

"A HABIT IS A CABLE; WE WEAVE A THREAD EACH
DAY, AND AT LAST WE CANNOT BREAK IT."

—Horace Mann

Maria Sosa knew she had to make a decision.
It was not one of those everyday minor decisions we all
make as we go about our lives. This was a life-changing
decision that would determine if her family would
survive the next few weeks.

Living in mountainous rural Colombia, Maria's life
was simple and meager. She raised chickens and sold
them for a little money that would purchase some of the
essentials required by her family. Her husband, Hugo,
worked for a land owner tending the cattle and crops.
Their home had no electricity, transport was by horse,
and to reach the nearest town it was a five-hour journey.
Maria and Hugo had three children—two boys, Elver
(eleven) and Juan (nine), and a daughter, Luz (seven).
Little Luz had been diagnosed with Reye's syndrome,
following a viral infection. This rare condition sadly
resulted in brain damage and a disability that restricted
her movement to a wheelchair.

To compound her challenges, Maria had recently given birth to another baby boy. The infant died after only three short weeks with the family. Hugo experienced so much distress over this that he suffered a major stroke which left him paralyzed, unable to speak, and with a walk that was reduced to a shuffle. He also suffered significant brain damage and was unable to work.

If all this wasn't enough to cope with, Maria had to be vigilant on another front. A local terrorist group, whose favorite tactic was taking foreigners hostage and demanding large ransoms for their release, was operating in the jungles nearby. They also kidnapped children and trained them to be terrorists, as well as demanding money from local area residents. Often Maria would have to surrender half of her chicken money when they came to call unexpectedly.

One day they wanted more than money. Young Elver was their target, a ripe young prospect to join their ranks in the jungle. Maria screamed and pleaded with them: "Don't take him away—he's my son!" Thankfully, they relented. This was Maria's defining moment, the moment when you trust your intuition, not caring or knowing what the outcome will be. You just know that you must act immediately! This was a choice that could change Maria's future.

Hastily she packed up a few belongings, gathered everyone together, and under the cover of nightfall, somehow shepherded her stricken family through the mountains to a small town. The all-night journey on foot was slow and arduous. They had to be careful not to make any noise in case the terrorists heard them. With the little money they had, Maria and her exhausted family boarded a bus to the Venezuelan border. There were several checkpoints there, and having no papers, Maria had to muster all of her persuasive skills to convince the guards to let them through. Hugo, her husband, was also very sick.

A local woman, whose daughter was from Colombia, noticed their plight and arranged for them to stay with her in Caracas. After months of applying for refugee status at various embassies, a door finally opened— Canada had accepted them! Maria had no idea where Canada was and had never been on a plane in her life. A few days later, she and her family arrived in Toronto on a very cold January day, determined to start a new life.

As of this writing, her boys are doing well in school, Maria is slowly learning English, and Luz, her daughter, is now walking, thanks to the care of some very skilled doctors and nurses. Life is still full of challenges as this new adventure unfolds, but Maria's immense gratitude shines through her eyes, with everyone she meets.

We all face defining moments that can transform our lives in positive ways, if we are prepared to step into our fear, and then focus and follow through with courage and determination.

Are you facing a defining moment that requires immediate action?

Your situation may not be as dramatic as Maria's; however, if it's significant to you, that's all that matters. Step out with boldness into the unknown and trust in yourself and intuition will carry you through. When your belief is strong and your action unstoppable, an unseen force supports your efforts—many call it divine intervention—and removes all obstacles. Your path becomes clear and unobstructed. Who knows what great rewards are waiting for you when you develop the habit of enthusiastic focused action. But like Maria, once you commit, there is no turning back. It's onward and upward!

While Maria's story is inspiring, here is the takeaway message that's important:

Life doesn't just happen to you. It's all about choices and how you respond to every situation. If you are in the habit of continually making bad choices, disaster often occurs. Your everyday choices ultimately determine whether you end up living with abundance or living in poverty. However, life never completely closes the door to opportunity.

To give you a simple visual, imagine you are holding a long white plastic chain that is twenty feet in length. The chain is made up of a few hundred individual links that are attached to each other.

Now imagine each link is a bad choice. Each bad choice is attached to another bad choice. A whole bunch of bad choices eventually becomes a habit. Now, imagine you are holding this plastic chain with your arms held high and you start passing the chain through your hands, from the first link until you come to about the middle of the chain. The last link that passed through looks no different from the very first link. That's just like a bad habit. We don't notice anything really changing— there are no negative results showing up. This could be a period of weeks or months. Keep passing the chain along until you are almost at the end—representing years. Suddenly you notice a very large knot in the chain. Do you know what that's called? A crisis! Heart attack, home foreclosure, divorce—and you didn't see it coming.

Consistent choices lay the foundation for your habits, as you'll find out in the next few pages. And your habits play a major role in how your future unfolds. This includes the habits you display to the business world every day, as well as the variety of behaviors that show up in your personal life.

Throughout this book, you'll find strategies that can be applied to both work and home. Your job is to review all of them and implement the ones that will give you the greatest rewards. By the way, all of these strategies work equally well for men and women. They are not gender specific. If you haven't noticed, one of the most exciting developments in the marketplace today is the rapid growth of women entrepreneurs.

In this chapter, we've laid out the most important elements about habits. First you'll discover how habits really work. Then you'll learn how to identify bad habits and how to change them. This will allow you to check out your own specific habits and determine which ones are unproductive. Finally, we'll show you a unique Successful Habits Formula, a simple but powerful strategy that will help you transform your bad habits into successful habits. Using this technique will ensure that you stay focused on what works, instead of what doesn't work.

SUCCESSFUL PEOPLE HAVE SUCCESSFUL HABITS

Unsuccessful People Don't!

How HABITS Really Work

YOUR HABITS WILL DETERMINE YOUR FUTURE

What is a habit? Simply stated, a habit is something you do so often it becomes easy. In other words, it's a behavior that you keep repeating. If you persist at developing a new behavior, eventually it becomes automatic.

For example, if you learn to drive a car with a standard gearshift, the first few lessons are usually interesting. One of the big challenges is figuring out how to synchronize the clutch and accelerator pedals so you have a nice, smooth gear change. If you release the clutch too quickly, the car stalls. If you press down too hard on the accelerator without releasing the clutch, the engine roars but you don't go anywhere. Sometimes the car jumps down the street like a kangaroo, surging and stopping as the new driver struggles with the pedals. However, with practice, the gear change eventually becomes smooth and you don't think about it anymore.

LES:
"For years I dabbled at playing golf and my scores proved it. I'd take an eight or a nine at several holes and end up with a score north of one hundred. Occasionally I took lessons and noticed some improvement. Then I wouldn't play for months and I'd still expect to produce a reasonable score. This is called living an illusion! I finally set a goal—to break ninety consistently. To accomplish this, I decided to create new habits; practice a little every day, study the top players, take regular lessons, and play twice a week. It's working—I just shot an eighty six!"

The great news is that you can reprogram yourself any time you choose to do so. If you're struggling financially, this is important to know!

Let's say you want to be financially independent. Doesn't it make sense to check your financial habits? Are you in the habit of paying yourself first every month? Do you consistently save and invest at least 10 percent of your income? The answer is either "yes" or "no." Immediately you can see if you are moving in the right direction. The key word here is consistent. That means every month. And every month is a good habit. Most people dabble when it comes to growing their money. They are very inconsistent.

Suppose you start a savings and investment program. For the first six months you diligently put your ten percent away according to plan. Then something happens. You borrow the money to take a vacation, and you tell yourself you'll make it up in the next few months. Of course you don't—and your financial independence program is stalled before it even gets off the ground! The solution is called a **no exceptions policy**. In other words, you commit to your better financial future every single day. It's what separates the people who have from the people who don't have. (In chapter nine, Taking Decisive Action, you'll learn a lot more about wealth creation.)

Let's look at another situation. If maintaining excellent health is high on your list of priorities, exercising three times a week may be the minimum standard to keep you in shape. A **no exceptions policy** means you will maintain this exercise habit no matter what happens, because you value the long-term benefits.

People who dabble at change will quit after a few weeks or months. And they usually have a long list of excuses why it didn't work out for them. **If you want to distance yourself from the masses and enjoy a unique lifestyle, understand this—your habits will determine your future.**

It's that important. Remember, successful people don't drift to the top. It takes focused action, personal discipline and lots of energy every day to make things happen. The habits you develop from this day forward will ultimately determine how your future works out. Rich or poor. Healthy or unhealthy. Fulfilled or unfulfilled. Happy or unhappy. It's your choice, so choose wisely.

YOUR HABITS WILL DETERMINE
YOUR QUALITY OF LIFE

Many people today are concerned about their lifestyle. Phrases like, "I'm looking for a better quality of life," or "I just want to simplify my life," are now commonplace. Recently, many people are rethinking their lives after experiencing devastating financial losses in the stock market or losing their homes to foreclosure. It seems the headlong rush for material success and all the trappings of a so-called successful life are now out of reach. Here's a critically important point to digest. To be truly rich includes not only financial freedom but developing rich, meaningful relationships, enriching your health, and enjoying a rich balance between your career and your personal life.

The nourishment of your own spirit or soul is also an essential requirement. This takes time to explore and expand. It is a never-ending process. The more you learn about yourself—how you think, how you feel, what your true purpose is and how you want to live—the more your life will flow.

Instead of just working hard every week or worrying about your job, you will begin to make better choices based on intuition and instinctively knowing the right thing to do. It is this higher level of awareness that determines your daily quality of life. In chapter ten, Living On Purpose, we'll show you a unique system that will make all of this possible for you. Reassessing your options regularly is a very good habit to develop.

THE RESULTS OF YOUR BAD HABITS USUALLY DON'T SHOW UP UNTIL MUCH LATER IN LIFE

Please make sure you are really alert before you read the next two paragraphs. If you're not, go splash some cold water on your face so you will not miss the importance of this fundamental concept.

More people than ever are living for immediate gratification. They buy things they can't really afford and put off payment as far down the road as possible. Cars, furniture, appliances, entertainment systems, or the latest "toy," just to name a few. People in the habit of doing this have a sense of playing catch-up all the time. There's always another payment next month. This often results in working longer hours or taking an additional job just to make ends meet, creating even more stress.

Taken to an extreme, if your expenses constantly exceed your income, you will have an ultimate outcome. It's called bankruptcy! When you develop a chronic bad habit, life will eventually give you consequences. And you may not like the consequences. Here's what you need to really understand: Life will still give you the consequences. Whether you like it or not isn't the issue. The fact is, if you keep on doing things a certain way you will always get a predictable result. Negative habits breed negative consequences. Successful habits create positive rewards. That's just the way life is. And sadly, in The Great Recession of 2008, millions of Americans discovered the harsh reality of this fundamental truth.

Let's look at a few other examples. If you want to enjoy longevity, you must have healthy habits. Practicing good nutrition, exercising and studying longevity play a major role here.

The reality? Most of the population in the Western world is overweight, under-exercised and undernourished. How would you explain that? Again, it's a live-for-the-moment attitude, with little or no thought given to future consequences. There's a long list when it comes to health. Here are a couple— working fourteen hours per day seven days a week will lead to eventual burnout. When you're eating fast foods or junk food on the run as a daily habit, the combination of stress and high cholesterol produces a much greater risk of heart attacks and strokes. These are life-threatening consequences, yet many people ignore the obvious and roll merrily along, undaunted by the fact that a major crisis may be looming just around the corner. For example, according to 2008 American Heart Association statistics, more than 82 million people have a significant risk for heart disease. The cost of this in 2007 was over $286 billion!

Look at relationships. Marriage is in trouble, with almost 50 percent ending up in divorce. If you are in the habit of starving your most important relationships of time, energy and love, how can you expect a happy outcome?

When it comes to money, your bad habits may lead you to a never-ending cycle of work in your later years, when you'd rather be enjoying more time off for fun.

Now here's some really good news:

YOU CAN TURN NEGATIVE CONSEQUENCES INTO POSITIVE REWARDS

Simply By Changing Your Habits Now.

JACK:

Personally, my best new habit is getting more sleep. I had been living on 6½ hours for a long time because I could. Between 6½ and 8 hours of sleep is when the human growth hormone kicks in, which keeps the body young and also builds muscle. That last hour and a half is also when the body does the most cleansing. The immune system does the most healing on the body in deep sleep, so I've just committed to sleeping more. I'm going to bed more at 11 PM and getting up at 7 AM. instead of going to bed at 1 AM and getting up at 7 AM.

The other big habit is, I'm networking more than I used to. I was so tied up reading to expand my knowledge base and doing searches on the internet that I wasn't building my relationships. If you don't talk to people, you don't have any kind of ability to deepen the relationship. If you continuously nurture your most important relationships, then when you need something, they're willing to help you because you're not just calling them only when you need them.

Another essential business habit in today's world is for people to become better storytellers. Good salespeople and good CEOs know how to tell a story, because what Velcro's to a person's mind is a story. I remember my dad telling me about the guy who started National Cash Register (NCR), the company where my dad worked. He was showing some Japanese prospects his cash registers and hoping they'd buy a bunch of them. These were the old style cash registers where you pushed down keys like the old typewriters. The drawer would pop open and the numbers would appear in the glass above. The owner was taking these people around illustrating how one of them worked—and it didn't work! Noticing a sledgehammer nearby, he picked it up and just beat the crap out of the cash register. Then he said, "That's what we do with cash registers that don't work at NCR. They never leave the building!" You tell that story to illustrate that you are committed to excellence.

Developing successful habits takes time

How long does it take to change a habit? The most common answers to this question are, "about twenty-one days," or "three to four weeks." This is probably true for making small adjustments in your behavior.

What you'll find is, that after twenty-one to thirty experiences with a new habit, it's harder not to do it than to do it. Before you can change a habit you need to first check how long you have owned it. If you have been doing something repeatedly for thirty years you may not be able to let go of it in a few short weeks. Acknowledge the fact that a deeply entrenched habit has long roots. It's like trying to sever a multistranded fiber that has molded itself, over time, into a single powerful rope. It's very hard to break. Long-time smokers know how difficult it is to break the nicotine habit. Many never do, despite the overwhelming evidence that proves smoking can significantly shorten your life expectancy.

As well, people with a long history of low self-esteem won't transform themselves into highly confident individuals, ready to take on the world, in twenty-one days. It may take a year or more to develop positive belief systems. These important transitions can affect both your professional and personal life.

Another factor about changing habits is the potential for slipping back into your old patterns. This can happen when stress levels rise or an unexpected crisis occurs. The new habit may not be strong enough to resist these circumstances, and more time, energy and effort will be required. To ensure consistency, astronauts use a checklist for every single procedure to ensure the same results every time. You can create a similar fail-safe system. It just takes practice. And it's well worth the effort, as you'll see shortly.

Imagine if you only changed four habits every year. Five years from now you would have twenty positive new habits. Now, here's the thing—would twenty positive new habits make a difference in your results? Of course. Twenty successful habits can bring you all the money you want or need, wonderful loving relationships, a healthier and more energized physical body, plus all sorts of new opportunities. And what if you created more than four new habits every year? Think of the possibilities!

Up to 47 percent of our everyday behavior is habitual

LES:

I remember losing my keys on a regular basis. At the end of the day I'd park the car in the garage, march into the house and toss my keys anywhere they happened to land. Later I'd be going out to a meeting and, of course, I couldn't find my keys. As the treasure hunt for my keys took place, my stress level would noticeably increase, and after the keys were finally found, I'd rush off to my meeting twenty-five minutes late, owning an attitude that would not be described as positive.

The solution to this recurring problem was simple. One day I nailed a block of wood to the wall facing the garage door. It had two hooks on it and a large label that said, "keys."

The next evening I came home, strode past my new parking spot for the keys, and tossed them in some remote corner of the room. Why? Because that's what I'd always done. It took me almost thirty days of forcing myself to hang them on the wall before my brain got the message:

"I guess we're doing something different now," and a new habit was finally formed. I never lose my keys anymore, but it took a considerable effort to retrain myself.

As mentioned earlier, many of our daily activities are simply routines. From the time you get up in the morning until you retire at night, there are hundreds of things you do the same way. These include the way you dress, get ready for the day, eat breakfast, brush your teeth, drive to the office, greet people, arrange your desk, check your email, set up appointments, work on projects, attend meetings, answer the phone and so on. If you've been doing these same activities for years, you have a set of firmly entrenched habits. They involve every area of your life including your work, family, income, health, relationships and many more. The sum total of these habits determines how your life operates. Simply stated, this is your normal behavior.

As creatures of habit we are very predictable. In many ways this is good because others may view us as reliable, dependable and consistent. (It's interesting to note that people who are very unpredictable also have a habit—the habit of inconsistency!)

However, with too much routine, complacency sets in and life becomes boring. We settle for less than we are capable of. In fact, many of the activities that make up our everyday normal behavior are performed unconsciously—without thinking. Here's the point: Your everyday normal behavior has a lot to do with the results in your life. If you're not happy with these results, something has to change.

NOTHING MUCH IN YOUR LIFE WILL CHANGE,
UNTIL YOU DO!

ONCE A NEW HABIT IS WELL-DEVELOPED, IT BECOMES YOUR NEW NORMAL BEHAVIOR

This is great news! By superimposing a new behavior on top of your present behavior, you can create an entirely new way of doing things. This new normal behavior then becomes your new standard of performance and productivity. In other words, you simply start replacing your old bad habits with new successful habits.

For example, if you always show up late for meetings, your stress levels are probably high and you feel unprepared. To improve this, make a commitment that you will arrive ten minutes early for every appointment during the next four weeks. If you discipline yourself to complete this process, you will notice two things:

1. The first week or two will be tough. In fact, you may need to give yourself a few mental pep talks just to keep yourself on track.

2. The more often you show up on time, the easier it becomes. Then one day it becomes normal behavior. It's like being re-programmed. And you'll discover that the benefits of the new program far outweigh the results of the old one.

By systematically improving one behavior at a time you can dramatically improve your overall lifestyle. This includes your health, income, relationships and time off for fun.

MARK:
Regarding health habits, I'm at the fittest I've ever been. I'm more conscious now, thanks to my wife Crystal's expertise and support. I'm more aware of the way that my body moves. I was starting to slump over because, you know, older people forget to take their vitamins and nutraceuticals and they forget to exercise at least an hour a day. Physically, you've got to have flexibility, and you've got to have balance. And each one of these requires a decision regarding the amount of effort you are going to expend to maximize your fitness as you grow older. I spend a lot of money on my health using acuscopes and myoscopes, which are sophisticated electronic instruments for energetic healing.

My best new habit regarding business is meditating every day in order to get in what I call an athletic zone, or the vortex, experiencing the "feeling" consciousness. This creates the habit of awareness, being where you want to be before you actually get there. You've got to be at the end result. For example, I could see *Chicken Soup for the Soul* was going to be number one while everyone was rejecting us, saying, "That will never work." However, we took ownership and it happened.

DECISIVENESS SEPARATES GREAT LEADERS FROM DREAMERS AND TALKERS.

How to IDENTIFY
Bad Habits

BE AWARE OF THE HABITS THAT
ARE NOT WORKING FOR YOU

Many of our habits, patterns, idiosyncrasies and quirks are invisible, causing renowned author Oliver Wendell Holmes to observe, "We all need an education in the obvious." So let's look more closely at the habits that are holding you back. You are probably conscious of a few right away. Here are some common ones we have received from clients in our workshops.

- Not returning phone calls on time.

- Being late for meetings and appointments.

- Poor communication between colleagues and staff.

- Never updating your website.

- Not allowing enough travel time when going to meet clients or prospects for outside appointments.

- Not attending to paperwork quickly and efficiently.

- Wasting time on the Internet.

- Allowing bills to go unpaid, resulting in high interest penalties.

- Not following up consistently on long overdue receivables.

- Talking instead of listening.

- Forgetting someone's name sixty seconds (or less) after being introduced.

- Hitting the snooze alarm several times in the morning before getting out of bed.

- Working long days with no exercise or taking regular breaks.

- Not spending enough time with your children.

- Having a fast-food meals program that often is Monday to Friday.

- Eating at irregular times of the day.

- Leaving home in the morning without hugging your wife, husband, children and/or dog.

- Taking work home with you.

- Being glued to your PDA when having dinner with your spouse.

- Making reservations at the last minute (restaurant, travel plans, theatre, concerts).

- Not following through on requests as promised.

- Not taking enough time off for fun and family— guilt free!

- Having your cell phone on all the time.

- Not deleting old emails.

- Controlling every decision, especially the small stuff you need to let go of!

- Procrastinating on everything from filing taxes to cleaning out your garage.

Now check yourself out by making a list of all the habits that keep you unproductive. Block off an hour so you can really think through this process. And plan it so you won't be interrupted. It's a worthy exercise and will give you a strong foundation for improving your results in the years ahead. In fact, these bad habits, or obstacles to your goals, really act as a springboard to your future success. Until you clearly understand what is holding you back, it's difficult to create more productive habits. The Successful Habits Formula at the end of this chapter will show you a practical way to transform your bad habits into successful strategies.

Another way to identify your unproductive behavior is to ask for feedback. Talk to people you respect and admire, who know you well. Ask them what they observe about your bad habits. Look for consistency. If you talk to ten people and eight of them say you never respond to important emails on time, pay attention. **Remember this—your outward behavior is the truth, whereas your inner perception of your behavior is often an illusion.**

If you are open to good honest feedback, you can make adjustments quickly and eliminate bad habits permanently.

YOUR HABITS AND BELIEF SYSTEMS
ARE A PRODUCT OF YOUR ENVIRONMENT

This is an extremely important insight. Understand that the people you hang around with and the environment you live in strongly influence what you do. A person brought up in a negative environment, continually subjected to physical or verbal abuse, has a different view of the world than a child reared in a warm, loving and supportive family. Their attitudes and levels of self-esteem are different. Abusive environments often produce feelings of unworthiness and a lack of confidence, not to mention fear. This negative belief system, if carried into adult life, can produce all sorts of unproductive habits including drug addiction, criminal activity and an inability to mold a steady career path.

Peer pressure also plays a negative or positive role. If you hang around people who are always complaining about how bad everything is, you may start believing what they say. On the other hand, if you surround yourself with people who are strong and positive, you're more likely to see a world full of opportunity and adventure.

Even if you were unfortunate enough to have a severely disadvantaged background, you can still make changes. And it may only take one person to help you make the transition. An excellent coach, teacher, therapist, mentor or positive role model can dramatically impact your future. **The only prerequisite is that you must commit to change.** When you are ready to do so, the right people will start showing up to help you. In our experience, that well-known saying, "When the pupil is ready the teacher appears," is true.

"'Parking,' yes. 'Belief Systems,' not so much."

How to CHANGE
Bad Habits

STUDY THE HABITS OF
SUCCESSFUL ROLE MODELS

As mentioned before, successful people have developed successful habits. Learn to observe what those habits are. Study successful people. As well-known business philosopher Jim Rohn said, "They leave clues." What if you were to interview one successful person every month? Take him or her out to breakfast or lunch and ask lots of good questions about their disciplines, routines and habits. What do they read? What clubs and associations do they belong to? How do they schedule their time? If you listen well and take good notes, you'll have a wealth of powerful ideas in a very short time. And if your request is sincere, truly successful people are happy to share their ideas. They enjoy the opportunity to coach people who are genuinely interested in improving their lives.

JACK AND MARK:
When we finished writing the first *Chicken Soup for the Soul* book, we asked all of the bestselling authors we know—Barbara De Angelis, John Gray, Ken Blanchard, Harvey Mackay, Harold Bloomfield, Wayne Dyer and Scott Peck—what specific strategies would be required to assure that our book would become a bestseller. All of these people were generous with their ideas and their insights. We did everything we were told. We made a habit of doing a minimum of one radio interview a day, seven days a week, for two years. We retained our own publicist. We sent out five books a day to reviewers and other potential opinion

molders. We gave newspapers and magazines free reprint rights to our stories. We offered motivational seminars to all of the people responsible for selling our books. In short, we asked what our bestselling habits should be and we put them into action. As a result, we have sold 500 million books to date worldwide. (To put this into perspective, at this writing, the entire Harry Potter series has sold about 450 million copies in at least seventy languages.)

The trouble is, most people won't ask. Instead, they come up with all sorts of excuses. They're too busy, or they rationalize that successful people wouldn't have time for them, and how do you find these people anyway? Successful people aren't standing on every street corner waiting to be interviewed. That's right. Remember, it's a study. That means you need to be resourceful and come up with ways to find where these successful people work, live, eat and hang out. Make it a game. Have fun. It's worth it! (In Chapter 5, which focuses on the habit of Building Excellent Relationships, you'll discover how to find and contact successful mentors.)

Here's another way to study successful people: Read their autobiographies and biographies. There are hundreds of them. These are wonderful true stories packed with ideas, and the books are in your local library, in bookstores, and downloadable online. Read one every month, and you'll gain more insights in a year than many university courses could offer.

Also, be alert for special documentaries that feature successful people. Another habit the three of us have developed is listening to motivational and educational audio programs when we are driving, walking or exercising. If you listen to an audio for thirty minutes each day, five days a week, in ten years you'll have been exposed to over thirteen hundred hours of new and useful information. This is a habit that almost all of the successful people we know have developed. (For some of the best, see our Resource Guide on page 343.)

Our friend Jim Rohn said, "If you read one book every month about your industry, in ten years you'll have read 120 books. That will put you in the top one percent of your field." Conversely, Jim wisely noted, **"All the books you haven't read won't help you!"** The internet is a wonderful source for inspirational videos, music, apps, and training programs. All this terrific information is out there waiting for you. So feast on it, and watch your awareness soar. Pretty soon, if you apply what you learn, your income will soar too.

DEVELOP THE HABIT OF CHANGING YOUR HABITS

People who are rich in every sense of the word understand that life is a learning experience. It never stops. Learn to constantly refine your habits. There's always another level to reach for, no matter how good you are right now. When you constantly strive to improve, you build character. You become more as a person, and you have more to offer. It's an exciting journey that ultimately leads to fulfillment and prosperity. Unfortunately, sometimes we learn the lessons the hard way.

LES:
On a routine visit to my doctor for a check up, I learned that my triglycerides were a little high as was my "bad" cholesterol. I was also advised to lose ten pounds of weight as my body mass index (BMI) was creeping outside the normal healthy adult range of 20–25. So what do you do when the evidence is there in black and white? Two choices. Ignore the numbers or start thinking about the consequences down the road—diabetes and heart disease quickly came to mind.

I've always believed in taking preventative action when it comes to my health. Waiting until a crisis occurred was never very appealing to me! However, I had allowed myself to slip into a few bad habits and ignored some early warning signals. It's easy to make excuses when you are busy in your business. I decided a few changes were necessary concerning my daily eating habits. Upon reflection, I realized my sugar intake was high. My healthy breakfast (I thought) consisted of three mixed cereals and three or four portions of fresh fruit. A nutritionist informed me this was far too much sugar to start my day. First wake-up call! On further reflection, I realized I was consuming more soda and high sugar drinks than normal. And in times of pressure deadlines at work, chocolate and cookies had become my daily comfort food. Adding this all up resulted in a case of the blindingly obvious! Too much sugar—more body bulge—negative test results.

Dear reader, if you find yourself in the same boat, take heart: there's a simple solution. For me, the new habits were to cut out the chocolate and cookies cold turkey and spread my eating throughout the day with smaller portions. And guess what happened? I lost sixteen pounds in two months and my triglycerides were back to normal, as was my BMI index.

My energy is great, I'm more focused and more confident now that I've taken better control of my health just by making a few adjustments. Was letting go of the sugary drinks and chocolate really tough to do? Surprisingly not, although I still enjoy an occasional cookie. I mean, life is meant to be enjoyed, right?

The big insight for me was to not become complacent regarding these important aspects of my life. Complacency precedes dangerous consequences. Stay alert!

The point of this story is to illustrate how life will always give you consequences related to your actions. So before you embark on a specific course, look ahead. Are you creating negative consequences or potential rewards? Be clear in your thinking. Do some research. Ask questions before you start any new habits. If you do this, you'll enjoy more of life's pleasures, and not be screaming for morphine to kill your pain!

Now that you understand how habits really work and how to identify them, let's conclude with the most important part —how to permanently change your habits.

As well as making a list of your bad habits, here's a few questions to stimulate your thinking.

- **Are my financial habits helping me reach my most important financial goals?**
  For example: Financial Freedom, that is, having the choice to do whatever I want without worrying about the cost.

- **Are any of my current health habits jeopardizing my future wellbeing?**
  For example: no exercise and consuming high calorie foods.

- **What communication habits do I need to improve?**
  For example: better listening, speaking clearly, being empathetic, less controlling.

- **What habits do I have that may be hurting my family relationships?**
  For example: not paying attention, being self-centered, perfectionism.

The Successful HABITS
Formula

This is a step-by-step method to help you create better habits. It works because it's simple. You don't need complicated strategies. This template can be applied to any area of your life, business or personal. If applied consistently, it will help you achieve everything you want. There are three simple fundamental steps:

1. CLEARLY IDENTIFY YOUR BAD OR UNPRODUCTIVE HABITS

It's important that you really think about the future consequences of your bad habits. These may not show up tomorrow, next week or next month. The real impact could be years away. When you look at your unproductive behavior one day at a time, it may not look so bad. The smoker says, "What's a few cigarettes today? It helps me relax. I'm not wheezing and coughing." However, the days accumulate and twenty years later in the doctor's office, the X-rays are conclusive. Consider this: If you smoke ten cigarettes a day for twenty years, that's seventy three thousand cigarettes. Do you think seventy three thousand cigarettes could have an impact on your lungs? Of course! In fact, the consequences can be deadly. **So when you examine your own bad habits, consider the long-term implications. Be totally honest. Your life may be at stake.**

Tobacco use is the leading preventable cause of death. On average, adults who smoke cigarettes die fourteen years earlier than non-smokers. Source: CDC

2. DEFINE YOUR NEW
SUCCESSFUL HABIT

Usually this is just the opposite of your bad habit. In the smoker's example it would be, "Stop Smoking." What are you actually going to do? To motivate yourself, think about all the benefits and rewards for adopting your new successful habit. This helps you create a clear picture of what this new habit will do for you. **The more vividly you describe the benefits, the more likely you are to take action.**

3. CREATE A THREE-PART
ACTION PLAN

This is where the rubber meets the road. In the smoking example there are several options. Read how-to-stop-smoking literature. Start hypnosis therapy. Substitute something else when the desire for a cigarette arises. Place a bet with a friend to keep you accountable. Start a fresh air exercise program. Use a nicotine patch treatment. Stay away from other smokers. The important thing is to make a decision about which specific actions you are going to implement.

You must take action. Start with one habit that you really want to change. You can apply this to any area of your life. Focus on your three immediate action steps and put them into practice. **Remember, nothing will change until you do.**

Insights

As we get older, the world continues to evolve, and along with it, so do our habits. Here are a few current habits that have become normal daily behavior across the globe: text messaging, online shopping, music and movie downloads, plus apps for just about anything we need.

However, what we have noticed is, the more connected we become electronically, the less connected we are physically and emotionally.

This has some serious consequences if we are not smart enough to look down the road. Throughout our own careers, we've discovered communication is one of the most important life skills. The habit of excellent communication is essential for businesses and individuals to thrive. Although group conference calls and video meetings undoubtedly save significant expense on travel and can create quicker action within teams, they will never be a complete substitute for sitting down face to face. This is especially true when presenting your product or service for the first time. There are so many subtle nuances that will not be picked up on a video screen.

When face to face, the presenter always has the advantage of creating direct emotional energy. The ability to respond immediately and confidently to unexpected objections, and ultimately to close the sale, is often related to the dynamic energy that has been created "live" in the room. Have you forsaken the power of personal presentations for the deceptive comfort of technology? This is especially valid if you are working on a major deal or building a relationship with an influential people-connector.

On the home front, statistics prove that families who are in the habit of eating together, especially at dinner time, communicate better and deepen their relationships. Families who are splintered and polarized have opposite habits. They often eat alone and allow their electronic devices to take priority. Many kids prefer playing a video game to family discussion. You can imagine the future consequences from this bad habit.

As we have said before, successful people and families have successful habits.

Is it time for you to change some of your current habits, especially the ones that may be driving a wedge into your most important relationships?

One of the things you really want to get clear about is knowing that anything you want to improve—your health, relationships, or even your golf game—requires a set of easy to measure, actionable habits. When the outcome you want is clear, then it's just a matter of commitment and following through each week on your best actions, until they become second nature. We want you to experience a transformation in your results and in your lifestyle. The next chapter will build on what you've learned about habits. It's all about focusing your power.

Expect some breakthroughs!

"POWER IS THE FACULTY OR CAPACITY TO ACT, THE STRENGTH AND POTENCY TO ACCOMPLISH SOMETHING. IT IS THE VITAL ENERGY TO MAKE CHOICES AND DECISIONS. IT ALSO INCLUDES THE CAPACITY TO OVERCOME DEEPLY EMBEDDED HABITS AND TO CULTIVATE HIGHER, MORE EFFECTIVE ONES."

—Stephen R. Covey

ACTION STEPS

Successful People I Want
to Interview

The Successful Habits
Formula

A. Successful People I Want to Interview

Make a list of people you respect, who have already done extremely well. Set a goal to invite each of them to breakfast, or lunch, or book an appointment at their office. Remember to take a notebook or a recorder with you to capture their best ideas.

	Name	Phone	Interview Date
1.	_____	_____	_____
2.	_____	_____	_____
3.	_____	_____	_____
4.	_____	_____	_____
5.	_____	_____	_____

B. The Successful Habits Formula

Look at the following examples. There are three sections—A, B and C. In section A, define the unproductive habit that is holding you back. Be specific.

Then consider the consequences if you keep repeating this behavior. Every action you take has consequences. Bad habits (negative behavior) produce negative consequences. Successful habits (positive behavior) produce benefits and rewards.

In section B, define your successful new habit. Usually all you need to do here is write the opposite of what you had in section A. If your bad habit was taking too much work home on weekends, your new habit could be to keep weekends free for fun and family. In section C, list the three action steps you will take to turn your new habit into reality. Be specific. Pick a start date and get going!

A. Habit That Is Holding Me Back

EXAMPLE:

Taking too much work home on weekends

CONSEQUENCES:

Family time restricted, feeling guilty, important relationships become polarized, marriage breakdown

B. Successful New Habit

EXAMPLE:

Completely free up weekends from work

BENEFITS:

More relaxed, rejuvenated and refreshed mentally, reduced stress levels, create unique family experiences

Three-Step Action Plan to Jump-Start My New Habit

1. Design my work better by not overcommitting.

2. Delegate secondary tasks to staff to free up my time.

3. Have my family keep me accountable. No golf if I don't follow through!

Start Date: February 3rd.

Habit That Is Holding Me Back

EXAMPLE:

Making bad investment decisions like get-rich-quick schemes or overly risky stocks

CONSEQUENCES:

Embarrassment, decreased net worth, increased family stress, need to work extra years to recoup losses

Successful New Habit

EXAMPLE:

Invest wisely in the areas that I know best

BENEFITS:

Peace of mind, security, confidence restored, better focus, healthy net worth, future freedom

Three-Step Action Plan to Jump-Start My New Habit

1. Find an excellent financial mentor whose advice I can trust.

2. Create a solid financial plan that is aligned with my new risk tolerance level.

3. Set up an auto debit plan to save 10 percent of my monthly income.

Start Date: Monday, 19th March.

On a separate sheet use the same format to determine your own new habit. DO IT NOW!

"You're right, I owe my success to luck!
I'm lucky that my alarm clock rings at 5:00 AM so
I can work 12 hours a day. I'm lucky that my car has
a stereo so I can listen to self-improvement tapes
while I commute. I'm lucky that my street is paved
so I can run three times a week. I'm lucky that . . ."

LIVING AND WORKING ON PURPOSE

TAKING DECISIVE ACTION

CONSISTENT PERSISTENCE

ASK FOR WHAT YOU WANT

THE CONFIDENCE FACTOR

BUILDING EXCELLENT RELATIONSHIPS

OVERCOMING SETBACKS

DO YOU SEE THE BIG PICTURE?

IT'S NOT HOCUS-POCUS, IT'S ALL ABOUT FOCUS

YOUR HABITS WILL DETERMINE YOUR FUTURE

You've completed the first step—well done!

It's Not Hocus-Pocus, It's All About Focus

> "LEARN HOW TO SEPARATE THE MAJORS AND THE MINORS. A LOT OF PEOPLE DON'T DO WELL SIMPLY BECAUSE THEY MAJOR IN MINOR THINGS."
>
> —Jim Rohn

The entrepreneur's dilemma.
If you own your own business, or are planning to in the near future, be aware of the Entrepreneur's Dilemma. (You can also adapt this if you're in management or any sort of supervisory role.) Here's the scenario: You have this great idea for selling a new product or providing a unique service. You visualize doing it better than everyone else, and of course you're going to make lots of money.

Initially, the main purpose of a business is to find new customers and to keep the ones you already have. Second, to make a fair profit. At the start, many small business ventures are undercapitalized. Consequently, the entrepreneur wears several hats, especially in the first year, and puts in long days and nights, with not much time for relaxing. However, it's an exciting time, putting deals together, meeting potential clients and improving the product line or service.

As a foundation is built, people and systems are put in place to create stability. Gradually the entrepreneur becomes more involved in day-to-day operations and administrative duties. What started out as an exciting venture becomes a daily routine, with much more time spent putting out fires, handling people problems, tax challenges and monthly cash flow.

Does this sound familiar to you? Well, you are not alone. In our combined 109 years of business experience, this is a very common situation. The dilemma is compounded because many entrepreneurs (and managers) are controllers. They find it difficult to let go, to allow other people to carry the load. Delegation is not their strength, and of course they are emotionally attached to their business. After all, they created it, weaned it, and nurtured it. They understand every detail and, in their minds, nobody else can do these important everyday tasks as well as they can.

This is the ultimate Catch-22. There are more opportunities on the horizon, and bigger deals to close, but you can't get to them because you're stuck with the day-to-day routine. It's frustrating. So you think, "Maybe if I work harder and take a time management course, I can handle everything." This won't help. Working harder and longer hours will not solve your dilemma. Trust us, we've been there more than once. So what is the answer? Here it is in one sentence: **You must invest most of your time every week doing what you do best, and let others do what they do best.**

That's it in a nutshell.

© Randy Glasbergen
www.glasbergen.com

GLASBERGEN

"I have some paperwork to catch up. If I'm not back
in two days, organize a search and rescue team."

Focus on those activities you do brilliantly, and from which you produce extraordinary results. If you don't, you'll probably create higher stress levels and ultimate burnout. Not a pleasant picture. Doing what you do best gives you energy, keeps you excited and frees you up to chase those new opportunities. But you're probably wondering how to handle all that stuff that's holding you back. You're right. It won't just disappear. Later in this chapter, you'll find out specifically how to deal with those monkeys and get them off your back.

Focus on Your Natural TALENTS

It's critically important that you understand this. To help you get the picture, let's take a look at the focused world of rock-and-roll music.

The Rolling Stones are one of the most prolific and enduring rock-and-roll bands in history. To date, their career has spanned almost fifty years. Mick Jagger and his three friends are now well into their sixties and still enjoy performing to sold-out stadiums around the world. You may not like their music, but it's hard to deny their success.

Let's go behind the scenes just before their concert begins. . . . The stage is set. It took over two hundred people to build this mammoth structure several stories tall and half the length of a football field. A convoy of more than twenty semi-trailers was required to haul it from the last location. Two private planes jet the key people, including the band, between cities. It's a huge operation. A world tour pulls in more than $80 million profit, so it's obviously worth the effort!

A limousine pulls up back of the stage. The four band members step out and wait expectantly for their cue call. They exhibit a hint of nervousness mixed with excitement as seventy-thousand people erupt into a deafening roar when their names are announced. The Stones walk on stage and pick up their instruments. For the next two hours they perform brilliantly, sending their legions of fans home happy and satisfied. After the final encore they wave good-bye, step into the waiting limousine and exit the stadium.

They are masters at applying the habit of Priority Focus. That means they only do the things they are brilliant at—recording and performing on stage—period. Notice this. After the initial planning, they don't get involved with hauling equipment, figuring out the complex itinerary, setting up the stage or doing the hundreds of other tasks that need to be performed efficiently to make the tour a smooth operation, and ultimately profitable. Other skilled people look after the details. The Stones simply concentrate on what they do best—that is, singing and performing.

There's a great message here for you, dear reader, and it's this: **When you focus most of your time and energy doing**

the things you are truly brilliant at, you eventually reap big rewards. This is a fundamental truth. And it's critical to your future success.

PRACTICE, PRACTICE, PRACTICE

Let's take a look at a few other examples. Sports is a good one. Every champion athlete focuses on his or her unique talents and continually refines them to an ever-higher level of performance. No matter which sport you choose, the big winners all have one thing in common. They spend most of their time focusing on their strengths, the things they are naturally good at. Very little time is wasted on unproductive activities. And they practice, practice, practice, often several hours every day, honing their skills.

LeBron James, currently the youngest basketball player ever to score 9,000 points in the NBA, has won numerous awards in his professional career. LeBron makes hundreds of jump shots per day, every day—it's his routine. Barcelona's soccer star Lionel Messi, currently the best player in the world, practices his dribbling techniques constantly. He's small in stature but he has perfected his technique so well that you would think the ball was stuck to his feet when he runs. When it comes to scoring goals, he makes the task look easy, often from the slightest of openings. At age twenty-four, he's won every major club trophy and was voted World Footballer of the Year, three years in a row.

Natural brilliance combined with the daily discipline to constantly hone their skills, is what separates these superstar athletes from everyone else.

Notice how these top performers spend very little time on their weaknesses. Many of our school systems could learn from this. Often, children are told to focus on their weaker subjects and not spend so much time on the ones they do well in. The rationale is to develop a broad level of competency in many subjects instead of focusing on a few. Wrong! As business coach Dan Sullivan says, "If you spend too much time working on your weaknesses, all you end up with is a lot of strong weaknesses!" This doesn't give you a competitive edge in the marketplace or position you to be wealthy. It just keeps you average. In fact, it's an absolute insult to your integrity to major in minor things.

It's important to clearly differentiate your areas of brilliance from your weaknesses. You are probably good at a lot of things, even excellent in some. Others you are competent at, and if you are honest, there are some things you are totally useless at doing. On a scale of one to ten, you could plot your entire range of talents, one being your weakest and ten being your most brilliant. All your biggest rewards in life will come from spending the vast majority of your time in the areas that score a ten on your talent scale.

To clearly define your areas of brilliance, ask yourself a few questions. What do you do effortlessly—without a lot of study or preparation? And what do you do that other people find difficult? They marvel at your ability and can't come close to matching it. What opportunities exist in today's marketplace for your areas of brilliance? What could you create using your unique talents?

DISCOVER YOUR BRILLIANCE

We are all blessed with a few God-given talents. A big part of your life is discovering what these are, then utilizing and applying them to the best of your ability. Some people never truly grasp what their greatest talents are. Consequently their lives are less fulfilling. These people tend to struggle because they spend most of their time in jobs or businesses not suited to their strengths. It's like trying to force a square peg into a round hole. It doesn't work, and it causes a lot of stress and frustration. For others, the discovery process takes years before their brilliance is revealed. Gord Wiebe fits right into that category.

In 1977, Gord left a job working in the rail yards of Winnipeg, Manitoba, and moved west to start a new life. Back then he had not yet discovered his true talents and capabilities.

Fast forward to today. At fifty-eight years of age, Gord is the major shareholder in a national manufacturing business that hit $190 million in revenues last year. How did this dramatic turnaround come about?

First, through the support and opportunity provided by a great mentor, his Uncle Harry, who had been working in the window business for several years. Harry was a passionate entrepreneur and decided to start his own residential window company. At that time, Gord was in his early twenties and describes his training in the business as minimal, but he developed some sales skills and enjoyed traveling around Southern Alberta, meeting people face to face. The company was growing, although the early business plan was based more on "a wing and a prayer." However, as young Gord discovered, passion drives momentum and momentum creates sales. Also a "customer first" focus built a strong base of happy customers.

The hiring of a progressive and talented vice-president pushed Gord into another steep learning curve that he handled in stride. A passion was now building inside him, wanting this fledgling company to overtake their biggest competitor who had monopolized the window business for years. The battle was on and Gord began to relish the challenges. His true talents were now coming to the fore. More offices were opened, more people were hired, and a new light commercial division was created to supplement their residential business. All Weather Windows (allweatherwindows.com) was now a major player by using innovative technology to stay ahead of the competition.

With the railroad days long behind him, Gord Wiebe says three core values have contributed most to his success.

1. A strong faith in God

2. An ongoing passion for the business

3. A total commitment to stick with it, through all the ups and downs that face every business

With more than one thousand people on the team and offices from coast to coast, hiring the right people became another important strategy. "The first indicator we look for when hiring is: Does this person demonstrate a passion for what they do? You find out pretty quick if someone has passion or not."

What stokes Gord Wiebe's passion today, after thirty-four years in the industry, is the exciting prospect of transferring the business on to the next generation. No doubt he is now relishing playing the role of mentor, with the knowledge that a caring uncle had once turned his life around when he needed it most. And in the process, he discovered how to release the talents that were within him all along. All he needed was an opportunity to express them.

Are you aligning your strengths and passions in what you do at work? This is what creates priority focus.

Make it a part of your everyday plan and you'll experience dramatic jumps in productivity and income. We have a practical method that will make this easy for you and will also clarify your unique talents. It's called the Priority Focus Workshop, and is outlined on page 59. You need to be absolutely clear about what really goes on during your typical week. This reality check is usually very revealing. Basically, you make a list of all the activities you do at work in a typical week.

Most people, when they add up their total, score between ten and twenty. One of our clients tallied a sixty-nine! It doesn't take a genius to figure out you can't do sixty-nine things each week and be truly focused. Even twenty activities is far too many. You'll be scattered all over the place and more prone to interruptions and distractions.

Many people are in shock when they see how much of their week is fragmented. "Overwhelmed," "out of control" and "stressed out" are typical phrases we hear a lot. However, completing the Priority Focus Workshop at the end of this chapter is a good starting point. At least you'll know where your time really goes. After completing the workshop, the next step is to list three things you are brilliant at doing in your business. Remember the definition of brilliant? These are activities you do effortlessly, that give you energy, and that produce the greatest results and income for your business.

By the way, if you are not directly involved with income-generating activities, who is? Are they doing a brilliant job of it? If not, you probably need to make some major decisions in the near future. Never forget, revenue comes from sales!

Now here's the next important question: In a typical week, what percentage of your time do you spend on your brilliant activities? Be totally honest. Often the answer is 15 to 25 percent. Even if 60 to 70 percent of your time is being used profitably, there's still a lot of room for improvement. What if you could refine this to 80 or 90 percent? Remember, your bottom-line income is directly linked to the amount of time spent in your areas of brilliance.

USE YOUR NATURAL GIFTS TO THE FULLEST.

They are the catalyst for your future success

The next step is to look at your original list of weekly activities and select three things you don't like doing, resist doing or are just no good at. There's no shame in admitting you have a few weaknesses. The most common answers here are paperwork, bookkeeping, setting up appointments or doing follow-up calls. All the little details that bring a project to completion are usually found on this list. Of course these need to be done, but not necessarily by you.

Have you noticed how these activities tend to drain your energy instead of expanding it? If this is true for you, wake up! When you keep on doing work that you detest, you need to remind yourself that this is futile. As renowned speaker Rosita Perez said: "When the horse is dead, get off!" Stop flogging yourself. There are better options.

Are You a STARTER or a Finisher?

This is a good time to consider why you like doing certain things and not others. Ask yourself this question: Am I a starter or a finisher? You probably do both to a degree, but what do you do more often? If you are a starter, you enjoy creating new projects, products and ideas that make things work better. The trouble with starters is that they aren't very good at finishing. All those little details we talked about earlier? That's boring stuff for starters. Most entrepreneurs are great starters. But after they get the ball rolling they tend to leave it and go on to something new. And what they often leave in their wake is a mess. Other people are then required to clean it all up. They are called finishers. Finishers love taking projects to completion. Often they aren't good at initiating the project (starters do that best); however, they are great at organizing what needs to be done and ensuring that the details are handled effectively.

So identify yourself. Knowing what your natural tendencies are is really helpful. If you're a starter, you can release the guilt you have about never getting things finished. Here's the key: Find a brilliant finisher to handle the details, and between you a lot more projects will be initiated and completed.

Let's give you a practical example. This book you're reading started out as an idea. Getting the book written—outlining the chapters, developing the content and having it all flow properly—is essentially the starter's job. Each of the three co-authors played an important role in this. However, to produce a finished product—including editing, printing, publishing and establishing distribution channels—required a lot of other people who are great finishers. Without them the original text would be collecting dust somewhere for years. So here's the next important question for you to consider: Who else could do the tasks you don't enjoy doing?

For example, if you don't enjoy doing the books, find an excellent bookkeeper. If you don't enjoy setting up appointments, have an experienced assistant help you. You don't like selling, or "motivating" people? Maybe you need a great sales manager who can recruit, train and track results of the sales team every week. If tax time frustrates you, use the services of an outstanding tax specialist.

Now, before you start thinking, "I can't afford all these people—it will cost too much," think again. How much time will you free up by effectively delegating the work you don't like doing in the first place? Either you delegate or you'll stagnate. You can plan to phase this help in gradually, or consider contracting the work out using part-time services to keep your overhead low.

One of our clients with a thriving home-based business found a unique combination. She hired a woman to come in on Wednesday mornings to do her books. The same person then cleaned her home in the afternoon. She really enjoyed both types of work, always did a great job, and it was cost-effective.

If You're Feeling SWAMPED, Get Help!

LEARN TO LET GO OF THE "STUFF" IN YOUR LIFE

If you're in a situation where your business is expanding and your role in the company requires you to focus better, a great way to handle the expanded workload is to hire a personal assistant. If you find the right person, your life will dramatically change for the better, guaranteed. So let's take a closer look at this key strategy. First, a personal assistant is not a receptionist, secretary or someone whose duties you share with two or three other people. A true personal assistant is someone who is totally dedicated to you. He or she is brilliant at doing the tasks you don't like to do, or shouldn't be doing in the first place. The main role of this person is to free you up from all of the mundane jobs and stuff that clutter up your week. Their role is to protect you so that you can focus entirely on your most brilliant activities.

The careful selection of this key person is critical to your future health. Select the right person and your life will become a lot simpler, your stress levels will noticeably diminish and you'll have a lot more fun. Select the wrong person and you will only compound your current problems.

Here are a few tips: First, make a list of all the tasks you want your assistant to be 100 percent responsible for. Most of these are the activities you want to discard from your own weekly list. When you interview, have the top three applicants complete a personal profile evaluation. There are several good ones on the market. (See Resource Guide, page 343.)

You can have a profile made up of the ideal candidate before you start your selection campaign. Run profiles on your top three interviews and compare these to the ideal candidate profile. Usually the person who is the closest match to your ideal profile will do the best job. Of course, you must take into account other factors, such as attitude, honesty, integrity, previous track record and so on.

Be careful not to select someone just like you. Remember, you want this person to complement your skills. Hiring someone with the same likes and dislikes as yourself will probably create a bigger mess.

A couple of other points worth noting: If you are a controller, someone who won't let go of things easily, it is essential that you surrender to your personal assistant! Before you panic about the word *surrender*, take a closer look. Controllers typically have a mind-set that says nobody can do these things as well as they can. That may be true. However, what if your assistant could do these tasks 75 percent as well initially? With proper training and good communication every week, your well-chosen assistant will eventually do these activities as well as you, and will outperform you in many of them. So give up the need for total control—it's holding you back. Gleefully surrender to someone with better organizational ability and a passion for looking after the details.

DILBERT *reprinted by permission of United Feature Syndicate, Inc.*

Just in case you're still hanging on to the notion that you can do it all, ask yourself, "How much am I worth per hour?" If you have never taken the time to do this, do it now. Check out the chart below.

How Much Are You Really Worth?

Your Income	Income Per Hour	Your Income	Income Per Hour
$50,000	$25	$140,000	$70
$60,000	$30	$150,000	$75
$70,000	$35	$160,000	$80
$80,000	$40	$170,000	$85
$90,000	$45	$180,000	$90
$100,000	$50	$190,000	$95
$110,000	$55	$200,000	$100
$120,000	$60	$500,000	$250
$130,000	$65	$1 million	$500

Based on working 250 days per year, eight hours per day.

Hopefully your dollar figure is high. Then why are you running around doing low-income activities? Give them up!

Last comment on personal assistants: It is absolutely imperative that you schedule time each day or at least once a week to discuss your agenda with your personal assistant. Communicate, communicate, communicate! The number-one reason these potentially great relationships fall apart is simply a lack of communication. Make sure your assistant knows what you want to spend your time on.

Also, allow reasonable time for your new "partner" to learn your systems. Indicate the key people you want to spend time with. Set up screening methods with your assistant that protect you from all the potential distractions and interruptions, so you can focus on what you do best. Be open to all input and feedback. Often, your assistant will create better ways to organize your office. Rejoice if this happens—you've found a real winner.

Now let's consider how you can implement the habit of Priority Focus into your personal life, so you have more time to relax with family and friends, or enjoy a particular hobby or sport.

No matter where you live, keeping a home in first-class condition requires maintenance. If you have kids, the problem is magnified three or four times, depending on their age and ability to destroy! Think of all the time spent in a typical week cooking and cleaning, washing up, fixing things, cutting grass, servicing the car, running errands and so on. Have you noticed there's no end to this? These activities have a habit of being continually recycled. It's the ongoing stuff of life. Depending on your mood, you enjoy it, put up with it or resent it.

What if you could find a way to minimize it, or even better, eliminate it? How would you feel? Free, more relaxed, able to enjoy more of the things you'd prefer to do? Of course!

What you're about to read in the next few minutes may require a new way of thinking, a leap of faith to some degree. However, focus on the rewards and benefits instead of the initial cost. They will far outweigh any investment you make. To put it simply, if you want to free up your time—get help. There's all sorts of good help available. Most of the help you require will be part time. For example, hire someone to do house cleaning once a week, or every other week.

LES:
My wife Fran used to think I was a plumber. If the tap in the kitchen was leaking, she'd ask me to fix it. Two hours later, with the floor flooded, bits of pipe lying everywhere, and the air blue with language unsuitable to print in this book, she realized she was wrong. Now we hire people who know what they are doing and pay them accordingly.

Is there a handyman in your neighborhood who is semi-retired and loves to fix things? Many experienced older people have terrific skills and are looking for little part-time jobs to keep them busy. These activities give them a sense of fulfillment. Usually, money isn't their primary need.

Make a list of all the things at home that need servicing, fixing or upgrading. You know, all those little jobs that you never seem to get around to because your time is all used up. Release your stress and hire someone.

You'll be making a contribution so that someone else can continue to use their skills. And you can eliminate hours and hours of frustration trying to do all those fix-up jobs that you're no good at, and don't even have the tools for. Maybe you weren't supposed to be a plumber, electrician, carpenter and all-around handyman.

What about outside the house? Cutting grass, weeding, trimming, watering plants and bushes, raking. Now here's a great opportunity for you. Check out the neighborhood. Look for an enterprising kid who wants to earn some money so he or she can buy a new bike, videogame or the latest iPod. Contrary to popular opinion, there are lots of young people who work hard and get the job done right. Find one. You are helping them provide value. And don't be cheap. A job well done deserves fair compensation.

If you are mentally blocking this idea, consider again. Think of all the extra time you'll have. You could reinvest those valuable hours into your own best money-making activities, or have real time to relax and re-energize with your family and friends. Maybe this new freedom from weekly "stuff" allows you to embark on that hobby you've always wanted to pursue, or enjoy more time for sports. And please, do it without feeling guilty. After all, you deserve time off, don't you?

Remember, you only have so much time every week. Life becomes more enjoyable when you are operating on a highly efficient, low-maintenance schedule. Now if you genuinely enjoy doing some of these tasks around the house (and you need to be totally honest about this), then go ahead. But only if it's truly relaxing or gives you a feeling of contentment.

The 4-D Solution

It's vital that you effectively separate so-called urgent tasks from your most important priorities. Putting out fires all day long in your office is, as time management expert Harold Taylor says, "Giving in to the tyranny of the urgent." That means every time a telephone rings you jump to answer it. When an email shows up on your computer you react to the request immediately, even if it does not require an immediate answer.

Instead, focus on your priorities. Whenever a choice to do or not do something has to be made, use the 4-D Formula to help you prioritize. You have four options to choose from:

1. Dump It
Learn to say "No, I choose not to do this." Be firm.

2. Delegate It
These are tasks that need to be done, but you are not the person to do them. Hand them over to someone else, with no guilt or regrets. Simply ask, "Who else could do this?"

3. Defer It
These are issues that you do need to work on, but not right away. They can genuinely be deferred. Schedule a specific time at a later date to handle this type of work.

4. Do It
Do it now. Important projects need your attention right away, so get started today. Move forward. Give yourself a reward for

completing these projects. Don't make excuses. Remember, if you don't take prompt action you'll end up with all those nasty consequences. Not a good outcome!

The Power of NO

Staying focused requires a measure of daily discipline. That means being more conscious every day of the activities you choose to spend your time on. To avoid drifting away from your focus, ask yourself at regular intervals, "Is what I'm doing right now helping me to achieve my goals?" This takes practice. It also means saying "No" a lot more. There are three areas to examine:

1. Yourself

The biggest battle going on every day is between your own ears. We talk ourselves in and out of situations constantly. Put a stop to this. When that little negative voice in the back of your head demands attention and tries to get to the forefront of your thinking, take a time-out. Give yourself a quick mental pep talk. Focus on the benefits and rewards of sticking to your priorities, and remind yourself of the negative consequences if you don't.

2. Other People

A variety of other people may attempt to destroy your focus. Sometimes they wander into your office for a chat because you have an open-door policy. Here's how to fix that—change your policy. Close your door for at least part of the day when you want to be left alone so you can concentrate on your next big project. If that doesn't work, you might put up a sign that says, "Do Not Disturb. Any Intruders Will Be Fired!"

MARK:

One of the great things I've learned to keep me focused is writing down exactly what I want to do. The more clarity you have about what you're going to do and really commit to, the more focused you become. I think God sends all these other cool, absolutely interesting, tantalizingly relevant distractions into our environment to see if we are really on purpose, what I call passionately on purpose. But you can't listen to everybody else's deal and attempt to do it. I spend most of my time saying "no" now, because people have known me as Dr. Yes. I'm saying "no" to more meetings unless they are in alignment with what I am currently focused on doing.

Distinguishing between a real opportunity that's on purpose for you and a bright, shiny object that's just a time-waster can be difficult. I decide based on the quality of the results that people have generated before they come to me. In other words, I want to know their track record. What have they achieved? Are they talkers or doers? Do they consistently make things happen? Do they have a big vision? If their track record is weak, then I prefer not to meet with them.

There are lots of very talented young people out there who can help you, too and who will re-energize your business if it's become a little flat.

3. The telephone

Perhaps the most insidious intrusion of all today is your PDA. Isn't it amazing how people allow this little piece of hardware to control their day? If you require two hours of uninterrupted time, turn off your iPhone, Blackberry, or whatever your particular preference is. Use your tech aid wisely—obviously there are times when you need to be available. Pre-schedule your appointments just like a doctor—2 PM to 5 PM on Mondays, 9 AM to 12 noon on Tuesdays. Then choose the most productive time to make your phone calls, for example, 8 AM to 10 AM. If you want to enjoy bigger results, there are times when you need to be secluded from the outside world. Give up the habit of automatically reaching for the phone every time it rings. Say "No." And take charge at home, too.

Our time-management friend Harold Taylor recalls an incident in the days when he was "addicted" to a ringing telephone. This was before cell phones became popular. On arriving home one day he heard the phone ring. In his haste to get there before it stopped, he broke down the screen door, gashing his leg in the process. Undaunted, he hurdled several pieces of furniture in a desperate bid to find out who was calling. Just before the final ring, he lifted the receiver, gasping, and said "Hello?" A demure voice replied, "Do you subscribe to the Globe and Mail?"

Here's another suggestion: To avoid those telemarketing calls, turn off your home phone at mealtimes. Isn't that when they call most often? Your family will appreciate the opportunity for some real discussion instead of these annoying intrusions. Don't allow your better future and your peace of mind to be put on hold through constant interruptions. Consciously stop yourself when you start doing things that are not in your best interest. From now on those wasteful activities are off limits. You don't go there anymore.

Be aware of old habits that may be pulling you away from your focus.

For example, excessive TV watching. If you're used to lying on the couch for three hours every night and your only exercise is pushing the remote control, you may want to take a look at that. Some parents understand the consequences of this and limit TV watching for their kids to a few hours on the weekend. Why don't you do the same for yourself? Here's a challenge for you. Take a whole week off from watching TV and see how much you can get done. You'll be amazed.

JACK:

The biggest personal insight I've had was understanding why I was so overwhelmed, and that's because I couldn't say "no" very well. What was really powerful for me was realizing that everything I didn't say "no" to but still hadn't done was creating my clutter. Books I'd promised people I'd read, letters I thought I should answer, etc. I did a visualization where I literally saw myself in my room, and every piece of paper was a pair of eyeballs looking at me pleading, "Please, give me attention." I realized I can't give attention to 20,000 requests a year. It's just not possible.

It's much better now. I'm not totally out of it, but I realized that I had this huge need to be seen as a nice guy. The fact is, I am a nice guy. I don't need to prove it to anybody, and I've learned how to say "no" to a lot more stuff and have better criteria for making decisions and not over-scheduling myself. I'm taking more time for my family, for myself, my own health, my own fun and my own exercise. There were months when I would never exercise because I'd be up every morning at 5 AM and go to bed at 11 PM and just be working all day long. Now I exercise every morning for at least an hour.

There are no magic formulas.

We hope you are getting the message that achieving what you want in life does not require magic formulas or secret ingredients. It's simply focusing on what works versus what doesn't work. However, many people focus on the wrong things. Those who live from paycheck to paycheck every month have not studied how to acquire financial intelligence. They have focused more on spending instead of acquiring a strong asset base for the future.

Many people are stuck in a job or career they don't enjoy because they have not focused on developing their areas of brilliance. There's a similar lack of awareness with health issues. The American Medical Association recently announced that 63 percent of American men and 55 percent of American women greater than twenty-five years of age are overweight. Even more concerning—one third of American adults are obese, meaning that their body mass index (BMI) is thirty or higher. However, children and youth are the main concern, since 12.5 million (17 percent) between the ages of two and nineteen are also obese. Obviously there are a lot of people out there focused on eating too much and exercising too little!

Here's the point. Carefully study what's working and what's not working in your life. What creates your biggest victories? What are you focusing on that's giving you poor results? This requires clear thinking.

IF YOU WANT FASTER RESULTS AND LESS STRESS, SHIFT YOUR FOCUS.

Insights

We made a strong statement in the original edition of this book that a lack of focus was the number one reason that stops people from getting what they want. Did you notice the same statement remains in this revised edition of *The Power of Focus*? I hope you get the point! Think about it: When you are pushing forward to hit a specific target, are you more likely to achieve it when your mind, body, spirit and resources are totally focused on the result, or when you are scattered and your attention is split in several directions?

It's a no brainer, right?

And yet what we find is a high percentage of company leaders—CEOs, entrepreneurs, professionals, managers, and salespeople—who are struggling to stay focused on their top priorities every week. Even though technology has given us better tools to avoid interruptions and distractions, we still languish at lower levels of focus. If you are struggling with this, read this chapter very carefully. More importantly, complete the appropriate Action Steps at the end of the chapter.

If you want more evidence, closely observe people and teams who are consistently successful. Sport provides wonderful examples of focus and discipline. In soccer, the worlds' most popular game, Manchester United recently became the most successful team in England by winning their nineteenth League Championship title in the 2010–2011 season. Along with all the many other trophies they have won over the years, one characteristic stands out that is wonderfully amplified by their iconic manager, Sir Alex Ferguson.

Now in his seventieth year, "Fergie" still has the same youthful enthusiasm, focus and drive that has served him well at United for the last twenty-five years. He says:

"Every year we have one focus—winning trophies!"

In the next chapter, we'll show you step by step how to develop what we call unusual clarity. You'll also learn how to set "big picture" goals. Then we'll equip you with a unique focusing system to ensure you achieve them. These strategies have worked wonderfully well for us. They will work equally well for you too.

> "FOCUS AND FOLLOW THROUGH NOW,
> OR EXPERIENCE THE DEVASTATING
> PAIN OF REGRET LATER."

—Les Hewitt

ACTION STEPS

The Priority Focus
Workshop

The Priority Focus Workshop

A practical six-step guide to maximize your time and productivity.

A. List all of the business activities at work that use up your time.

For example: phone calls, meetings, paperwork, projects, sales, follow-up procedures. Subdivide major categories such as phone calls and meetings. Include everything, even the five-minute tasks. Be specific, clear and brief. Use additional paper if you have more than ten.

1. _____   6. _____
2. _____   7. _____
3. _____   8. _____
4. _____   9. _____
5. _____   10. _____

B. Describe three things that you are brilliant at doing at work.

1. _____
2. _____
3. _____

C. Name the three most important activities that produce income for your business.

1. _____
2. _____
3. _____

D. Name the three most important activities that you don't like to do, or are weak at doing.

1. _____
2. _____
3. _____

E. Who could do these for you?

1. _____
2. _____
3. _____

F. What one time-consuming activity are you going to say "No" to or delegate right away?

_____
_____
_____

Take time to reflect on your answers to these questions. Then make a few practical decisions that will free up more time to do what you do best.

LIVING AND WORKING ON PURPOSE

TAKING DECISIVE ACTION

CONSISTENT PERSISTENCE

ASK FOR WHAT YOU WANT

THE CONFIDENCE FACTOR

BUILDING EXCELLENT RELATIONSHIPS

OVERCOMING SETBACKS

DO YOU SEE THE BIG PICTURE?

IT'S NOT HOCUS-POCUS, IT'S ALL ABOUT FOCUS

YOUR HABITS WILL DETERMINE YOUR FUTURE

Your momentum is picking up—on to number three.

Do You See The Big Picture?

"THE FUTURE BELONGS TO THOSE WHO BELIEVE
IN THE BEAUTY OF THEIR DREAMS."

—Eleanor Roosevelt

Peter Daniels is an unusual man whose life reads like a Horatio Alger story.
Born in Australia, his parents were third-generation welfare recipients used to being poor. Peter attended elementary school in Adelaide. Because of a learning disability, he found it difficult to understand and assemble words. Consequently he was labeled stupid by teachers who were either too busy or didn't care enough to find out why he struggled. One teacher in particular, Miss Phillips, would make Peter stand in front of the class where she would berate him with, "Peter Daniels, you're a bad boy and you'll never amount to anything."

Of course this did nothing for his self-esteem. As a result, he failed every grade in school. One of his earliest career choices was to become a bricklayer. A few years later, married with a young family, he decided to go into business for himself. The first venture failed miserably and he was broke within a year. Undaunted, he saw another opportunity and channeled his energy into making it a success. A similar fate awaited him; he was broke within eighteen months. With steely determination to overcome these setbacks, Peter again launched himself into the competitive world of business, only to end up broke for a third time. He now had the unbelievable track record of going broke three times within five years.

Most people would give up at this point. Not Peter Daniels. His attitude was, "I'm learning and I haven't made the same mistake twice. This is excellent experience." Asking his wife Robena to support him one more time, he decided to sell residential and commercial real estate. One skill Peter had honed over the years was his ability to persuade. He was a naturally good promoter. Much of this came from the necessity to deal with a constant stream of creditors who wanted payment. During the next ten years the name Peter Daniels became synonymous with residential and commercial real estate. Through careful selection and astute negotiation he accumulated a portfolio worth several million dollars.

Today Peter Daniels is an internationally acclaimed businessman who has created successful ventures in many countries around the world. His friends include royalty, heads of state, and the leading movers and shakers of the commercial world. He is also a philanthropist who is passionate about helping others, and whose wonderful generosity has funded many Christian endeavors.

When asked what turned his life from triple indebtedness to unprecedented success, he replied, "I scheduled time to think. In fact, I reserve one day a week on my calendar just to think. All of my greatest ideas, opportunities and money-making ventures started with the days I took off to think. I used to lock myself away in my den with strict instructions to my family that under no circumstances was I to be disturbed." The same strategy worked for Einstein who actually did his pondering in a special thinking chair.

And it transformed the life of Peter Daniels from school failure to multimillionaire. By the way, Peter has now written several bestselling books, one of which was titled *Miss Phillips, You Were Wrong!*, a reminder to his old teacher not to give up too quickly on her students.

Developing Unusual
CLARITY

Another reason why Peter Daniels enjoys continuous success is his ability to create exciting pictures of the future. Most people don't have a clear picture of what they want. At best it's fuzzy. What about you?

Do you schedule time regularly to think about your better future? You may say, "It's okay for Peter Daniels, but I could never find a day each week to think. I need an extra day just to keep up with my present commitments."

Well, could you start with five minutes and gradually build it to an hour? Wouldn't that be a good use of your time, spending sixty minutes each week creating an exciting picture of your future? Most people spend more time planning a two-week vacation than they do designing their life, especially their financial future.

Here's a promise: If you make the effort to develop the habit of unusual clarity, the payoff for you down the road will be tremendous. Whether your desire is to be debt-free, enjoy more time off for fun, build wonderful loving relationships, or contribute to a worthy cause, you can achieve all of this, and more, if you have a crystal-clear picture of what you want.

In the next few pages, you'll discover a comprehensive strategy that will give you a "big screen" picture of the years ahead. In the following chapters you'll also learn how to strengthen and support this future vision through the use of specific mentors. In fact, you'll develop a solid fortress of support that will render you impenetrable to negativity and doubt.

So let's get started.

BY THE WAY, HAVE YOU NOTICED THAT KIDS HAVE UNUSUAL CLARITY? HERE'S SOME PROOF:

"I've learned that you can be in love with four girls at the same time."

—Age nine

"I've learned that just when I get my room the way I like it, Mom makes me clean it up."

—Age thirteen

"I've learned that you can't hide a piece of broccoli in a glass of milk."

—Age seven

SOURCE: *Live and Learn and Pass It On* by H. Jackson Brown Jr.

The Purpose of
GOALS

Are you a conscious goal-setter? If you are, great. However, please read the information we are about to share. Chances are you'll benefit from the reinforcement, plus this expanded vision of setting goals may give you new insights.

If you don't consciously set goals, that is, you don't have a written plan, or set targets for the weeks, months and years ahead, then pay very close attention to this information. It can dramatically improve your life.

First, what is the definition of a goal? If you're not clear on this, you may get derailed before you start. We've heard lots of answers over the years. Here's one of the best:

A GOAL IS THE ONGOING PURSUIT OF A
WORTHY OBJECTIVE UNTIL ACCOMPLISHED.

Consider the individual words that make up this sentence. "Ongoing" means it's a process, because goals take time. "Pursuit" indicates a chase may be involved. There will likely be some obstacles and hurdles to overcome. "Worthy" shows that the chase will be worthwhile, that there's a big enough reward at the end to endure the tough times. "Until accomplished" suggests you'll do whatever it takes to get the job done. This is not always easy, but essential if you want a life full of outstanding accomplishments.

Setting and achieving goals is one of the best ways to measure your life's progress and create unusual clarity. Consider the alternative—just drifting along aimlessly, hoping that one day good fortune will fall into your lap with little or no effort on your part. Wake up! You've got more chance of finding a grain of sugar on a sandy beach.

The Top-10 Goals
CHECKLIST

Talk show host David Letterman created wacky top-10 lists that people actually paid money for. Here's a list that has a lot more value—a checklist to make sure you're using a successful framework to set goals. It's like a smorgasbord. So pick out what seems to fit you best and use it.

1. Your most important goals must be yours.

This sounds obvious. However, a common mistake made by thousands of people is to allow their main goals to be designed by someone else. This could be the company you work for, your industry, your boss, your bank or mortgage company, or your friends and neighbors.

In our workshops we teach people to ask themselves the question, "What do I really want?" At the end of one of these sessions a man came up to us and said, "I'm a dentist. I only went into this profession because my mother wanted me to. I hated it. One day I drilled through the side of a patient's mouth and ended up having to pay him $475,000."

Here's the point: When you let other people or society determine your definition of success, you're sabotaging your future. So put a stop to that right away.

Think about this for a moment. The media has one of the strongest influences on you when it comes to making decisions. And most people buy into it daily. In fact, if you live in a fairly large city you are bombarded with at least twenty-seven hundred advertising messages every day. There are constant radio and TV commercials, plus billboards, newspapers and magazines contributing to this onslaught. Our thinking is consciously and subliminally being influenced non-stop. The media defines success as the clothes we wear, the cars we drive, the homes we live in and the vacations we take. Depending

67

on how you measure up in these categories, you're branded a success or a failure.

Do you want more evidence? What's on the front of most popular magazines? A cover girl—someone whose glamorous figure and hairstyle are perfect, with not a wrinkle in sight. Or a male hunk whose muscular torso wasn't formed by merely working out five minutes a day on a miraculous exercise machine. What's the message? If you don't look like this you're a failure. Is it any wonder that many teenagers struggle with eating disorders like bulimia and anorexia, when peer pressure doesn't tolerate anyone who's remotely out of shape or who has average looks. This is ridiculous!

Decide now to create your own definition of success and stop worrying about what the rest of the world thinks. For years, Sam Walton, the founder of Wal-Mart, one of the largest and most successful retail store chains in history, enjoyed driving an old Ford pickup truck even though he was one of the wealthiest men in the country. When asked why he didn't drive a vehicle better suited to his position, he'd reply, "Well, I just like my old truck." So forget about image and set goals that are right for you.

By the way, if you really want to drive a luxury car, or live in a beautiful home, or create an exciting lifestyle, go for it! Just make sure that it's what **you** want, and that you're doing it for the right reasons.

2. Your goals must be meaningful.

Inspirational speaker, Charlie "Tremendous" Jones, recalled the early days of his career like this: "I remember when I was struggling to get my business off the ground. There were long nights at the office when I'd take my jacket off, roll it up to make a pillow and grab a few hours sleep on my desk." Charlie's goals were so meaningful that he did whatever it took to help his business grow. If that meant spending a few nights sleeping in the office, so be it. That's total commitment, a crucial ingredient if you want to become the best you can be. In his early thirties, Charlie went on to build an insurance brokerage that produced more than $100 million per year in revenue. And that was back in the day when $100 million was still a lot of money. Now governments talk in trillions!

When you prepare to write down your future goals, ask yourself, "What's really important to me? What's the purpose of doing this? What am I prepared to give up to make this happen?" This thinking process will increase your clarity.

It's critically important that you do this. Your reasons for charting a new course of action are what give you the drive and energy to get up in the morning, even on the days you don't feel like it.

Ask yourself, "What are the rewards and benefits for this new discipline?" Focus on the exciting new lifestyle you can enjoy by committing yourself now to consistent action.

If this doesn't get your adrenaline pumping, visualize the alternative. If you just keep on doing the same things that you've always done, what will your lifestyle be like five years from now, ten years from now, twenty years from now? What words will describe your future financial picture if you don't make any changes? What about your health, relationships and the amount of time you have off for fun? Will you be enjoying a lot more freedom or still be working too many hours a week?

AVOID THE "IF ONLY" SYNDROME.

Master philosopher Jim Rohn astutely observed that there are two major pains in life. One is the pain of discipline; the other is the pain of regret. Discipline weighs ounces, but regret weighs tons when you allow your life to drift along unfulfilled. You don't want to look back years later, saying, "If only I had taken that business opportunity; if only I had saved and invested regularly; if only I had spent more time with my family; if only I had taken care of my health. . . ." Remember, it's your choice. Ultimately, you are responsible for every choice you make, so choose wisely. Commit yourself now to creating goals that will guarantee your future success and peace of mind.

3. Your goals must be specific and measurable.

Here's where most people lose it. It's one of the main reasons individuals never achieve what they're capable of. They never accurately define what they want. Vague generalizations and wishy-washy statements aren't good enough. For example, if someone says, "My goal is to be financially independent," what does that really mean? For some people financial independence is having fifty million in secure assets. For others it's earning $100,000 a year. For someone else it's being debt-free. What is it for you? What's your number? If this is an important goal for you, take the time now to figure it out.

Your definition of happiness requires the same scrutiny. Just "wanting more time with my family," doesn't cut it. How much time, when, how often, what will you do with it, with whom? Here are three words that will help you achieve more clarity: **Be more specific.**

LES:
One of our clients in The Power of Focus Coaching Program indicated his goal for better health was to start exercising. He was feeling sluggish and wanted more energy. "Start exercising" is a very poor definition of this goal. It's too

general. There's no way to measure it. So we said, "Be more specific." He added, "I want to exercise thirty minutes a day, four times a week."

Guess what we said next? You're right. "Be more specific." By repeating this question several times his health goal was redefined as follows: To exercise for thirty minutes a day, four times a week, Monday, Wednesday, Friday and Saturday from 7 AM to 7:30 AM. His routine consists of ten minutes stretching and twenty minutes on his exercise bike. What a difference! Now we can easily track his progress. If we show up at the scheduled times to observe, he will either be doing what he says, or not. Now he's accountable for results.

Here's the point: When you set a goal, challenge yourself with the words, "Be more specific." Keep repeating this until your goal is crystal-clear and measurable. By doing this, you'll dramatically increase your chances of achieving the desired result that you want.

REMEMBER, A GOAL THAT IS NOT MEASURABLE IS JUST WISHFUL THINKING.

4. Your goals must be flexible.

Why is this important? There are a couple of reasons. First, you don't want to design a system that is so rigid and cast in stone that you feel suffocated by it. For example, if you design an exercise program for better health, you may want to vary the times during the week and the type of exercise, so it doesn't get boring. An experienced personal fitness coach can help you customize a program that's fun, has lots of variety and still guarantees the results you want.

Here's the second reason: A flexible plan allows you the freedom to change course if a genuine opportunity comes along that is so good you'd be crazy not to pursue it. A word of caution here. This doesn't mean you start chasing after every idea that comes by your door. Entrepreneurs are famous for getting distracted and losing their focus. Remember, you don't need to be involved with every new idea—just focusing on one or two can make you happy and wealthy.

"D'yer ever feel you're on the verge of an incredible breakthrough?"

5. Your goals must be challenging and exciting.

Many business owners seem to "plateau" a few years after the start of a new venture. They lose the early excitement that was originally fueled by uncertainty and the risks involved to get their product or service into the marketplace. They become operators and administrators and much of the work seems repetitive and uninspiring.

When you set goals that are exciting and challenging, you acquire an edge that prevents you from settling into a life of boredom. To do this you must force yourself to jump out of your comfort zone. This might be a little scary because you never know for sure if you'll land on your feet. Here's a good reason to push yourself—you will always learn more about life and your capacity to succeed when you are uncomfortable. Often when your back is up against the wall of fear, the greatest breakthroughs occur.

John Goddard, the famous explorer and adventurer, the man *Reader's Digest* called "the real Indiana Jones," is a wonderful role model for this concept. At the tender age of fifteen he sat down and made a list of 127 challenging lifetime goals he wanted to accomplish. Here are a few of them: Explore eight of the world's major rivers including the Nile, the Amazon and the Congo; climb sixteen of the highest mountains including Mount Everest, Mount Kenya and the Matterhorn; learn to fly a plane, circumnavigate the globe (he did this four times); visit the North and South Poles; read the Bible from cover to cover; play the flute and violin; and study primitive cultures in twelve countries including Borneo, the Sudan and Brazil. By the time he turned fifty he had successfully completed more than one hundred of the goals on his list.

When asked what caused him to create this fascinating list in the first place, he replied, "Two reasons. First, I was fed up with adults telling me what to do and what not to do with my life. Second, I didn't want to be fifty years old and realize I hadn't really accomplished anything."

You may not want to challenge yourself the way John Goddard did, but don't settle for mediocrity. Think big. Create goals that get you so excited you can hardly sleep at night. Life has a lot to offer—why shouldn't you enjoy your fair share?

6. Your goals must be in alignment with your values.

Synergy and flow are two words that describe any process moving effortlessly forward to completion. When your goals are in synch with your core values, the mechanism for this harmony is set in motion. What are your core values? Anything you feel strongly about that resonates at a deeper level of your being. These are fundamental beliefs that are well-developed and have molded your character for years. Honesty and integrity, for example. (You can make your own list on page 90.) When you do something that contradicts these values, your intuition or gut feeling will serve as a reminder that something isn't right.

Suppose you owed a lot of money and there is incredible pressure on you to repay the loan. In fact, the situation is almost unbearable. One day a friend approaches you and says, "I've figured out a way for us to make some easy money. All we need to do is rob the bank! The biggest monthly deposits are being made tomorrow. I've got a foolproof plan—we'll be in and out of there in twenty minutes." You now have an interesting dilemma. On the one hand, your desire to ease your financial concerns is strong and getting your hands on that much money may be very appealing. However, if your honesty value is stronger than your desire for the money, you won't rob the bank because you know it's not the right thing to do.

And even if your "friend" did a super sales job and actually convinced you to go ahead with the heist, afterwards you'd be churning inside. That's your honesty factor reacting. The guilt would haunt you forever.

When you harness your core values to positive, exciting, purposeful goals, decision-making becomes easy. There is no internal conflict holding you back—this creates an energy surge that will propel you to much higher levels of success.

7. Your goals must be well balanced and integrated.

If you had to live your life over again, what would you do differently? When people in their eighties are asked this question, they never say, "I'd spend more time at the office," or "I'd go to more board meetings."

No, instead they clearly indicate they'd travel more, spend more time with their family and have a lot more fun. So when you're setting goals make sure you include areas that give you time to relax and enjoy the finer things in life. Working yourself to a standstill every week is a surefire way to create burnout and ill health. Life's too short to miss the good stuff.

8. Your goals must be realistic.

At first this sounds contradictory to the previous comments about thinking big. However, a measure of reality will ensure that you get better results. Where most people are unrealistic about their goals is in determining the amount of time it will take to achieve them. Make a point of remembering this important sentence:

THERE ARE NO SUCH THINGS
AS UNREALISTIC GOALS, ONLY
UNREALISTIC TIME FRAMES.

If you're earning thirty-thousand dollars a year and your goal is to be a millionaire in three months, that's definitely unrealistic. When it comes to new business ventures, a good rule of thumb is to double the time you think it will take for the initial start-up. Usually there are legal holdups, government red tape, financing challenges and a multitude of other things that tend to slow you down.

Sometimes people set goals that are pure fantasy. If you're four feet tall, you probably will never play professional basketball. So by all means think big and create an exciting picture of the future. Just make sure your plan isn't far-fetched and that you allow a realistic amount of time to get there.

9. Your goals must include contribution.

There's a well-known Bible phrase that says, "Whatever a man sows, that he will also reap." (Galatians 6:7). This is a fundamental truth. It seems if you hand out good things and you consistently sow well, your rewards are guaranteed. That's a pretty good deal, isn't it?

Unfortunately many people who strive for success—usually defined as money and things—miss the boat. There's just no time or room in their lives to give something back to society. Simply put, they are takers, not givers. And if you always keep taking, you will most certainly lose out in the long run.

Contribution can take many forms. You can give your time, your expertise and you can, of course, give financially. So make it a part of your ongoing goals program. And do it unconditionally. Don't expect a payback immediately. That will come in due course, often in the most unexpected ways.

10. Your goals need to be supported.

This last part of your goals checklist is controversial. There are three points of view. Some people advocate telling the whole world about what they are going to do. They rationalize that it makes them more accountable. It's pretty hard to back down when the world is watching to see if you'll really do what you said. There's a lot of pressure when you choose this strategy, and certain individuals thrive on it.

Dr. Robert H. Schuller is a good example. He told the world he was going to build a beautiful Crystal Cathedral in Garden Grove, California. At the time the projected cost was more than twenty million dollars. Many observers laughed and scoffed at his idea and said he couldn't do it. He went ahead and did it anyway—the Crystal Cathedral was dedicated debt-free. The cost? Just under thirty million dollars.

One of Schuller's comments said it all "I think when you have big dreams you attract other big dreamers." And he did. In fact, several people donated more than one million dollars each to help the project succeed.

Here's the second option. Set your own goals, keep them to yourself and get on with the job. Actions speak louder than words, and you'll surprise a lot of people.

Third, and this may be the wisest strategy. Selectively share your dreams with a few people you trust. These are carefully chosen proactive individuals who will support and encourage you when the going gets tough. And if you have big plans you'll need their help, because you are bound to run into a few roadblocks along the way.

"... And that, in a nutshell, is my marketing plan.
Any questions?"

Note: This cartoon is actually a pretty accurate picture of some people's marketing plans. They are literally all over the map! The same applies to setting goals. We've seen many businesspeople with their goals scribbled illegibly on notepads and scraps of paper. They jot down any idea that comes into their heads. There is no system, no clear definition of what they really want. Then we have the people who love to play with the latest mind-mapping software. Give them an hour and they'll create a mass of "tentacles" that crawl right off the screen. As the cartoon shows, it's all a big blur. Designing the life of your dreams deserves a little more attention and planning than that, don't you agree?

Your Master PLAN

Now that we have laid the groundwork, it's time to get started on your own master plan. This is the exciting part—actually creating your better future, and the clarity to go with it. This is your big picture. There are six major steps. We suggest you read through all six first and then set time aside to implement each strategy.

1. Review the Top-10 Goals Checklist.

Use this checklist as your frame of reference when you sit down to create your actual goals. It will help you design a crystal-clear picture. It is summarized on page 90.

2. Decide What You Want to Accomplish and Why.

To get your juices flowing, make a list of all the things you want to accomplish in the next five years. Have fun with this, and open your mind to all the possibilities. Create a childlike enthusiasm—do not place any restrictions on your thinking. Be specific and personalize your list by starting each sentence with "I am" or "I will." For example—"I am taking six weeks vacation every year." or "I will save or invest 10 percent of my net income every month." To help you, here are a few important questions to help you focus:

- What do I want to do?

- What do I want to have?

- Where do I want to go?

- What contribution do I want to make?

- What do I want to become?

- What do I want to learn?

- Who do I want to spend my time with?

- How much do I want to earn, save and invest?

- How much time do I want off for fun?

- What will I do to create optimum health?

To ensure that you enjoy a healthy integrated lifestyle, choose some goals in each of the following areas—career and business, financial, fun time, health and fitness, relationships, personal, and contribution, plus any others that are of special significance to you.

Prioritizing your list

Now that you have stretched your imagination, the next step is to prioritize. Take a look at each of your goals and determine a realistic time frame for accomplishment.

Write a number beside each goal—one, three or five years. This will give you a general framework to work from.

In his great book, *The On-Purpose Person*, author Kevin W. McCarthy describes an excellent technique to help you prioritize. He calls it the tournament draw. This is a format used for all sorts of competitions—from spelling bees to tennis tournaments to the Super Bowl playoffs. Prioritize your choices by making separate draw sheets for your one-year, three-year and five-year goals.

THE MAIN DRAW[1]

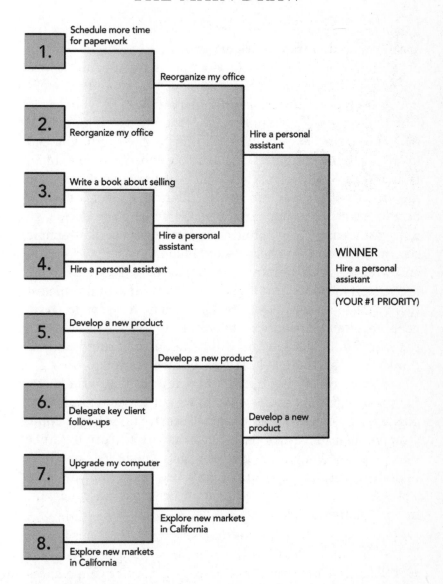

---

1 *The Main Draw concept: The On-Purpose Person, Kevin McCarthy, used by permission of NavPress. All rights reserved. 1-800-366-7788.*

THE MAIN DRAW

List each of your one-year goals on the left-hand side of the sheet. Make the draw sheet big enough to accommodate all of the items on your list—for example, sixteen or thirty-two lines deep. (We are assuming you will have more than eight one-year goals.) This is the preliminary draw. Now you decide which goals are most important; that is, which ones will move on to the next round. Repeat this process until you end up with the final eight. These have now become your Main Draw. Again, you must select which of these eight are more important, all the way through to the final winner. This will be your single most important priority. To help you decide, go with gut feeling. Your intuition is rarely wrong. This simple system forces you to choose what is most meaningful to you and what is less important. You can, of course, complete the less important goals later if you wish. Now repeat this for your three and five year goals. We know that these longer term goals are often more difficult to create. However, it's well worth the extra effort. Those years will be upon you faster than you think! Make sure you at least have a three year plan.

Here's one other vital tip: Before you prioritize, write down the most important reason that you want to accomplish each goal, and the biggest benefit you will receive upon completion.

As we mentioned before, big reasons are the driving force that keep you going when the going gets tough. It's a good use of your time to clearly identify your reasons before you start. This will ensure that your Main Draw goals really are the most important ones on your list.

3. Create Inspiring Pictures.
To improve your focus on the new lifestyle you want, create inspiring pictures of your most important goals. This is an enjoyable process and the whole family can join in.

The internet provides great resources for finding pictures. At websites such as gettyimages.com, you'll find thousands of photos. Just Google what you are looking for and select the images that suit you best.

For example, if a trip to Australia and New Zealand is one of your "must do" goals, find great pictures of what you want to see and the activities you'd like to enjoy. Create a Power Point display with your PC or use Keynote on Apple, using the various goal categories that are most important to you as a framework. You can also attach positive statements to these to give added emphasis to your pictures, such as "I am enjoying a one-month vacation with my family in Australia and New Zealand." Include the date you want to go. Look at your pictures often to actively engage your subconscious. Believe, with all the emotion and passion you can muster, that your goals will be achieved.

See it—Believe it—Achieve it!

MARK:

In terms of following through on your vision, I've met many people who have done this through one of my most passionate projects called *The Richest Kids in America*. I've interviewed 101 smart, profitable young entrepreneurs who are out there blazing their own trails of success. They are all confident, forward-thinking goal setters who are making a significant impact in the world of entrepreneurship. Here's one example: Chauncey Cymone Holloman is a poet and lyricist who created her own company, Harlem Lyrics LLC, in 2003, at the age of fifteen. Her business today is worth $1.2 million.

Chauncey says, "The idea for unique greeting cards for teens came to me when I was shopping for a greeting card for my best friend. I wanted a special card for her because she was turning sixteen and I wanted something to say exactly how much she meant to me and how close we were. I went from card to card and they were either way too mature with a very, very adult mind-set or they were very, very immature. So I went to my mom that night and told her about this huge gap in greeting cards. There are no greeting cards specifically for teenagers, and especially urban teenagers. She told me that this sounded like a good idea and a good concept and she told me to submit to her a business plan. I was fifteen at that time, so of course I did not know what a business plan was, but I looked up the definition and later I handed one to her. It is pretty much how Harlem Lyrics got started."

Harlem Lyrics was created to express exactly how teens view the world. The cards capture the "voice" or vernacular of today's youth by embedding popular slang in its content. Chauncey says, "It is my dream that through the voices of my characters, we will inspire and empower more young girls to find their voices." Chauncey created five teen characters whose voices echo the personalities of mainstream urban youth.

She says, "Harlem Lyrics got part of its name from the Harlem Renaissance Era, which put a worldwide spotlight on the 'voice' of Black America. Lyrics was derived from the lyrical writings of the hip hop era, which continued in the spirit of highlighting our views about self, others, and relationships. From our content and illustrations, we bring to you the undeniable swagger of hip hop."

The company, based in Arkansas, started out as an Afro-centric greeting company. Today, it is a gift, fashion, and entertainment business focused on trendy and urban themed products. From her funky colorful website, (officialharlemlyrics.com), to clear business principles and strategies, Chauncey Holloman is a young woman who knows what she wants and is making it happen. Her motto is: **"Be Bold! Express yourself. Find out what your God-given talent is and make it profitable."**

Chauncey was able to see the bigger picture when confronted with this opportunity. She was not finding what she needed or wanted as a consumer. This was a problem to her and she figured to other teenagers as well. Looking at it from the perspective of wanting to solve it, she had her big idea moment. She became the solution.

I have heard many people say, "I had that same idea" when a new problem-solving concept, product, or business is revealed to the public. And I always say, "I am sure you did. But you continued to let it be a problem. Why is that?" Most people will come up with a list of excuses and I just chuckle to myself because I know firsthand what it takes to be an enlightened thinker and problem solver.

Now, here are the three remaining strategies to help you create unusual clarity.

4. Capture your Best Ideas

Create a special file on your laptop, tablet, or smart phone where you can store your best ideas and insights. The founder of The Virgin Group of Companies, Richard Branson, just uses a little notebook to scribble down his thoughts. This is a powerful way to expand your awareness. Did you ever have a big idea in the middle of the night? You sit straight up in bed and your mind is racing. Usually you only have a few seconds to capture that idea before you lose it, or your body says, "Go back to sleep; it's three o'clock in the morning!" In fact, you may drift back to sleep, wake up hours later and have completely forgotten what your great idea was.

A BRILLIANT IDEA WITHOUT ACTION IS LIKE ROGER FEDERER[2] PLAYING TENNIS WITHOUT A RACQUET!

This is why capturing ideas is so valuable. By recording your best thoughts you never need to rely on your memory. You can review your ideas any time you want. Use this for business ideas, sales tips, presentation skills, money-making projects, quotes you have read, or stories that will help you explain something better. Just keep your ears and eyes open every day and listen to your own intuition.

For example, if you have just finished a great sales presentation where everything went exactly as planned and you closed a big deal, capture your best thoughts. What did you say that worked so well? Maybe you asked a specific question that prompted the buying decision, or gave a better explanation of your benefits and services. Replay the presentation in your mind and capture what worked.

It's also beneficial to record or video your presentation. Invite someone who you really respect to go over it with you and then you can brainstorm how to improve it. Keep practicing. Movie star Robin Williams averages thirty takes per scene, until both he and the director are satisfied with his performance.

Did you ever screw up an important presentation? That's also a good time to capture your thoughts on what you did wrong. You might highlight these and add, "Never say this again!" In both examples, by writing down your thoughts while they are fresh in your mind, you reinforce what worked and what didn't work. This gives you incredible clarity.

Here's another valuable suggestion to heighten your awareness. First thing in the morning, for five minutes, record your

---

2 *Roger Federer currently holds the record for most major titles on the Professional Tennis Association circuit, sixteen in total.*

feelings. Words to describe feelings include anxious, sad, happy, excited, bored, angry, enthusiastic, frustrated, energized. Write in the present tense as if you are having a conversation with yourself. Use "I" language: "I am feeling anxious today because my daughter is driving on her own for the first time," or "I feel excited because I'm starting a new job this morning." When you consistently get in touch with your feelings you are more connected to everyday situations and more aware of what's really going on in your life.

5. Visualize, Think, Reflect, and Review.

The power of visualization is often seen in sports. Olympic athletes mentally run the event in their minds several times just before they perform. They totally focus on a positive result.

Olympic gold medalist Mark Tewksbury, the Canadian who won the 200-meter backstroke swim at the 1992 Olympic Games in Barcelona, Spain, actually stood on the winners' podium on the eve of the race and visualized a come-from-behind winning performance. He heard the roar of the crowd, could see where his family was sitting in the stands and saw himself triumphantly accepting the gold medal. The next day he swam the race exactly as imagined and won by a fingertip!

Remember, if you copy the techniques of champions you too can become a champion. Use your positive imagination to create these winning pictures.

The sharper these images are and the more intense you feel, the more likely you are to create the desired result. It's a powerful process. So follow through with this and you'll find this clarity will give you a distinct edge in the marketplace.

6. Develop Mentors.

Another wonderful way to ensure major improvements in your productivity and vision is to enlist the aid of people who have vast experience in areas where you need the most help.

When you surround yourself with a carefully chosen team of experts, your learning curve increases rapidly. Very few people do this consistently. Again, if you dare to be different you'll reap the rewards down the road. The alternative is to figure everything out yourself using trial and error. It's a slow way to move forward because you run into many roadblocks and distractions. On the other hand, cultivating advice and wisdom from specific mentors propels you to faster results. You'll learn all about this in Chapter 5, Building Excellent Relationships.

Insights

We are still amazed at the number of people from all walks of life who spend little or no time designing their future. More accurately, many people don't know how. They don't have a process or a system to guide them. And they allow their busyness to become an excuse for not taking the time to learn how to plan ahead. If anything is backward, that line of thinking certainly is!

What we've observed more recently, however, is the fact that those who do set clear goals often don't have enough desire, drive and persistence, when it comes to following through.

The truth is, we need to be inspired for those important attributes to kick in. As Dr. Wayne Dyer says, "Inspiration is when an idea takes hold of you and moves you to a place you were meant to be. Motivation is when you have an idea and your Ego is what's pushing you to achieve the goal." This is a very important, yet subtle, distinction.

When you are truly inspired, your energy flows almost effortlessly. You will experience joy in the challenge and the doing. Roadblocks often melt away. The right people will show up to guide you and help you along.

One of the critical aspects of gaining inspiration is to create a quiet time. As author Fran Hewitt says in her gift book for women,

The Ego and the Spirit, "Our inner guidance sits in the silence waiting for us to turn down the noise. Follow what your Spirit says, instead of listening to your perfectionist Ego."

Whether you need inspiration to reach another level in your career or business, or become a better spouse, friend, or parent, we know from our own experiences that the most valuable source of ideas comes from inside, when we are tuned in, receptive, and alert. Turning off the noise and being still, accelerates this process.

When this new state of awareness is practiced you will start receiving "flashes" or "insights" that are important. These need to be acted on immediately because they are usually a vital step in helping you get what you want. For example, you may have a strong feeling to call your best friend and you do, only to learn that she was in a serious car accident and the sound of your voice was really comforting. Or, you have this urge to contact a client you haven't heard from in six months and they are ready to place a large order with your company. Don't hesitate when you receive those insights. They are unusual moments of clarity and can disappear as fast as they first surfaced.

To make this easier, develop the habit of turning down the pervasive noise of life every week. Schedule some quiet time to meditate, reflect, or just be still in the silence.

"IF YOU GO TO WORK ON YOUR GOALS,
YOUR GOALS WILL GO TO WORK ON YOU.
IF YOU GO TO WORK ON YOUR PLAN, YOUR PLAN
WILL GO TO WORK ON YOU. WHATEVER GOOD
THINGS WE BUILD, END UP BUILDING US."

—Jim Rohn

ACTION STEPS

The Top-10 Goals Checklist

Know what you
want and why

Capture your Best Ideas

The Top-10 Goals Checklist
To maximize your results, remember your goals must be:

1. Yours.
2. Meaningful.
3. Specific and measurable.
4. Flexible.
5. Challenging and exciting.
6. In alignment with your core values.
7. Well balanced and integrated
8. Contributing to society.
9. Realistic.
10. Supported.

LIST YOUR CORE VALUES BELOW:

e.g., Honesty, integrity, strong family, faith, creativity, independence.
As much as possible, align your goals with your core values.

_____

_____

_____

Know what you want and why

Use the questions below to help you clarify and prioritize your goals.

- What do I want to do?
- What do I want to have?
- Where do I want to go?
- What contribution do I want to make?
- What do I want to become?
- What do I want to learn?
- Who do I want to spend my time with?
- How much do I want to earn, save and invest?
- How much time do I want off for fun?
- What will I do to create optimum health?

To ensure that you enjoy a healthy integrated lifestyle, choose some goals in each of the following areas—career/business, financial, fun time, health/fitness, relationships, personal and contribution, plus any others that are of special significance.

We strongly recommend that you schedule at least one full day to complete this critically important Action Step.

Capture your Best Ideas

Review step four. To do this, use your PDA, laptop, notebook, or an elaborate engraved journal. Develop the habit of capturing your best ideas, thoughts and insights. This is not a "Dear Diary." Use it for business strategies, money-making ideas, stories that illustrate a point, marketing concepts and whatever else you think is important. If you enjoy structure, create tabs for specific topics. The most important thing, however, is to train yourself to start writing. Start this week.

LIVING AND WORKING ON PURPOSE

TAKING DECISIVE ACTION

CONSISTENT PERSISTENCE

ASK FOR WHAT YOU WANT

THE CONFIDENCE FACTOR

BUILDING EXCELLENT RELATIONSHIPS

OVERCOMING SETBACKS

DO YOU SEE THE BIG PICTURE?

IT'S NOT HOCUS-POCUS, IT'S ALL ABOUT FOCUS

YOUR HABITS WILL DETERMINE YOUR FUTURE

You've built a solid foundation—well done!

Overcoming Setbacks

"YOU'RE A WINNER. THE TESTS OF LIFE ARE NOT MEANT TO BREAK YOU, BUT TO MAKE YOU."

—Norman Vincent Peale

Have you ever experienced a sudden or unexpected reversal in fortune?

For example, you got hit with a surprise tax bill that crushed your profits for the year, or the bank called your loan because you missed a few payments, and they panicked. At least, that's your story!

And sometimes the stock market falls out of the sky overnight and 25 percent of your net worth disappears. We have all experienced setbacks at some point in business. Over the long haul it's just part of the game. Markets go up and markets go down. Recessions roll in and out; we can even track them in detail for the last hundred years.

In this chapter you'll learn why some people handle setbacks successfully, whereas others often quit. We'll also dig deeper into different aspects of focus and how those can derail you even further when facing a setback. And of course we'll discuss a few of our own personal experiences along with other enterprising souls who have turned their setbacks into huge victories.

There are two polar opposite choices you can make when confronting a setback or crisis.

1. Embrace the challenge with a "bring-it-on" attitude.
2. Bury your head in the sand and hope it all goes away.

People with the first approach seem to actually relish challenges that force them to stretch and test their capacity. Others, when faced with a crisis just decide to make the best of it, even if they don't have all the answers or an action plan. It's one step at a time and let's see where the next step leads. The second approach is reserved for those who simply won't respond to any type of challenge and unfortunately suffer the consequences later.

Our friend W. Mitchell certainly wasn't expecting his life to change dramatically as an outgoing young man who loved his job as a grip man on the famous San Francisco cable cars. At age twenty-eight, he was good looking, single and enjoyed daily interaction with the tourists. Mitchell had a couple of specific goals he was working on. One was to obtain his pilots' license and the other was to buy a beautiful big Honda motorcycle. Finally, he reached the point where these two goals came to fruition in one memorable day.

That day, after completing several flying lessons, was the day he got to fly solo—no instructor, just himself, the plane and a big sky to explore. Mitchell completed his flight, no problem, and was exhilarated after a successful landing. He then enjoyed a leisurely ride on his new shiny motorcycle into town. What a day this was turning out to be!

While going through a green light at an intersection, Mitchell didn't see the laundry truck that smashed into him, hurling him and his motorcycle underneath the vehicle. In seconds the gas cap came off and the mixture of fuel and heat ignited Mitchell in a ball of fire. He would have died if not for the brave intervention of a car salesman standing at the corner, who ran furiously from the dealership with a fire extinguisher and put out the flames. Mitchell was rushed to the hospital with serious injuries. His face had been burned off and his hands were reduced to stumps. A life that had looked so promising had almost been snuffed out in seconds. Several months ensued during which Mitchell experienced a very painful and slow rehabilitation process. Plastic surgery was required to rebuild his face. The burns to his body were so severe that wearing any sort of clothing was torturous to his sensitive skin.

But, despite all of this, Mitchell was alive. There were other challenging situations such as school children taunting him with cries of "Monster! Monster!" as he walked by the school yard. Mitchell had a new life, a very different one from his original dreams and aspirations.

He moved to a little town in Colorado called Crested Butte and by sheer determination managed to get his private pilot's license restored. So life was getting better. Mitchell went into business with two friends and started Vermont Castings, ironically a wood burning stove company! The business was very successful and Mitchell became chairman of the Board. One cold, crisp winter day, four and a half years after the fiery crash in San Francisco, Mitchell took a few friends for a ride in a plane. However, just after the aircraft lifted into the air, Mitchell knew something was wrong; the plane wasn't flying properly. It stalled, meaning the wings actually stopped flying, and instead of Mitchell being able to make an emergency landing, the plane just fell back onto the runway. Fearing fire, he urged his passengers to get out quick, which they did, but the pain in Mitchell's back prevented him from joining them. It turned out he was paralyzed and was told he'd never walk again!

How would you react in Mitchell's situation? Is this fair? One tragic accident is bad enough, but to be slammed with another debilitating experience would be too much for most people.

Mitchell says it was more than tough. Here's the aftermath of that event. W. Mitchell went on to be elected mayor of Crested Butte. The campaign button he wore on his lapel read, "Not just a pretty face!" He then won a famous victory over the world's biggest mining company by preventing them from destroying the beautiful mountain that was a backdrop to the town. W. Mitchell went on to host his own radio show and now travels all over the world inspiring audiences with his timeless message:

"It's not what happens to you, it's what you do about it that counts."

His book with the same title, is a must read. You'll find it at www.wmitchell.com.

Oh, and in case you're wondering what the initial "W" stands for, Mitchell's response is—"Wonderful!"

Cultivate a Champion Mind-set

As Mitchell's incredible story proves, you can find another way to live your life, even when you feel like you've been knocked senseless. Mitchell looked at life this way: "Before my accident, I used to be able to do 10,000 things. Now I can only do 9,000. I choose to focus on the 9,000 that I can still do and let go of the 1,000 that are no longer available to me." Many people would do the opposite with a lesser setback. They'd spend years lamenting what they had lost and lose sight of the fact they still had other options. Others allow the unexpected to blight their progress in sales.

> **LES**
> I once talked to a young realtor who had two good sales almost wrapped up, towards the end of the month. In fact, he was so confident the transactions would close, he had spent a good chunk of the anticipated commission earnings before the papers were signed. Not a good plan! Both deals fell apart. I asked him how long it took him to recover from this setback. His answer shocked me. He said, "Almost a full month."
> In contrast, I spoke to the number one performing realtor in the same office, who had held that title for two consecutive years. When I relayed the story about losing two deals in a month, and asked what his recovery time would be, his response was: "Naturally I'd be disappointed, but within twenty-four hours, I'd be out making calls again." Big difference!

What is your typical response time when faced with a similar situation? Too long? Or do you bounce back on your feet fast? Your bounce-back ability has a lot to do with your future success. There's one thing we know for certain. If you have big dreams and big goals, you will hit some big roadblocks. People with great bounce-back ability have champion mindsets. In other words, they think differently compared to average performers. And when it comes to results, they far outdistance those average performers.

So how do you cultivate a champion mindset? As we discussed in the last chapter, you must have big reasons to succeed. Setting goals is important but why those goals are important to you is a major factor when it comes to achieving them.

Consider Lance Armstrong, professional cyclist, who successfully battled cancer and went on to win seven consecutive Tour de France championships, the most grueling and competitive cycling competition in the world. To this date, that record has never been beaten and maybe never will. When asked if he would rather be known as a cancer survivor or a record-winning athlete, Lance indicated that his victory over a fast growing cancer was a lot more meaningful. His "why" was to prove to the world that with discipline, determination and commitment, you could conquer the biggest challenges that life serves up. And by doing so, hopefully inspire others to achieve their own victories. That's a big WHY!

As Pastor Andy Stanley says, "When your vision is clear, you limit your options and your decisions become easy." In other words, you have left little choice but to push forward and eventually succeed. When you have a champion mindset, decisions are easier when faced with a setback because there's no way you are giving up on your goal. Champions treat challenges like a contest, one they are determined to win. (You'll learn more strategies about this in Chapter 8, Consistent Persistence.)

Overcoming Recessionitis

Setbacks occur in many forms. They can threaten your health, your relationships, your financial security, and of course your career or business. Often the elephant in the room shows up as a full blown recession. The economy tanks and suddenly jobs, real estate and under-capitalized businesses get hit like a tsunami—full force! And surprisingly few people see the warning signs.

As authors of this book and risk-taking entrepreneurs, we've all made some bad decisions. And sometimes the economy has floored us with a sucker punch we didn't see coming.

LES:

In 1980, I was doing great working as an independent distributor for an international direct sales company. I had broken the company's sales records and been the number one distributor in the country for three consecutive months. As a result, my wife Fran and I won several trips to exotic locations in France, the Bahamas and California. And the money was a blessing—my income had soared in the last eighteen months. Overall, life was very good.

Two years later, the company I worked with had hit the skids. Another recession had rocked the economy with interest rates sitting at 22 percent toward the end of that year. I had to close my office, even though there were still four years left on the lease, and the landlord wasn't prepared to let me walk away without payment. After jumping through hoops to solve that particular challenge, I ended up working with an executive search company as a commission-based consultant. Within six months they went into receivership and I was on the street, out of a job.

My wife wasn't working either. We had a three-year-old daughter and a three-month-old baby boy to care for as well. What do you do when your world collapses? You focus on practical solutions, instead of becoming sick with worry and constantly fighting negative emotions. Worry only creates more tension and that never produces the creativity required to get back on your feet again.

My wonderful mentor, Jim Rohn, who gave me great advice over many years, suggested one strategy that was life changing. He said, "Make a list of ten options to improve your situation. Force yourself to come up with ten and put them in writing. The first two or three may not be what you want to do, however, keep going and you may have a great idea when you get to number eight or nine."

I followed Jim's advice, spending a couple of hours in my basement late one night, racking my brains to complete my list. Sure enough, just as he said, a big idea popped out towards the end of my list. It was a business called Achievers Canada and from that moment of desperation, the idea blossomed and I was able to build one of the largest seminar companies in the country. This provided me and my family with multiple revenue sources and a wealth of knowledge that became a major stepping stone for the work I do today. Use the Action Steps section at the end of this chapter to formulate your own ten best options list.

Here's what I learned. We have a far greater capacity to survive and thrive than you can ever imagine. Tough times challenge you to step up and dig deep into that inner sanctum, where new ideas lie waiting for you to bring them to life. Don't let a few roadblocks stop you from creating the life you deserve. Rise to the challenge and blast through them!

Recession
WARNING SIGNS

- **The stock market has been buoyant for too long** with many companies having a super-high paper value but no real profits. A correction is bound to happen. Think: the dot com bubble in 2000–2001.

- **You and your team have become complacent, lulled into a false sense of security.** You haven't noticed the shifting sands of change that could sink your product or service. Think, digital technology swallowing up the video tape and DVD industry.

- **Debt loads are unreasonably high** in business and in personal households. Unmanageable debt in the last few years has brought countries such as Greece, Italy, Ireland and even the United States to their knees.

- **Governments ignore the mounting debt crisis despite the warnings.** When trillions becomes a mainstream word, look out! If you were thirty years old and someone gave you a dollar every second, it would take fifty two years before you received one trillion dollars—mind boggling!

- **When major corporations are focused on greed, the consequences are inevitable.** Hello, Lehmann Brothers, WorldCom, Enron and a host of others who ended up in the corporate graveyard. Unfortunately the victims are usually everyday taxpayers who had little or no say in the matter.

When you boil it all down, it's apparent that **a lack of focus** is at the core of any recession. When your focus is centered on the wrong things—ego, politicking and lining your own pockets—you automatically hit the off switch for what you should be focused on, that is, adding real value to the people you serve in the form of excellent products and services.

Recession BUSTERS

Here are a few storm-proofing strategies to better prepare you for the next recession. Yes, there will be another one—check your history.

- **Build reserves**
  Don't put up with a feast or famine existence—you're smarter than that! People who weather the recessionary storms have developed the habit of saving or investing a healthy percentage—20 percent or more—of their profits. Remember Peter Daniel's story in Chapter 3? He went broke three times in five years. That was enough. Solid reserves are now a major plank in his international business fortress. You do the same.

- **Learn your lessons and don't repeat your mistakes**
  When you are in the eye of the storm and your financial ship is being beaten and battered, you probably aren't too focused on the lessons you need to learn. You're just trying to survive. Understandable. However, at a later date, make sure you do figure out what you could have done better and use it wisely.

- **Be alert**

  Like a captain on a ship you must be looking ahead for any sign of trouble. One reason why the Titanic sank on her maiden voyage in 1912 was due to the fact there were no binoculars available for the man whose job was to watch out for icebergs. Don't be unprepared. Talk to experienced people. Read relevant articles in your industry. Discuss the trends. In business, leaders sink or swim based on their ability to accurately predict the future.

- **Avoid negative news**

  The media and naysayers love negative news. A recession to them is like going to a banquet with an unlimited supply of food. Don't join the line up! Focusing on the recession only helps to create the recession. Instead, focus on not participating.

- **Trust your intuition**

  Sometimes, too much consensus divides opinions to the point where poor decisions or no decisions are made. Not good! Go with your gut when you feel the need to make course corrections, especially if you are in charge. If you need to persuade the decision maker, deliver a compelling, emotional presentation backed up with irrefutable evidence.

- **Stick to your knitting—avoid bright shiny objects!**

  When you expand too quickly or diversify too much, you can be stretched so thin that you become extremely vulnerable to a turbulent economy. Think Warren Buffet and other stalwarts who stick to what they know best. You don't need to jump on every new opportunity that comes along. This is difficult for entrepreneurs because a boring profitable business quickly loses its excitement. All of us like adventure, living on the edge, even if it costs us in the end. Say no more!

In America, 13.5 million days of work are lost per year due to work related depression, stress and anxiety.

On the surface, it's easy to see why recessions cause stress. However, there may be deeper reasons for this, too.

JACK:
Experiencing a turbulent economy is stressful. I know. I've been there more than once—it's *really* stressful!

The mental stress that occurs is often created by having negative beliefs. These are usually "shoulds" or "should-nots" that block the natural flow of your energy, and that becomes stressful. I'll give you an example. I had a student, who as a child, heard her Dad talking about how things were difficult and they might not be able to feed all the children in the family, because there was a recession in England. She decided at the age of six that she was going to be one of the ones that got fed. Her Dad was just blowing off steam, but she heard it and her little mind went, "Oh my God, if he's not going to feed all the kids, I want to be one of the ones he feeds." So she became the perfect exemplary child. She got A's in school, took all the extracurricular activities in high school—became student president, did volunteer work, made her bed, cleaned up after herself in the kitchen, dressed nicely, but underneath she was a nervous wreck! She was always afraid something bad was going to happen, if she wasn't good.

When I was counseling with her awhile ago, I said, "What would you like to achieve from this coaching program?" and she said, "I want to get more done." I said, "Tell me about your life as it is now." She explained that she had three different jobs and was on five boards of directors. I said, "I have a shocking possibility for you. I don't think your life is about getting more done. I think it's about exploring why you think you have to get so much done in the first place, and perhaps lopping off some of it so you can have a life." We did an age regression technique where she went back to age six and remembered the event with her parents during the recession. She was able to realize how bad a decision that was to make at the age of six. She then made a new decision that she didn't have to be perfect in order to succeed in the world. She resigned from three boards and dropped one of her jobs. Now she's much happier and a lot more balanced.

Letting go of limiting beliefs about who you should or shouldn't be is really important. Sometimes it's imposed by our parents that you should be this way. Sometimes it's an inner decision you make on your own. There's so much stress in the world right now. We see it when the economy slows. We see it in road rage. We see it in over-population.

I went to New York a couple of years ago. I was there for three days and I was starting to go really crazy because of all the horns honking and people screaming at each other! You get in a taxi and it's not moving. You're late for a sales appointment, when every deal is vital. I went to a yoga class on the third day. We meditated for ten minutes at the end. When I walked out, horns were still blowing but to me it was just background noise. I was so relaxed I wanted to hug the bus driver! So it's not the stressor—it's our response to it. Thinking we have to get there on time or something bad will happen creates stress. We really need to release the stressful thinking. Bryon Katie's book, *Loving What Is,* is really helpful. You can download free worksheets on her website; www.thework.com.

If the turbulence in your life seems too much; stop, breathe, pause and read this:

Reverse Living

Life is tough.
It takes up a lot of your time, all your weekends,
And what do you get at the end of it?
. . . death, a great reward.
I think the life cycle is all backwards.
You should die first; get it out of the way.
Then you should live twenty years in an old-age home.
You get kicked out when you're too young,
you get a gold watch, you go to work.
You work for forty years until you're
young enough to enjoy your retirement.
You go to college, you party until you're ready for high school,
You become a little kid, you play, you have no responsibilities,
you become a little boy or girl, you go back into the womb,
you spend your last nine months floating.
And you finish off as a gleam in someone's eye.

—*Norman Glass*

Source: *Chicken Soup for the College Soul*

Are you smiling now? Oh come on, just a little smile. Put some humor in your life and your stress will start to dissolve.

Special Note: Understand that these warning signs and strategies to keep you out of trouble also apply to your personal and family life as well as your business or career. Be vigilant on all fronts.

MARK:

A lot of people ask about the cause of The Great Recession in 2008. My take on it is, there was no accountability and no responsibility from people who were self-interested at the top of the corporate money tree. Two must-see movies that will really open your eyes to this are *Inside Job* and *Too Big to Fail*. I believe the impact of this economic shake up has caused some good things to happen. People are finally realizing if you are suffocating in debt, way over your head, that's the road to ruin. As my friend Peter Daniels says, "Unhealthy debt binds people and destroys initiative." So take responsibility. Educate yourself financially. Learn how to manage your cash flow. Don't be lulled into bad decisions by taking bad advice from people with no real experience.

Schwadron is reprinted with permission from cartoonstock.com

Find Another WAY

Sometimes a setback can appear like an unscalable mountain and you don't have the equipment or the fortitude to start the climb. For example, your company folds or you suddenly lose your job and months later you are still unemployed. It's easy to stay stuck. The bigger danger is that the emotional stress becomes greater and self-worth issues come to the forefront. Tension at home rises, arguments ensue and with no obvious solutions in sight, life can become pretty miserable. Compound these events with a home foreclosure notice from the bank and now life seems totally unfair. This is where resentment and rage can eliminate solution-based thinking. You've had enough. This isn't right. Why me?

In that case, the reality is you've got to find another way. Step back, regroup, refocus and retrain for another opportunity, if necessary. Understand you may need to take three steps backwards before you can move forward in a new direction. As described earlier, look at ten possible options. That's a great place to start. Here's another technique we've used successfully to conquer setbacks.

The Problem SOLVER

This is a ten step process in a logical order that starts with clearly defining your challenge and concludes with a victory celebration. That's how confident we are that The Problem Solver really does what it says.

All of the steps are laid out for you to work through in the Action Steps at the end of this chapter. The main reason for writing this book was to give you practical resources that have been tested in the real world of business and everyday life. Please test them yourself instead of embarking on a whole trial and error expedition which might take you around in circles, instead of climbing your mountain. All of us have played that game before. As you'll learn in Chapter 5, there are smarter ways to get things done. Using the leverage of other people's experience is one of them.

Surrender to a Higher Power

LES:

The look on the surgeon's face said it all. Avoiding eye contact, he slowly said, "I'm afraid it's cancer. And the prognosis isn't good, with so many lymph nodes positive—two to five years!" I stood there in disbelief. My thirty-three-year-old, wonderful wife Fran, had just been given a death sentence. The biopsy results told the truth. Indisputable. This wasn't in our plans. My fledgling seminar business was just starting to thrive, our kids were three and six years old, and we had lots to look forward to. Now what? If you've been in a similar situation, you know that fear washes over you pretty fast. Fear of the unknown. What do we do? Who can help? Is this really happening?

In the months that followed, Fran was a champion. She took on the challenge, researching alternative therapies, undergoing radiation and chemotherapy, fighting the mental demons that sought to extinguish her hope.

One day it was all too much to bear. As she attempted to have a nap in the bedroom, she described what happened: "I was literally shivering with fear about the thought of leaving my family. My eyes were closed but I was fully conscious. I started praying to God, asking for help to at least not be burdening my family with a long, drawn-out illness. Within five minutes I felt a strong sensation, like someone was wrapping me in a warm protective blanket, starting at my feet and slowly covering my body. Then a wonderful calm came over me and I felt strong. It was as if someone had whispered, 'It's okay, you'll be all right. Move on with your life.' So I did."

People of faith call this divine intervention. All I know is that miracles do happen and we were the grateful benefactors at the time. That was twenty-five years ago and we are both thankful for every new day.

Be PREPARED!

This famous Boy Scouts motto sends a strong message to everyone who may be on the verge of business, personal or financial turbulence. There are two realities here. For clarity, let's use an airline pilot's example. All pilots receive weather warnings before takeoff or during flight. If you fly often, you've likely heard this message from the flight deck. "Looks like we're in for a little bit of a bumpy ride, so please fasten your seat belts and stow your tray tables until the seat belt sign is turned off."

As passengers, we're now prepared for some turbulence. Usually it's not that bad and sometimes we hardly notice any change at all because the pilot announces later that he or she made a few adjustments and was able to rise above the storm clouds or detour around them. If there was a big storm brewing directly ahead, you're thankful that the pilot was thinking quickly to avert potential danger. In these situations the pilot has control. Are you as prepared as those pilots are when they take to the skies? Do you stop to check if you are on track each week, pausing long enough to see if there are any storm clouds on the horizon at home or at work, so you can make the necessary corrections well in advance? Don't allow your busyness to weaken your defenses or lessen your awareness. Be prepared!

The second reality is, sometimes in life we don't receive any warnings. We have no control. Have you ever been on a flight and suddenly the plane dropped thirty feet? Talk about panic! Did the plane stall? Are we going down? And there's nothing you can do. Here's the message:

EXPECT THE UNEXPECTED.
Focus on what you can control and acknowledge what's out of your control.

In business, we see a lot of people stewing over things they cannot prevent. This creates much discussion around the water cooler. Don't waste your time and energy. If you're not the boss and head office keeps making changes you don't like, either suck it up or find another opportunity with a better environment. On some occasions there are extenuating circumstances that motivate certain people to turn the old rules upside down.

Luan Mitchell, no relation to W. Mitchell who you read about earlier, is a remarkable woman who has faced plenty of her own setbacks.

The last born of five children, with a nineteen-year spread between the first and herself, Luan started waitressing at the age of twelve at one of her mother's restaurants. Later she became a competitive gymnast and in her early twenties won a beauty pageant as well as volunteering regularly in her local community soup kitchen and at church events.

Luan met and married Fred Mitchell, a businessman who ran a family meat packing company and was fourteen years older than herself. Fred had a big vision for expanding the company, but just before they were married Fred was diagnosed with cystic fibrosis, which is often terminal in young adults. This was devastating news and made worse with the knowledge that they most likely couldn't have children. Plus, Fred's ability to continue as CEO of the business looked short term at best.

This created major ripples of concern in Fred's family. What happens if Fred dies? Would Luan, an inexperienced outsider, get the company?

Before the wedding, Luan signed a prenuptial agreement that in effect shut her out of the business. Not a great start to married life! Their honeymoon was spent in the hospital. Fred's health quickly deteriorated. One ray of sunshine was, Luan had a very healthy nine pound baby boy and would later be blessed with two more children. She also became a daily caregiver, learning to do all of the percussion therapy that was required to clear Fred's lungs three or four times a day. One night as she was lying in bed nursing her baby son, she felt something warm on her right shoulder. It was blood. She looked over and Fred was hemorrhaging badly. At the hospital, the staff basically threw up their arms and said, "This guy is not going to make it." And Fred said, or rather gurgled, "I'm not going anywhere. I have things to do!" Seeing his determination changed Luan's life.

Miraculously, Fred ended up having a heart and double lung transplant. He donated his healthy heart to a fifty-two-year-old woman, saying later that Luan was the only woman in the world who literally allowed her husband to give his heart to another woman! That sense of humor and willpower helped Fred and Luan through a very tough battle.

During all of this, another battle for control of the business was going on with the family. This erupted into an ugly lawsuit that dragged on for two years. At the end of the first year, although back on his feet, Fred was broke and out of a job. He and his young family drove from state to state in their van, desperately looking for work. Finally, the legal settlement gave Fred half of the company and he immediately placed Luan on the Board of Directors. The company was teetering on bankruptcy. Fred was determined to rebuild, then the next setback arrived without warning. The bank called their 33 million dollar line of credit!

Let's pause here for a minute. What would you do in this situation? Fred's health was still a big issue and Luan had no business experience. And now the wolves were at their door looking for the scraps.

In Luan's words, here's what happened:

"We hit the road and sold our story to potential investors, anyone who believed in us. One day the banker came to put the key in the lock and close the company.

They had aimed their financial bazooka at us and our hard working employees. Well, they had to take that key right back, because to their shock, we presented them with a check for 33 million dollars! Fred won the Turnaround Entrepreneur of the Year award by Ernst and Young. We were getting ready to accept that award, and he went for a health check-up. And he died—suddenly he died! I put my fist through the wall. I thought somebody had hit me with a cosmic two by four, right between the eyes."

Now what? Would *you* have thrown in the towel here and finally surrendered?

Fighters don't quit. If anything, this made Luan more determined to succeed, if for no other reason than to make sure Fred's dream for his company came true.

And so other battles began. Now with three kids in tow, Luan had to take on the shareholders who obviously didn't want her anywhere near the business. Get this. On the morning of Fred's funeral, they deliberately called a Board of Directors meeting. In her early thirties, Luan was now the majority shareholder. Here was her response. "If you have this meeting, I'll be bringing my children. And at the funeral afterwards, you'll have to explain to everyone why I look like a scarecrow; why I didn't have time to do my own hair and dress my children for their daddy's funeral, because you schmucks called a board meeting!"

The meeting was canceled.

Despite more pressure from the shareholders to sell—"What does a little blonde piece of fluff like you know about running a meat packing company with a slaughterhouse?"—Luan hung on. She won the support of every employee and as a united team they went to work. Luan built a 45 million dollar expansion to the plant and opened up new markets in Japan and the Asian rim. The staff expanded to 2,000 people and the company shifted from bankruptcy and soft receivership to half a billion dollars in revenue within two and a half years. Luan Mitchell is now recognized as one of the most accomplished women in the world. She has an intimate understanding of competitiveness and the global pressures in today's tough business climate.

She has won all sorts of awards for her business acumen, including being named Canada's number one female entrepreneur of the year, three years in a row, by *Profit* and *Chatelaine* magazines. In 2005, she was named Woman of the Year by the American Biographic Institute. She is also a bestselling author. Luan has now become an in-demand speaker all over the world, on entrepreneurship and bounce-back ability. A far cry from a teenage beauty pageant participant.

Here's a few extra lessons she imparted to us:

- Don't let age be your cage.
- Allow yourself to learn; don't go through life with your emergency brakes on.
- Stand up for what you believe, or you will find yourself falling for anything.
- Most of all, believe in yourself and your incredible ability to succeed.

If you are not inspired after reading that story, we are! All of these real life examples throughout this book are here for you to digest, so you can extract strategies that will help you on your journey through life. Remember, one well-implemented idea can significantly accelerate your awareness and success. So don't delay, grab the opportunity. And don't allow the negative voices to hold you back.

Insights

You've learned that overcoming setbacks is an ongoing process. Maybe the only way you might avoid this reality is to become a hermit, but even that has its challenges. Life is for living large, not for retreating into a cave. However, the truth is, some of these obstacles can be terrifying when you feel out of control. It's worth repeating; these are just individual events, they are not your whole life. Look for the lessons in the experience once the turmoil has died down. These are the important building blocks that strengthen your character and your ability to overcome bigger challenges later. And above all, understand that the one thing you do have control over is your attitude. Work on it every day. Do everything you can to create a champion mind-set. In Chapter 6, you'll find lots of strategies to boost your confidence.

But first, let's show you how to develop excellent relationships and build a veritable fortress of support around you. When you have strength in numbers, setbacks are easier to handle and overcome. Read on!

"DON'T BE DISTRACTED BY CRITICISM.
REMEMBER, THE ONLY TASTE OF SUCCESS SOME
PEOPLE HAVE IS WHEN THEY TAKE
A BITE OUT OF YOU."

—Zig Ziglar

ACTION STEPS

Ten Best Options

The Problem Solver

Ten Best Options

No matter how difficult your challenge may be, make a list below of your ten best options. The first few may not be what you want but write them down anyway. Be creative, think outside the box. Ask yourself some "what if" questions. Be open to the unexpected. Often the best solution will be one of your later insights. Complete all ten before you review your list.

1. _____
2. _____
3. _____
4. _____
5. _____

6. _____
7. _____
8. _____
9. _____
10. _____

Now choose the one that seems to fit best and start formulating an action plan.

The Problem Solver

When you're experiencing a significant setback, use the Problem Solver below to help you solve it. This is a series of ten questions that will guide you step by step to the outcome you want. For best results, it's important to go through the entire written process. Use it often—your decisiveness will dramatically improve when you do.

1. **What is my challenge?**
   Accurately define your situation. Remember to be clear, brief and specific.

2. **Decide to confront the issue and deal with it.**
   Making a decision to move through your fear is a major step forward. For your good health and peace of mind, decide now.

3. **What is the desired result I want?**
   Again, clearly define the preferred outcome. Visualize closure, and describe the major benefits when you have dealt with this particular setback.

4. **In one word, describe how you will feel when you have successfully overcome this setback.**

5. **What information do I need that will help?**
   Learn more by reading, researching, reviewing contracts, or other important documents.

6. **What can I do myself?**
   List the specific actions you are capable of doing well.

7. **Who else can help me?**
   Consider someone else's expertise that you need, but don't have the skills or experience to perform yourself.

8. **Now, what specific action steps am I going to take?**
   This is your game plan. Think through each step to final closure.

1. _____
2. _____
3. _____

9. **When am I going to start?** _____

   date: _____

   What's a realistic time line to bring this situation
   to closure?

   date: _____

   Get started!!

   Remember, peace of mind is on the other side of fear.

10. **Review your results and celebrate!**

LIVING AND WORKING ON PURPOSE

TAKING DECISIVE ACTION

CONSISTENT PERSISTENCE

ASK FOR WHAT YOU WANT

THE CONFIDENCE FACTOR

BUILDING EXCELLENT RELATIONSHIPS

OVERCOMING SETBACKS

DO YOU SEE THE BIG PICTURE?

IT'S NOT HOCUS-POCUS, IT'S ALL ABOUT FOCUS

YOUR HABITS WILL DETERMINE YOUR FUTURE

Almost halfway there—stay focused!

Building Excellent Relationships

"IT TAKES A LOT OF LIFE EXPERIENCE
TO SEE WHY SOME RELATIONSHIPS LAST AND
OTHERS DO NOT. BUT WE DO NOT HAVE TO
WAIT FOR A CRISIS TO GET AN IDEA OF
A PARTICULAR RELATIONSHIP. OUR BEHAVIOR
IN LITTLE EVERYDAY INCIDENTS
TELLS US A GREAT DEAL."

—Eknath Easwaran

Chris Keating is a dynamic, thirty-year-old entrepreneur who creates memorable artwork for families. His company, Towne Photography, is recognized as the best place in Calgary to go for family portraits. Business and marketing came naturally to Chris. At the age of ten, he thought that recess time in the schoolyard was dull. There was nothing to do and no facilities in the big dirt playground. So he decided to liven things up by creating a game called Cherry Bombs. Chris had observed that the fruit from nearby Oriental cherry trees froze in the cold weather and thawed when it warmed up, leaving them soft inside with a thin skin. He picked off the cherries and packaged them in Ziploc bags and asked his friends to buy them; ten in a bag for twenty-five cents. The cherries were perfect for throwing at people. And so one of the first paintball games was invented! The kids loved this game. It was fun and it was great exercise as everyone was chasing or running away from each other. The cherries left a small red mark on clothing but the kids didn't care. And so they bought more and more cherries.

Chris's thriving little business ended abruptly when some parents complained about the cherry stains and Chris's mom discovered a cardboard box under his bed containing 150 dollars in profit from this startup business. She thought these were ill-gotten gains—he was taking money from his friends with no just cause. Obviously entrepreneurship was not in the genes of his parents, both being professional academics.

However, just getting good grades at school was never a focus for Chris. As he says, "That never worked for me." Upon leaving school, he took a job as a laboratory technician in a petroleum company. For the first three months this line of work held his interest, but then it became monotonous. He was transferred to the imaging department where his job was photographing rocks. So he called a friend who was a photographer to learn more about cameras. His first assignment was to "hold her bag" that weekend at a wedding where she was the official photographer. A week later he attended a one-day course she had organized, paying eighty dollars for the tuition. After the program Chris knew that photography was what he wanted to do for the rest of his life.

The next day, he went to the bank and obtained a credit card with a five-hundred-dollar limit. He bought four hundred and twenty dollars' worth of camera equipment and used the remaining eighty dollars to print his own personal business cards. He was in business! A few years later, after struggling in the early days, Chris discovered a niche that motivated him—family portraits. Sadly, at age ten, during the year of his Cherry Bomb "adventure," Chris's parents divorced and he experienced the trauma of a broken family. This weighed heavily on him. He asked himself, "How can I make a difference in the lives of families, to emphasize the importance of a loving close-knit family and the joy it creates?" From that point on, memorable artwork for families became his passion.

Chris says, "My unique advantage is that I create an emotional connection with the family during their first visit." At the Design Appointment, Chris starts by explaining that he wants to create a powerful memorable experience for everyone and encourages them to become totally involved. This is very different from the usual approach. Questions such as, "What background do you prefer?" never arise. Chris views himself as a commissioned artist and quickly instills a high level of trust that he will produce a result that the family will be thrilled to receive. And he delivers every time.

His fees now range from two thousand to fifteen thousand dollars or more, per family, a far cry from the twenty-five cent bag of cherries he sold in the school playground! Today he is recognized as an industry leader. His practical content and entertaining style have taken him all over the world speaking to audiences of professional photographers.

Chris has also expanded his impact on the non-professional camera-carrying world by doing fifteen-city nationwide tours where his sold-out photo workshops receive rave reviews. These lead to a four-day photography extravaganza in Havana, Cuba. During his first trip there with his students, he was arrested for photographing government buildings, but that's another story! Chris is focused on being a good role model for his own family, primarily his wife Carolynn and their three young boys. Last year they enjoyed sixteen weeks of vacation.

As a successful young entrepreneur, Chris has remained humble and passionate about his artwork. He says, "Photography is incredibly easy. All you have to do is dedicate your life to it." His unique self-designed websites are well worth a visit: www.TownePhotography.com and www.PhotographicResource.com.

A major factor in Chris's success is his ability to build excellent rapport with his clients and to transform this into long-term repeat business. As he says, "I genuinely like the people who have given me the privilege of coming into their lives and allowing me to create something special that will be long-lasting and memorable."

In business, building great relationships is an essential core strategy, as Chris ably demonstrates. Now let's look at why some relationships remain strong and sustainable whereas others collapse completely.

The Double SPIRAL

Relationships can be very fragile. Many marriages don't survive, families are broken up and often kids are raised with only one parent to support them. What causes these relationships to fall apart when there is so much joy and love at the beginning?

It's helpful to look at your life as a spiral. Sometimes you are in an Upward Spiral. That's when things are going well, your confidence is high and life is rewarding. Your most important relationships are healthy and flourishing. The opposite is the

Downward Spiral. This is when things start to unravel, a lack of communication occurs, stress increases and life becomes a constant struggle. Relationships are polarized during the Downward Spiral.

Nature gives us dramatic versions of these spirals. A tornado is a powerful example. Spiraling down from the sky, these dark funnels hit the ground sucking up everything in their path with devastating results. The Michael Crichton/ Steven Spielberg movie *Twister* provided a close-up view of these awesome spirals, and the incredible energy they contain.

Another example of a Downward Spiral is a whirlpool. On the outer edge of the whirlpool the water doesn't look too dangerous. If you are not aware of the powerful forces at the center, however, you can be pulled down very quickly.

UNDERSTANDING THE DOWNWARD SPIRAL

Let's look at how the Downward Spiral shows up in real life. To clearly understand the potential impact this can have on your current and future relationships, think of a relationship you have been involved in that didn't work out. You need to re-create in your mind all the steps that caused this relationship to fall apart. Visualize clearly what happened.

Go back as far as you can and relive it. What was the first thing that happened? What happened after that? Then what happened? To understand the full impact of this, be sure to complete the Action Steps at the end of this chapter. Recording each individual step of your Downward Spiral all the way to the lowest point will help you understand the pattern.

For example, in a marriage the husband becomes self-centered and doesn't help around the house anymore. He spends more time at the office, leaving early in the morning before the kids are up and arriving home late in the evening. Communication is limited to business and finances. Maybe money is tight and there isn't enough to cover the mortgage, car payments, children's dance lessons and dental bills. Gradually the tension builds up, arguments occur more often and each partner blames the other for the situation they are in. The Downward Spiral is now gaining momentum, just like being drawn into the center of the whirlpool. Either, or both, may seek solace by drinking, going out with the boys (or girls), gambling, or, in the worst cases, abusing each other physically and mentally. At this point, the relationship has been sucked dry and the Downward Spiral is at its lowest point. Separation often occurs, ending in divorce, and another family is placed on the broken-home list, a statistic that seems to be growing annually.

When you carefully reflect on what causes relationships to fall apart, you can take steps to heal them. Even if the relationship is past saving, you'll be better prepared for the next one, and able to prevent the same pattern from materializing. Awareness is always the first step to progress. You can also use this spiral technique to review your most important business relationships. Here's a common scenario:

Two people form a partnership. They have a great idea for a new product or service and they pour a lot of time and energy into their exciting new venture. Because they're so busy making things happen, no legal partnership document was ever prepared or signed. They are good friends and they intend to do that down the road. Also, there are no clear job descriptions or methods for compensation and profit sharing.

Let's look down the road a few years. The partnership is now struggling because one person is a controller and won't allow his partner to make any decisions without his permission. Finances are tight and there's weekly bickering about the way revenues should be spent. One person wants to reinvest their earnings in the company so it can grow, whereas the other has a pay-me-first attitude. Gradually the rest of the staff is pulled into the conflict and two distinctive political camps emerge. A crisis develops and one partner wants out of the business, but there is no shotgun clause, and of course no agreement that would make this easy. The partners both dig their heels in and finally they set up their own legal teams. The battle is on. Often the attorneys end up with most of the money, the business collapses and two more people are heard to proclaim, "Partnerships never work!"

Here's a tip: If you are currently in a business arrangement with one or more partners, or are considering one in the future, always plan your exit strategy first, before you get too involved. Make sure it's in writing. And beware of emotional attachments. The undisputed fact that your new partner is a nice guy, or your best friend, is no reason to sidestep a written agreement. Lack of foresight and preparation ruins more businesses today than anything else.

Now that you've looked closely at how the Downward Spiral can show up in your life, learn from it. Because we are creatures of habit, there's a good chance that you will repeat the same behavior in your next important relationship. Really understand this. It's critically important for your future health and wealth. If you find yourself going into the same Downward Spiral, immediately take a mental time-out. Interrupt the pattern with clear thinking and decide to make positive adjustments. Changing your behavior is the only way you will get a different result. Here's how: Use a new template. That is, superimpose an Upward Spiral for excellent relationships on top of your Downward Spiral, the one that got you into so much trouble.

"WHEN YOU ARE IN CONFLICT WITH SOMEONE,
THERE IS ONE FACTOR THAT CAN MAKE THE
DIFFERENCE BETWEEN DAMAGING YOUR
RELATIONSHIP AND DEEPENING IT.
THAT FACTOR IS ATTITUDE."

—William James

UNDERSTANDING THE UPWARD SPIRAL

Let's analyze how this Upward Spiral works so you can reap the rewards quickly. Repeat the process as before, except this time you are going to focus on a relationship that you gradually nourished, expanded and enriched, until it blossomed into a wonderful long-term friendship or business relationship. Go back in your mind and replay all the significant things that happened from the time you first met until the relationship fully matured. Most people don't do this, so you will enjoy a tremendous advantage in the marketplace when you develop an accurate blueprint that you can duplicate many times in the future. Powerful relationships ensure powerful results.

Here's a positive example to help you win. Dave owns an engineering business. He adapts ideas from clients and helps them create new products. Innovative design and efficient workmanship are Dave's areas of brilliance. Over the past twenty-two years he has honed these skills to a high level. Along the way, he's also learned how to treat people properly. He has a loyal customer base and pays attention to simple things like returning phone calls promptly and following through with his clients' requests.

When a new client approached him one day with an idea for a rubber extrusion product, he was happy to help. The young man had big visions. He dreamed of his own manufacturing facility that would supply some of the world's largest users of his unique product. Dave provided his expertise and made subtle changes to the prototype. These refinements made it less costly to make and more robust. This new alliance between the young entrepreneur and the experienced engineer blossomed over the next few years into an enjoyable, mutually rewarding friendship. Each in their own way helped the other to higher levels of creativity and productivity. Eventually the young entrepreneur's dream was realized. Because of his larger vision and persistence, he secured several exclusive multimillion dollar contracts. All along he stayed in touch with Dave for advice.

As his business grew, so did Dave's. One day, reflecting on his incredible success, he made an important phone call that would enrich their special relationship even further. He offered Dave a percentage of all his future profits. It was his way of saying, "Thank you for believing in me, for helping me get started and for pushing me through the tough times."

All excellent relationships have a starting point. Often the first few interactions are not memorable. However, you soon develop a good feeling about the other person. Maybe it's his integrity, enthusiasm, positive attitude, or just that he does what he says he is going to do. A bond develops, and each new step strengthens the relationship further, making it more and more special.

Do you get the picture? When you review in detail how you developed your best relationships, it provides a unique process for creating bigger and better future relationships. Knowing what works and what doesn't work will help you avoid costly mistakes that create a Downward Spiral. The good news is, you can apply this template for excellent relationships to any area of your life. It works for personal and family relationships as well as for professional and business alliances.

Develop the habit of constantly reviewing your Double Spirals—use them to protect you from any negative downward pull, and to guide you into the positive world of truly special and loving relationships.

JACK:

I learned a lot about building business relationships from author and speaker Ivan Misner. Ivan wrote a book called *Networking Like a Pro*. He taught me something called visibility, credibility, and profitability. When most people are building business relationships, they try to turn them into profitable relationships too quickly. What's important to know is you have to first be in a state where you meet people. That's why networking and going to association meetings, clubs, chambers of commerce, and to church and so forth are all great ways to be visible.

That's something Larry Benet taught me. He's a connection expert. He says, "Whenever you meet someone–it doesn't matter who it is–ask them, "What's the one or two most important projects you're working on right now?" (You can also ask them what are the top two initiatives or challenges you're facing.) "How could I help you?" Then if they tell you something you could actually do, go ahead and do it. Send them an article. Connect them with somebody who can help them. Spend some time coaching them or whatever it might be. Now you've created credibility. You are a credible resource in their life. If you approach that person three months later and ask them for a favor (Could you introduce me to someone? Would you be willing to give me an endorsement? Would you be on my board of advisors?), there's a relationship already established that you can build on. I don't think I knew that ten years ago. My attitude was, "We're all in the business of doing business; let's get on with it." You must create a relationship first. I think that's a big piece. Ask the questions, "What are you focusing on? How can I help you?" and then deliver real value. If you are not doing this, then start as soon as possible; otherwise you may be missing out on some of your best business opportunities.

Say "No" to TOXIC People

Before we move on, please heed this important advice—**avoid toxic people!** Unfortunately, there are a few people out there who see the world as one big problem, and in their eyes you're part of it. You know the type. No matter how well things are going, they focus on the nitpicking little negative details. And they do it constantly. It's a habit that totally destroys relationships. One blast of negative energy from their lips can erase that smile on your face permanently. These people are poisonous to your health. You need a long-range antenna to keep them outside your boundaries at all times.

You may be thinking at this point, "Easier said than done. Do you mean if my friend, who I've known for years, is always complaining about his job and how awful things are financially, and nobody wants to help him out, that I should just turn and walk away when he talks like this?" No—run! As fast as you can, and as far as you can. His constant negativity will drain the life out of you.

Now please understand, we're not talking about someone who has a genuine challenge and needs real help. We're referring to those chronic whiners who take great pleasure in dumping all their negative garbage on your plate at every opportunity. They also inform you, with a not-so-subtle cynicism, that you can't do this and you can't do that, especially when you have a really great idea. They delight in bursting your positive bubble. It's the highlight of their day. Don't put up with it anymore.

Here's where the real power is: It's always your choice. You can choose the type of people you want in your life. And you can choose to pursue new opportunities. Maybe you just need to make some better choices. It's that simple. If it means letting a few people go, well, you'll get over it. In fact, take a close look now at your present relationships. If someone is dragging you down all the time, make a decision. Let go and move on.

Here's an interesting voicemail message we heard of from Pastor Henry Schorr:

"Thanks for calling. I've been away making changes in my life. Please leave a message. If you don't hear back from me, you are one of the changes. Enjoy your day!"

The Three Big
QUESTIONS

Now that you've had a chance to understand your Double Spiral, and an opportunity to clean house regarding the negative people in your life, here's another great strategy that will benefit you immensely. It's called the Three Big Questions.

Business mogul Warren Buffet is one of the best-known and most successful investors in the world today. His company, Berkshire-Hathaway, has grown from a few private clients with modest holdings to a multibillion-dollar enterprise. Mr. Buffet is famous for careful analysis and for investing in long-term opportunities. He rarely sells his stock after making an investment. His intensive preparation includes a thorough analysis of the numbers, especially the company balance sheet. If these are to his liking, he spends considerable time meeting key people in the organization, getting to know how they run the business. He observes their philosophy and how they treat their staff, suppliers and clients. When he has these tasks completed, Buffet asks himself three questions concerning the key people: "Do I like them? Do I trust them? Do I respect them?"

If any one of these questions results in a "No," the deal is off. It doesn't matter how good the numbers look, or the potential for growth. These three simple, powerful questions are the foundation for Warren Buffet's relationships. Adopt them as your own. They will ultimately determine how rich you become.

A few years ago, Buffet was the wealthiest man in America. He recently relinquished this title to Bill Gates, founder of Microsoft. It's interesting to note that despite the age gap, these two phenomenally successful entrepreneurs are close friends. Who you hang around with does make a difference.

The next time you are about to enter into an important business or personal relationship with people you don't know very well, do your homework first. Look for clues that demonstrate their integrity, honesty and experience. Watch how they treat other people. Little details will offer big insights: Are they in the habit of saying "Please" and "Thank you," especially to people in service positions, such as waiters and waitresses, bellhops and cab drivers? Are they down-to-earth with others, or do they have a need to impress people? Take sufficient time to digest their overall behavior before you make a commitment. And always refer to the Three Big Questions. Pay attention to your intuition. That gut feeling will guide you. Don't let your heart rule your head. When we are too emotionally involved, we often make bad decisions. Give yourself time to think before rushing into any relationship. Look at this another way: Why would you choose to build relationships with people you don't trust, don't respect or don't like? Going ahead when your instinct is telling you not to is a formula for disappointment or even disaster.

There are lots of excellent people out there to enjoy your valuable time with. So whether it's marriage, a business partner or hiring a sales team, choosing the right people is critically important to your future health and wealth. Choose carefully.

**The true joy in life comes
from spending time with people
who constantly inspire, nourish,
and replenish your soul**

Core Clients and
THE DOUBLE WIN

The next step in developing the habit of Excellent Relationships is learning to nourish your most valuable relationships in a win-win atmosphere. A lot has been written and spoken about the philosophy of win-win. In our experience, most of it is just surface talk. Win-win is essentially a philosophy of how you live your life. In business, win-win means having a genuine concern for the other person; that they win as much as you do, whether it's a sale, employee contract, negotiation or important strategic alliance.

Sadly, the attitude of many people in business has been to grind every last cent out of every situation. These so-called guerrilla tactics cause a lack of trust, cynicism, questionable ethics and a high level of anxiety in the marketplace. The result is win-lose. On the other hand, win-win doesn't mean giving the farm away every time you make a deal. That's lose-win, with the other person receiving too much, which could eventually put you out of business.

There's also another category called lose-lose. This happens when both parties are too stubborn or too egotistical to create a winning solution. A common example is contract negotiations between management and unions. If a stalemate occurs, the eventual result may be a long, drawn-out strike where nobody really wins.

In your personal life, win-win is the foundation for warm, loving relationships. It's a husband wanting to create a win for his wife and family. He's willing to pitch in and do an equal share of household duties and help with the children's extracurricular activities, especially when his wife is also working full time. Win-win is a wife giving solid support to her husband as he strives to build a new business or start a new career, and is willing to accept a few sacrifices along the way.

Win-win is giving to your community, being an outstanding neighbor and being less self-centered. For win-win to really work, you must practice it every day. This takes time, and challenges you to make a serious commitment to building these important alliances.

Now let's look at another crucial element in growing your business—building excellent **Core Client Relationships**.

Your core clients are people at the heart of your business. They buy from you consistently and are a main source of revenue. They are also happy to provide excellent referrals for new business, because they genuinely love your products and outstanding service.

Amazingly, many people today don't even know who their core clients are. Core clients are your passport to future growth. Unfortunately, these important relationships are often taken for granted. The attitude is, "She always orders two thousand units every month. We need to focus on new business."

NOT EVERY DEAL IS WORTH SAVING

New business is important. Staying in touch with your best clients is more important. It's a lot more difficult to find new customers than it is to keep and serve your old customers.

Also, be aware of the time you spend on people who are peripheral clients. The word peripheral is worth noting. It means at the outer edge, unimportant or not worth mentioning. Another term is dispensable. Do you have any peripheral clients in your business? If you're not sure, here's how you can spot them. They commonly take a lot of your time and energy and give you very little business in return. Sometimes they give you no business at all. But they will question you on every little detail, and they'll place unreasonable demands on your time. Of course, you may not want to turn any business away from your door. But what is it costing you in time and energy to dabble in minor results? Some deals just aren't worth the effort.

Let's look back to your core clients. There's one critical element you need to understand about these people. You don't ever want to lose them. Here's the big question. How much real time do you spend with your most important core clients?

This is worth studying. Our research indicates that very little time is allocated to core clients. Consequently, these relationships never mature to their full potential. On the bottom line, that means a lot of money is squandered.

Now that you know who these important people are, pay more attention to them. The long-term rewards are well worth the effort. Your business will increase, and you'll also minimize the likelihood of losing any of these top clients to your competitors.

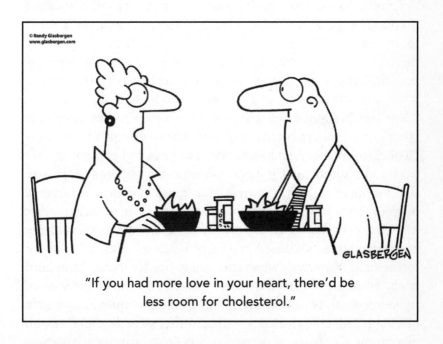

"If you had more love in your heart, there'd be less room for cholesterol."

Now let's take a look at your most important personal relationships. These include family and friends, mentors, spiritual advisers and anyone who is special in your life outside of the business world. Again, think carefully about who qualifies to be on this unique list of core people. Then write down their names. If you are tempted to skip over this exercise, stop! Procrastination is your greatest enemy. Don't put off your better future. Do each step as soon as you finish reading this chapter. Remember, this book is a work in progress. By the time you finish it you will have kick-started many of these exciting new habits. Your life will be richer and eminently more satisfying. Take a close look at this list and review the amount of time you spend with these people. Is it sufficient? Do you enjoy quality time, or just a few seconds on the telephone? Who else do you spend your personal time with? Are they robbing you of time that would be better spent developing your core relationships? If you answered "Yes" to this last question, what are you going to do about it? Maybe it's time to say "No" to those people who distract you every day. They're not on your most-important-people list, so why are they stealing your time? From now on, protect your family time and personal time. Be polite but firm.

We briefly mentioned win-win as it relates to the people in your life. It's important to really understand what this means. Bestselling author Stephen Covey provides a good analogy. He says you should treat your most important relationships like a bank account. For example, the more deposits you make in your core relationships' bank account, the stronger these associations become. In the process you become more valuable to these people.

Normally, money is what you deposit at the bank. However, with your core relationships you can make a variety of deposits. With your core clients in business, you will probably offer special services and all those little extras that define you as unique. These may include golf outings, dinners or special trips. Other healthy deposits include allocating time to share ideas or advising how to handle certain challenges. Maybe you consistently provide good referrals to expand their business. Sometimes it's making them aware of a great book, or emailing an article about their favorite pastime or hobby. You could also connect them to people who have a unique service or product. The more you know about the people on your core client list and core personal list, the more you can help them. And the true spirit of win-win means that you make these deposits unconditionally. In other words, don't give to get something back. Just experience the sheer joy of giving.

If you don't already have one, create an information file for every one of your core clients and core personal relationships. Find out everything you can about these individuals. Include their likes and dislikes, favorite restaurants, birthdays, anniversaries, kids' names, favorite hobbies, sports and pastimes.

Business guru Harvey MacKay, the founder and chairman of the $100 million Mackay Mitchell Envelope Company in Minnesota, calls his information file the MacKay 66, because there are sixty-six questions that his sales team asks to gain an in-depth knowledge of every important client. Most people don't keep files like this because they are not really serious about win-win. It takes considerable time and effort to cultivate highly successful relationships. It means that you will often be required to go the extra mile. This way of living gradually becomes your new normal behavior. You do it without thinking. When win-win behavior becomes truly embedded in your everyday life, the floodgates of opportunity will open up for you like never before. You will indeed be richer for it, and we don't just mean financially.

LES:
Here's a humorous win-win story that shows preparation pays off:
    A wealthy, outgoing Texan was visiting Dublin, Ireland, for the first time and was keen to experience the local social

scene and make a few friends. It was Saturday evening and he walked into a corner pub that seemed lively. The place was packed with lots of Guinness being quaffed by the thirsty locals.

Wanting to engage with people and impress them, too, the Texan loudly announced that he would give one thousand Euros to the first person who could drink ten pints of Guinness, one after the other. Nobody responded. In fact, one man beside him walked out of the pub. The Texan was dumbfounded because he knew the Irish were famous for the ability to "hold their drink."

Fifteen minutes later, after sitting alone at the bar, he felt a tap on his shoulder. When he turned around, a little Irishman, about seventy years old, asked him, "Excuse me sir, is the bet still on?" The Texan said, "It most certainly is." The word went quickly around the bar that old Mickey Malone had accepted the bet. The barman carefully set up ten pints of Guinness on the counter. Mickey rubbed his hands together and went to work. One, two, three, four, five, six, seven pints—a quick breath—eight, nine— his audience was now urging him on, cheering, yelling and stamping their feet—and finally, ten. He did it! The crowd exploded in a roar that could be heard two blocks away.

The Texan, duly impressed, peeled off ten crisp one hundred Euro notes, and stopped as he reflected momentarily. "Say, weren't you the fella that walked out of the pub when I announced the bet?" Mickey looked at him, rather sheepishly, and said, "Yes, sir." "Well, why did you leave?" the tourist asked. "Oh, I just went over to the pub across the street to see if I could do it first!"

. . . And Then SOME

Win-win is a great way to live, and true friendships take time to mature. Value the ones you have and do whatever it takes to make them even richer. Here's a powerful strategy that will make it easy. It's called the And Then Some technique.

Let's say you want to expand an important personal relationship with your husband or wife. If you are not married, you can apply this technique to almost any meaningful relationship, so adapt it accordingly. In fact, pick someone you'd like to enjoy a deeper level of friendship with. To show you how it works, we'll use the husband and wife example.

Imagine it's the end of the week, and David the good husband has arrived home from work. His equally good wife Dianne has dinner ready, and they both enjoy an excellent meal. David compliments her and then poses the following question: "Dianne, on a scale of one to ten (one being pathetic and ten being wonderful), how would you rate my performance as a husband during the last week?" This is a serious question. Dianne reflects for a moment and says, "I'd give you an eight."

David accepts the answer without comment, and asks the And Then Some question: "What would I have needed to do to make it a ten?"

Dianne answers, "Well, I would have really appreciated you helping John with his homework on Wednesday. I was under pressure to be at my computer class by 7 PM, and I felt guilty leaving without him being looked after properly. Also, you promised to repair the tap in the bathroom this week. It's still dripping. I'd really like it fixed, please." David simply says, "Thank you, I'll be more attentive next time."

Then the roles are reversed. When Dianne asks David to give her a score out of ten, David awards her a nine. Now it's her opportunity to ask the And Then Some question. "How could I have scored a ten?"

David gives her sincere feedback. "You were great, but there was one little thing. Remember you promised to record the football game for me when I was away Monday and Tuesday? I know it just slipped your mind, but I was looking forward to watching the highlights when I got home. I was really disappointed." Dianne listens, offers an apology and makes a commitment to record requests like this in her daily planner.

Before you say, "That sounds great, but it would never work for me," stop and think. You're right, very few people use the And Then Some technique, and even fewer do it on a weekly basis. The most common excuses are, "I'm too busy," "That's silly," or "Get real, my husband (or wife, or friend) would never agree to that."

BE TOTALLY OPEN TO FEEDBACK

Here's what these well-worn excuses are really saying: "My partner and I are not open to feedback, because our relationship has not matured to that level." Regularly giving and receiving honest feedback is one of the best ways to enrich your marriage, friendship or business relationships. It's the hallmark of human beings who have a high level of awareness and a unique sensitivity to the needs of others. Because of this maturity they enjoy honest, open and fulfilling alliances with the most important people in their lives. You can also use this technique with your children and other family members. Your kids will tell you the real story—they don't pull any punches!

By asking a few simple questions every week, you can learn more about yourself from people who care enough to give you honest feedback. Instead of becoming defensive like most people, accept the information as a gift. It will help you become more genuine and trustworthy.

And Then Some means you are willing to learn more, do more, and put more into the relationship because it's important to you.

In the process, both parties are rewarded and strengthened. Consider the benefits of applying the And Then Some technique in your professional life. If you own the company, you could ask your key people, "On a scale of one to ten, how do you rate me as a boss? What can I do to become better—to rate a ten?" Managers could do the same with their sales or administrative teams. What about your core clients? Here's a great opportunity to understand the strengths and weaknesses of your business, and how to improve those areas that are not performing well. Remember, your core clients may also include suppliers, or your outside support team.

If this technique is new to you, the first few attempts may be awkward or uncomfortable. That's normal. Any new habit takes a lot of practice and perseverance before it finally clicks. Hearing the truth from people you respect and love also takes some getting used to. Sometimes the truth hurts; you may need to swallow your pride a few times in order to enjoy the future benefits. One other note here—if you are giving critical feedback, always do this in private. On the other hand, give praise in public. People need and enjoy well-deserved recognition of any kind. Simply stated, criticize in private; praise in public.

MARK:
Here's what I've learned regarding family life, and I've had to learn this the hard way before being able to implement it on a regular basis.

To prevent important relationships from falling apart, it really helps if you can sit down together, eyeball to eyeball, soul to soul and heart to heart, and communicate clearly. Both people must be open-minded; they're not trying to not be in a relationship. They want to be in it and make it work, that's what the decisive power is, the commitment to make it work. In my previous marriage, I got addicted to work and I started thinking I was the most important guy in the world. Boy, do I know different now! I know how important I'm not. I mean, I can put my fist in a bucket of water, pull it out, and the water doesn't know my fist was there! Make sure your ego doesn't overrule your heart. This approach also helps in solving business relationships that need repair, especially in partnership situations.

REMEMBER, FOR THINGS TO CHANGE

You've Got To Change.

In this next section we will introduce a powerful formula that can be life-changing for you. As authors of this book, we have all been blessed with great people who have guided us, inspired us and corrected us on our journey in business, as well as in our own personal relationships.

There are two ways you can approach building a successful life. You can either decide to go it alone and be a controlling individualist, or you can decide to have other people give you some assistance. The first option requires a lot of trial and error. You will learn the hard way, take your fair share of bumps and bruises, and maybe ultimately get what you want . . . or not!

The second option is where you use strategic leverage to help you avoid some of life's difficult detours. How? By finding people who will be willing to mentor you. Over many years, our own success was accelerated by the expertise provided by wonderful people. We encourage you to pay particular attention to what you are about to read next. It can save you years of trial and error.

How to Find Great
MENTORS

Surrounding yourself with well-chosen mentors can dramatically change your life. A mentor is someone with vast experience or a unique talent, who is willing to share ideas with you on a regular basis. You, as the mentee, the recipient of this great information, have a responsibility to use it wisely by furthering your career and financial status or by enhancing your personal or family life. It's like a teacher-student relationship, except that you have the benefit of one-on-one tutoring. And the big bonus is that you normally don't pay for any of the lessons. What a deal!

Here's a proven three-step method to help you enjoy the considerable advantages of mentorship:

1. Identify the target.

Select one specific area of your life that you want to improve. There may be several, but for the purpose of getting started, choose only one. Here are a few ideas—growing your business, sales, marketing, hiring excellent people, preparing financial statements, learning new technology, investment strategies, accumulating wealth, eliminating debt, eating and exercising for optimum health, being an excellent parent, or doing effective presentations.

2. Select your mentor candidates.

Think about someone who is exceptionally experienced or talented in the area you have selected for improvement. It could be someone you know personally, or it could be a leader in your industry. Maybe it's someone who is recognized as a top authority on this topic—a well-known writer, speaker or celebrity. Whoever it is, make sure he or she has a proven track record and is truly successful.

3. Create your strategic plan.

If you don't already know the whereabouts of your proposed mentor, how are you going to locate this unique individual? And when you do, how will you make contact? The first thing to realize is that you are probably never more than six people away from anyone you want to meet, including your new mentor. That's exciting to know—treat it like a game. There may be six doors you need to open before you have all the information you need. Who could open the first door for you? Proceed from there, and keep asking. You'll be surprised how quickly the other doors open up once you put the word out.

You may be looking at the name of your proposed mentor and second-guessing yourself with thoughts like, "I don't even know this person and she certainly doesn't know me. And if she did, she probably wouldn't give me any of her valuable time." Stop right there! The following story is big proof that finding and contacting mentors is well within your capabilities.

LES:
One of our clients, an ambitious, proactive young woman named Ashley Meszaros, was struggling in her new business. She had launched a telephone answering service called We An-Ser Communications and soon realized there was a lot more to running this business than she had initially contemplated. Despite having made a significant financial investment in professional equipment, she had no trained staff and had never been in sales before. Her previous job working as a safety officer in a local company had, as she puts it, "become stale." She had also remortgaged her home to finance the telephone equipment and her husband, Mike, was also changing careers.

However, Ashley is a go-getter who doesn't stand still for long. She realized she needed help, unlike many other entrepreneurs, those rugged individuals who steadfastly resist the thought of surrendering to anyone else's expertise. That's when she hired me as an executive coach. I suggested she find a mentor, someone experienced in her industry, who could help her avoid a lot of unnecessary trial and error. This immediately struck a chord, as she knew someone who ran a similar business. After providing a little instruction on the best way to contact this person, I encouraged her to make the call. This new potential mentor had built a very successful business over many years and had experienced just about every situation imaginable as her company grew. She also lived almost a thousand miles away so there were no concerns about competing with each other.

When Ashley called, the woman immediately said she'd be happy to help. They arranged to have a regular call on the first Wednesday of each month at 1:30 PM. In order not to waste time, Ashley emailed her some questions a few days before calling. The impact was immediate. Ashley says, "After the first call, I couldn't sleep for a week! I had so many great ideas from my new mentor. And I followed through on all of them. She really helped me with sales tips, presentation skills, hiring staff, setting up special accounts, preparing proper fee schedules, handling difficult customers and running an efficient office. And she didn't charge me a cent!"

Over several months their relationship became closer and Ashley was able to pass on some of her own ideas that were welcomed and proved valuable. A true WIN-WIN was established.

It all started with that one phone call. So let's analyze how you can enjoy similar success. The most important thing is to be sincere. Sincerity goes a long way in helping you get what you want in life. Here's what Ashley said when she first got through on the telephone, "Hello, Mrs. Armstrong (not actual name), would you consider being my mentor. All that would mean is spending ten minutes on the phone with me once a month, so I could ask you a few questions. I'd really appreciate it. Would you be open to that?"

When you ask that closing question, the answer will usually be "Yes" or "No." If it's "Yes," control your excitement and ask another question. "When would be a good time to call you in the next few weeks?" Then confirm a specific time for your first mentor meeting. Follow up with a handwritten "thank you" note right away.

If the answer is "No," politely thank the person for their time. Depending on how firm the refusal was, you could ask if it would be okay to call back at a more convenient time to reconsider your request. Otherwise move to plan B—call the next person on your list.

Let's review the key elements in the phone call. First, get right to the point. Busy people appreciate this. Don't socialize. Stick to a well-prepared script using a relaxed conversational tone. It only takes a minute. Also, it is important to control the conversation. Say what you want to say, ask the closing question and then shut up. At this point, you allow your potential new mentor to speak. If you follow this sequence, your success ratio will be high. Here's why: First of all, when you ask someone to be a mentor, it is the ultimate compliment. Second, they are rarely asked. And if you do it with total sincerity, having reminded them of their own earlier challenges, you will often receive a positive response.

Before you make the call, it's useful to have as much information as possible. If you don't know the person, go on the Internet and do some research. Find out about their role in the business. Use social media also to further your search.

Remember, you can have several mentors. You can select people for any area of your life that you want to improve. They may live in another city or country, or they may be half an hour's drive away. So get started and have fun. These unique relationships can dramatically accelerate your progress. Trial and error is one way to gain experience, but it's hard work figuring everything out on your own. Tapping into other people's successful formulas and adapting their ideas is a lot smarter. It's usually who you know that opens up the doors for bigger and better opportunities. Treat it like a "connect-the-dots" game. Successful people are well-connected. Simply follow their moves. To help you further, you will find a step-by-step Action Plan for Developing Mentor Relationships at the end of this chapter.

MAKING YOURSELF BULLETPROOF

Now we want to share with you another important building-block in developing the habit of Excellent Relationships. It's called Building Your Own Fortress. The definition of a fortress is a structure that is impregnable, a sanctuary or a place of refuge. Within a fortress you are protected from the storms of business and life. Here's how you can build one.

It's like building a championship football or hockey team. Each player has a role to play, and the team is only as good as its weakest member. The team is molded by the coach. He or she is at the center of the action. The combination of uniquely gifted team players and a coach who can create and implement a successful game plan produces triumphant winners.

Consider yourself as the coach. Two major questions you need to address at this point in your life are, "Who is on my team?" and "Do they perform at the level I require to achieve my dreams and goals?" This is all about setting very high standards so that you can enjoy a lifestyle that gives you total freedom, ongoing prosperity and a unique sense of worth. When you need help, you'll have the best people to assist you. This is an ongoing process, not a quick fix.

THE FORTRESS

Your Unique Total Support System

Use the following categories to guide you in the building of your Fortress. These are not ranked in any specific order of importance.

1. The Family Unit.

2. Specific Mentors and Coaches.

3. Health and Fitness Team.

4. Business Support Team (Interior).
   (e.g., Administrative Staff, Sales and Management Team.)

5. Business Support Team (Exterior).
   (e.g., Banker, Lawyer, Suppliers.)

6. Core Clients.

7. Personal Mastermind Group.

8. Personal Development Library.

9. Spiritual Adviser.

10. Other Strategic Alliances.
    (e.g., Networking Groups, Passive Income Pipelines.)

11. The Sanctuary. (Your own personal retreat, or getaway location.)

Here's how it works: Take a close look at your important relationships—the people who support and help you throughout the year. Separate them into two main categories: business/career and personal. Make a list of these important people. In your business/career list, examples would include your banker, lawyer, accountant, bookkeeper, tax specialist, suppliers, financial adviser, management staff, sales team, administrative staff, personal assistant and secretary/receptionist. In the personal category, the range is much broader: doctor, chiropractor, medical specialist, massage/physiotherapist, personal fitness trainer, nutritionist, dentist, dermatologist, financial consultant, hairstylist, dry cleaner, plumber, electrician, travel agent, realtor, insurance agent, car dealer, tailor, gardener, home help, babysitter and anyone else whose expertise you might need.

Obviously you don't interact with all of these people every week. The question is, when you do require their help, do they consistently do a brilliant job for you? Sometimes the person you select doesn't do a very good job. To avoid this, take time to check the person's history. Brilliant people do brilliant work. They do it on time and they do it consistently. They make you feel good in the process, and they charge a fair price. These are people you can always rely on to get the job done right.

How many don't deserve to be on your team because their performance is not good enough? Be totally honest. How many gaps are there on your team? This is easy to determine. These are the times you rush to the Internet hoping to find someone at the last minute. Often the person you select doesn't do a very good job because you didn't have time to check their background and references.

From now on, don't make decisions "on the run." And don't tolerate sloppy workmanship, tardiness, exorbitant pricing or any sort of hassle that will create more stress in your life. You don't need that. Go online for references or ask your friends. Do your homework. Do the research. Be patient, and gradually surround yourself with a first-class team of people who will make your life joyful and rich beyond measure. Start right away. You'll be amazed at how this will transform your relationships.

Insights

What we've realized more than ever in business is that relationships take time to blossom. A lot of people don't understand this. They tend to focus on the deal, closing the sale and moving on. In personality profiling, they are classified as hunters not nurturers. Hunters are important. They are keen to get out there and do what it takes to secure a sale. Nurturers take the long-term approach because they want to develop long-term business. The ideal would be a combination of both.

What hat do you wear in this arena? Do you need to shift your focus or make any adjustments?

Cultivating "champions" in the business world takes time. These are people who will become your greatest door openers, who can lead you to amazing opportunities. Be patient; keep adding value to them and the rewards will eventually flow. Make sure you study the WIN-WIN section in this chapter.

The same principles apply for creating excellent relationships at home. Here's a tip: **If you want a strong marriage, work at it every day.** That's even more important as the relationship gets older. Always be on guard against the scourge of broken relationships—complacency! And if you want a further incentive—divorce these days can be very, very expensive. Some people never recover financially, never mind from the emotional scars.

To sum it all up, pay more attention to the important people in your life. Create time for them regularly and be sincerely interested in their needs and wants. The payoff is huge and making money is a very small part of it. In the next chapter you'll learn all about building and maintaining a high level of confidence—an essential ingredient for long term success.

"TRUST IS THE GLUE OF LIFE.
IT'S THE MOST ESSENTIAL INGREDIENT
IN EFFECTIVE COMMUNICATION AND THE
FOUNDATIONAL PRINCIPLE THAT HOLDS
ALL RELATIONSHIPS TOGETHER."

—Stephen R. Covey

ACTION STEPS

The Double Spiral

Building Your Fortress

Developing Mentor Relationships

Make sure you complete these exercises. If you skip over them, you're probably not serious about developing excellent relationships. Don't sell yourself short. Make the effort now to learn about yourself and the impact you have on other people.

1. The Double Spiral

FAILED RELATIONSHIPS—Mentally revisit a significant relationship that didn't work out. Starting at number one, identify each step in the process that caused the relationship to fall apart. Be specific.

1. _____
2. _____
3. _____
4. _____
5. _____

EXCELLENT RELATIONSHIPS—Mentally revisit one of your greatest relationships. Starting at number one, identify each step in the process that caused this excellent relationship to expand.

5. _____

4. _____

3. _____

2. _____

1. _____

2. Identifying Core Clients

Write down the names of your ten most important business relationships. These are the people who bring you most of your sales and income. They love your products and service. They give you repeat business and are happy to refer you. (Note: if you are a manager or supervisor, the team of people you look after would be part of your core client list.) Please take sufficient time to think about this. These people are the building blocks to your better future. Treat them well! The most important people are your core clients. The word core means at the center, the heart or essence of anything valuable.

Now record how much time you spend with each of these people in a typical month. What does this tell you? What adjustments do you need to make?

1. _____ 6. _____

2. _____ 7. _____

3. _____ 8. _____

4. _____ 9. _____

5. _____ 10. _____

DEVELOPING MENTOR RELATIONSHIPS

What specific areas of expertise do you want to improve?

1. Check the most important

- ❏ Expanding My Business
- ❏ Sales and Marketing
- ❏ Health and Fitness
- ❏ Hiring Excellent People
- ❏ Balanced Lifestyle
- ❏ Financial Strategies
- ❏ Communication Skills

- ❏ Developing Strategic Alliances
- ❏ Eliminating Debt
- ❏ New Technology
- ❏ Parenting
- ❏ Other _____
- ❏ Other _____

2. List the top three areas of expertise you want to improve, and name two possible mentors for each.

1. _____   _____
                                _____
2. _____   _____
                                _____
3. _____   _____
                                _____

3. From the list above, select the most important area you want to work on right away, and your preferred mentor.

_____

4. Take a sheet of paper and use the example on pages 145-146 to create your own script for your first contact. Practice on the phone with a friend. Rework this until it begins to flow.

Now Pick a Time and Date and Make the Call.

If you are not able to speak to the person right away, keep calling until you do connect. Persistence really pays off. Remember, just one excellent mentor relationship can help you jump to a whole new level of confidence and awareness.

LIVING AND WORKING ON PURPOSE

TAKING DECISIVE ACTION

CONSISTENT PERSISTENCE

ASK FOR WHAT YOU WANT

THE CONFIDENCE FACTOR

BUILDING EXCELLENT RELATIONSHIPS

OVERCOMING SETBACKS

DO YOU SEE THE BIG PICTURE?

IT'S NOT HOCUS-POCUS, IT'S ALL ABOUT FOCUS

YOUR HABITS WILL DETERMINE YOUR FUTURE

You made it—now keep going!

The Confidence Factor

"I AM CONVINCED ALL OF HUMANITY
IS BORN WITH MORE GIFTS THAN WE KNOW.
MOST ARE BORN GENIUSES AND JUST
GET DE-GENIUSED RAPIDLY."

—Buckminster Fuller

In 1999, South African President Nelson Mandela celebrated his eightieth birthday.
For almost twenty-six of those years he was confined to a prison cell because of his outspoken views about apartheid. During this time Mandela's confidence must have been severely tested. It is a tribute to his faith and conviction that he ultimately triumphed and went on to be elected to his country's highest office.

Confidence is a habit that can be honed and strengthened every day. During this process you will be challenged by fear, worry and uncertainty. These elements constitute the ebb and flow of life. It's a constant struggle, a mental battlefield that must be won if your life is to be filled with abundance.

To start, carefully read the words spoken by Nelson Mandela at his inaugural speech. This is a man who accepted the challenge and won. Digest each sentence slowly. Use them as a strong foundation for your next level of achievement.

Our deepest fear is not that we are inadequate.

Our deepest fear is that we are powerful beyond measure.
It is our light, not our darkness that frightens us.

We ask ourselves, who am I to be brilliant, gorgeous, talented and fabulous?
Actually, who are we not to be?

You are a child of God.

Your playing small doesn't serve the world.

There's nothing enlightened about shrinking so that other people won't feel insecure around you.

We were born to make manifest the glory of God that is within us.

It's not just in some of us, it's in everyone.

And as we let our own light shine, we unconsciously give other people permission to do the same.

As we are liberated from our own fears, our presence automatically liberates others.

Source: A *Return to Love* by Marianne Williamson
(as quoted by Nelson Mandela in his inaugural speech, 1994)

This chapter contains many practical strategies that will boost your confidence to an all-time high. It is important that you utilize these on a daily basis. Confidence is the all-important factor you need to protect yourself from the slings and arrows of negativity. In the absence of confidence, fear and worry are ready to take control. Progress is held in check and momentum grinds to a halt.

So let's tackle this essential habit with gusto and a commitment to stamp out the negative forces once and for all. First, you need to clean up any unfinished business that's holding you back. Make that your starting point.

Resolving Unfinished BUSINESS

Unfinished business is a term describing all of the messes in your life that you haven't dealt with. You may be struggling with legal, financial, relationship, organizational, health or career messes, to name just a few. When you allow these to build up, they can overwhelm you. The reason many people won't deal with this unfinished business is fear. Fear breeds doubt, and doubt leads to a loss of confidence. It's a vicious cycle. If left unchecked, a downward spiral begins and is soon gaining momentum. Suddenly life is out of control. This excess baggage is like a dead weight around your neck. It can bring you to a standstill.

The result is a tremendous drain on your energy. Some people have accumulated so much unfinished business over the years, it feels like they're pulling an elephant along behind them. There are three ways to handle this:

1. You can play the denial game.

Some people pretend it's not really happening. For example, a man worrying about his debt-load refuses to look at the real numbers in the hope that they will somehow disappear. Rather than change bad habits, such as spending more than he makes, he finds it easier to live in a fantasy world. Denial usually results in major consequences of the variety you won't like.

2. You can go into limbo.

Life sort of stops and you tread water. You don't fall back, but you don't make any progress either. It's frustrating, and of course the unfinished business is still there waiting to be dealt with later. Being in limbo keeps you stuck.

3. You can confront the issue head on.

This seems like the obvious course of action, yet many people choose the previous two options. Why? We usually don't like confrontation—it's uncomfortable and there's a certain amount of risk involved. Sometimes it can be painful, and may not work out the way you want it to. Here's a phrase that will help you: **Step into your fear.**

PAINFULLY OVERCONFIDENT IN HIS NEW INVENTION, TOG MISCALCULATES THE EFFECTIVENESS OF HIS CLUB-PROOF VEST.

Most of the time fear only exists in our minds. Our imagination is powerful. Small issues often get blown out of proportion, and we create mental pictures that are ridiculous when compared to the facts. A friend in Arizona, George Addair, told us about a firefighter who attended one of his self-knowledge workshops. He said, "Firefighters deal with fear every time they prepare to enter a burning building. Just before they go into action they experience it—the uncertainty of not knowing if they'll survive or not. An incredible transformation takes place as soon as they go inside the building. They literally step into the fear, and because they do, the fear disappears. They are 100 percent in the present moment. They are then able to concentrate on fighting the fire, evacuating people and doing all the things they were trained to do. By confronting their fear, they can focus on the immediate situation and get the job done."

Another important factor is the energy you consume when you live in fear. You can't afford to have all that vitality bottled up. It restricts your capacity. If you want to gain confidence, accelerate your progress and restore your energy to maximum levels, you must confront your fears. Make a decision now to deal with your unfinished business once and for all. Give it your best shot. Put it behind you, and move on.

Make this a habit. Be aware that unfinished business is an ongoing reality. Every week something will happen that needs to be resolved. Don't allow these things to fester. Handle them promptly, with confidence. Your life will become refreshingly simple and uncluttered when you do.

Common fears	Strategic plan to counteract fear
Poor health	Learn more about good health habits, nutrition, exercise and your genetics.
Losing your job	Become so valuable that you can't be fired. And if you are, your special skills will open up new opportunities. Keep refining your strengths. Focus on your brilliance; develop excellent connections.
Loneliness	Surround yourself with positive, supportive people. Be a giver. To attract friends, become a friend.
Uncertainty about the future	Most of the jobs in the future haven't even been invented yet. Focus on developing your greatest talents. Design exciting goals.
Dying	It happens to all of us. Have faith. Live every day to the fullest. Explore spiritual truths.
Failure	The spiritual side of you proves there is a bigger plan. God gave you talent. Seek it out. Surround yourself with winners. "Failure" is an opportunity to learn. Making mistakes is essential for long-term success.
Making major decisions	Think on paper—plan ahead—seek good advice. (See Chapter 9, Taking Decisive Action).
Rejection	Don't take it personally, especially if you're in sales. We all experience some form of rejection every week. Become thick-skinned.

Common fears	Strategic plan to counteract fear
Conflict	Step into the fear. Look for a win-win solution. Accept that conflict is a part of life. Take a course in conflict resolution.
Ignorance/Lack of knowledge	Practice the habit of learning something every day. Read, study, become more conscious. Remember: The use of knowledge is your greatest power. Learn more. Become an expert in what you do best.
Losing your family	Continually nourish your most important relationships. Build a lifetime of positive memories you can cherish forever.
Public speaking	Join Toastmasters, take a Dale Carnegie course, join the National Speakers Association (see Resource Guide for details), choose a great mentor, write out a ten-minute speech on your favorite subject. Practice. Accept opportunities to speak when asked. Hire a speech coach.
Poverty	Learn about money and how it works. Check your belief system. Find an excellent financial coach. Set specific goals to save and invest a portion of everything you earn. (See Chapter 9, Taking Decisive Action.)
Success	Embrace the fact that success comes from study, hard work, good planning and taking risks. You deserve it if you do all of this.

JACK:

To expand your confidence, stop focusing on what you don't have. Start focusing on what you want. Your brain has the ability to focus on the past, to focus on the present, or to focus on the future. You want enough focus in the present that you don't crash into a truck while you're driving, but the real focus is, "Where am I headed?" "Where do I want to get to?"

Captain Chesley Sullenberger, who famously landed his crippled plane in New York on the Hudson River, had lost engine power. He said, "Well, what do I have? I've still got wings. I've still got flaps. I have a river over here. This is all I've got. I'm going to work with that." He focused on the outcome he wanted, to land the plane safely. He didn't focus on crashing! If you focus on what you do have and what you want, you can create a vision for yourself, produce a plan and go for it.

The Law of Attraction says that if I'm focused on not having a job, I'm going to get more of not having a job. Focus on, "Hey, I'm going to have a job. The perfect job is coming. There may be twenty percent unemployment in our town because the factory closed, but eighty percent of the people are still working. It's not my job to figure out how to employ everyone in town. It's my job to figure out how to employ me. I want to be one of the eighty percent."

The Twenty-Five-Cent
CHALLENGE

Our friend Wayne Teskey had a Mastermind Group consisting of four other business friends. They are a dynamic bunch of entrepreneurs who used to meet monthly to share ideas and offer support to each other. At one meeting they agreed that life had lost some of its challenge. Their businesses were doing well, but they needed a new stimulus. They came up with an idea that would test their confidence and cause them to stretch out of their all-too-familiar comfort zones.

The plan was to fly from Edmonton, their home city, to Toronto, more than three thousand miles away, on a one-way ticket with only twenty-five cents in their pockets. Upon landing, they each had to figure out how to get back home with no credit cards, no checks and no friends to help them out. To make it more interesting, they agreed to use at least three modes of transport. In other words, if one person was able to arrange a flight home, part of the journey had to include two other forms of transportation—train, bus, car, bicycle or on foot. Also, they could not tell anyone the nature of their challenge.

Picture yourself in this situation. What would you do? It would obviously require creativity, innovation, courage and a strong belief in your ability, as well as money, to successfully make the trip back home.

Unknown to this madcap group, a friend had alerted the local media in Edmonton as well as major radio stations and newspapers. Upon arrival in Toronto, they were met at the airport by several photographers and reporters, all intrigued by this unique adventure. Now there was real pressure to perform!

It took most of the group about a week to get home, and everyone accomplished his goal. There were some interesting stories. One person took the long route by hitching rides. Stopovers included Minneapolis, where he worked as a croupier in a casino. He came back with more than seven hundred dollars. Two of the other members talked their way into staying at one of Toronto's finest hotels at no charge. Others found odd jobs.

EVERYTHING YOU WANT IS ON THE
OTHER SIDE OF FEAR.

Wayne had fun on the street asking well-heeled businessmen, "Do you have any money that you don't plan on spending today?" If the answer was "Yes," he'd continue with a big smile, "Can I have some of it, please?" Some people actually paid up!

Back in Edmonton, the story gained front-page coverage. In fact, the group created more publicity than many expensive advertising campaigns. The "Masterminds," as they were now affectionately known, unanimously agreed that the trip was one of their all-time greatest learning experiences. They discovered that no matter how little they had, it was possible to not only survive, but to prosper. Confidence levels soared and their twenty-five-cent challenge created bigger and better business opportunities in the months that followed.

Forgive and FORGET

You have an incredible capacity and ability to overcome life's greatest challenges. Embrace this reality, and use it the next time a crisis occurs. In fact, celebrate the opportunity to perform at a higher level. When you break through the wall of fear, the rewards are many. You will enjoy peace of mind and the ability to dream and design an exciting future without being shackled by worry and guilt. When you continually clean up your unfinished business, life becomes simple and uncluttered. This gives you a surge of new energy.

All of this breeds confidence. It's critical that you understand one thing—confidence grows by doing, not by thinking. Only action produces results. As Sheryl Crow sings, "A change will do you good." To produce a different result, you need to change something. It all starts with you. Until you change, nothing else will change. Procrastination is a one-way ticket to staying stuck. It's an excuse not to perform.

Here's a big point about unfinished business. You really need to grasp this, so stay focused. To release yourself totally from the baggage of the past, you must learn to *forgive*. Read it again: **You must learn to forgive**. There are two sides to this. First, you need to forgive the people who obstructed you in the past—parents, friends, relatives or teachers. In fact, anyone who undermined or abused your confidence verbally, physically or mentally. No matter how traumatic the experience, to be free you must forgive them. This may not be easy, but it's essential if you want to have peace of mind and a happier future.

How do you do this? Write a letter, make a phone call, have a face-to-face conversation, whatever it takes, but it is of paramount importance that you settle the issue within yourself. Just let it go, and move on.

Second, forgive yourself. Silence forever those negative thoughts of guilt. The past is history. You will never be able to change it. Instead, accept the fact that whatever you did, your choices were based on your level of knowledge and awareness at the time. The same goes for your parents. Don't blame them for your upbringing—they did what they did based on their circumstances, belief systems and parenting ability.

Look at the word forgiveness. In the center are four letters, give. There's the clue. You must give to be free. The biggest gift you have to offer is love. Remember, you can't give what you don't already have. If you don't have love within you, how can you give it? It starts with forgiving yourself. You must move past the "It's not my fault," and the "Poor me" syndromes, or you'll never enjoy real love in your heart. This takes a special type of awareness. It's living at a higher level. To do this effectively requires detaching yourself from the past events of your life, so you can be free to give without conditions.

Too many people never let the real person within them come alive. Consequently, they live a dormant and unfulfilled existence. Instead of gloriously stretching and challenging themselves to be all they can be, they flounder in the everyday stuff of life. You can be different! Make a decision now to remove yourself from this futility and explore the unique talents you've been given. They are within you, just waiting to be let loose.

LES:

My friend and award-winning author, Annette Stanwick, faced one of the most challenging days of her life when she received the news that her brother Soren had been brutally murdered. Distraught with grief, she struggled to understand why this young man had been senselessly struck down in the prime of his life. Equally heartbreaking was the fact that the perpetrator had not been found.

Almost two years later the police finally announced they had arrested the killer. Shortly afterwards, Annette was asked if she would like to make an impact statement at the trial. She agreed. The tension in the courtroom was palpable as Annette had to deliver her comments while facing her brother's murderer. His name was Travis and Annette saw a quiet, frightened young man standing in front of her. Summoning up her courage, she delivered an emotional, heartfelt statement that let Travis know clearly the devastation he had caused Annette and her family.

The greatest impact came as a total surprise to everyone in the courtroom that day, when she looked Travis in the eye and said, "I forgive you for what you have done." This took tremendous courage. However, Annette said later that the sense of freedom that embraced her almost immediately was life changing and opened up unexpected opportunities. One of those was to visit several penitentiaries and counsel prisoners who had received life sentences. Her book, *Forgiveness: The Mystery and Miracle*, has also inspired thousands of other people to forgive and let go of their pain.

Annette's story reinforces how our response to situations can be a catalyst for new energy and opportunity, or, a way to stay stuck in our pain. Visit www.annettestanwick.com.

A Winning ATTITUDE

Attitude has a lot to do with your success and your ability to get what you want. As you are probably aware, attitude can change quickly. In fact, every day your attitude is severely tested. One of the greatest examples of losing confidence occurred at the 1996 Masters Golf Tournament in Augusta, Georgia. Australian Greg Norman, a premier golfer and one of the favorites to win the championship, had performed brilliantly. At the end of the third day, he was six strokes ahead of his nearest rival, and with only one more round remaining, Norman seemed a cast-iron certainty to wear the famous green jacket presented to the winner on Sunday afternoon. All he needed was an average performance to secure the win. Inexplicably, however, his game collapsed during the final round. Within twenty-four hours his six-stroke lead evaporated, and he ended up losing by five strokes to Nick Faldo, who had quietly chipped away at Norman's seemingly insurmountable lead. Indeed, it was Faldo's persistence and confidence that eventually caused the upset. In fact, Faldo has made a habit of coming from behind to win, having won back-to-back Masters (1989–90) in similar fashion.

As the final round progressed, Greg Norman's attitude noticeably deteriorated. The confident stride seen the day before changed to slumped shoulders, and a blank expression appeared in his eyes as he saw his long-time dream to become Master's champion disappearing. His plummeting downward spiral was a poignant reminder of how fickle confidence can be. Strong and positive one day, in total disarray the next. To combat this, let's look at some practical strategies that will help boost your confidence.

Six Confidence-Building
STRATEGIES

1. Every day remind yourself that you did some things well.

Instead of dwelling on what didn't work or the tasks you didn't finish, focus on what you did accomplish. Don't minimize these. Give yourself a mental pep talk at the beginning and end of the day. Coach yourself, just like you would help someone else to overcome a challenge.

2. Read inspiring biographies and autobiographies.

We want to reinforce this one more time. Read books, articles and magazines. Build a file of those stories that inspire you most. Download documentaries, ebooks, audios and videos. Go to the movies—there are a lot of great stories out there. Find out about people who started with nothing, or who had devastating setbacks, and still found a way to win. Remember, your capacity far exceeds your current level of performance. Life without challenges is an illusion. Accept the fact that you will have ups and downs, just like everyone else. Your confidence grows when you actively take on the challenges of life. You won't win them all, but with the right attitude you'll win more than enough.

3. Be thankful.

No matter how bad your circumstances may be, there's probably someone worse off than you. If you doubt this, volunteer your time in an acute-care burns ward at the children's hospital. Put things into perspective. Think of all the things (and people) you take for granted that are not available in other countries. Most of your problems will pale in comparison when you take a mental snapshot of all the benefits you enjoy every day.

4. Build excellent support around you.

If you need a boost, refresh your memory by reviewing Chapter 5, Building Excellent Relationships.

5. Push yourself to accomplish short-term goals.

There's no greater way to build confidence than getting things done. Create an environment of accomplishment every week. Focus on your three most important targets. Every day do something that moves you closer to finishing a project, closing a sale or expanding a relationship. Don't allow yourself to be distracted or interrupted. By doing so you'll eliminate the feelings of guilt and failure. Take one small step at a time.

Make sure these mini goals are realistic. Self-rejection can shatter your confidence, so don't beat yourself up when everything doesn't come together as planned. Be flexible. And when others say "No" to you, don't take it personally. Accept the fact that you need to lose sometimes before you can win.

6. Do something good for yourself every week.
Find a way to celebrate your weekly accomplishments.

Don't you deserve it? If you said "No," go back to step one and start again!

THE ROAD TO CONFIDENCE IS PAVED WITH WEEKLY VICTORIES

Learn To Applaud Them.

Believe in your own CAPABILITY

The real root of being a confident person is your ability to believe in yourself. Let's look at this in more detail now:

JACK:
Many of us have beliefs that limit our success—whether they are beliefs about our own capabilities, beliefs about what it takes to succeed, beliefs about how we should relate with other people, or even common myths that modern-day science or studies have long since refuted. Moving beyond your limiting beliefs is a critical first step toward becoming

successful. You can learn how to identify those beliefs that are limiting you and then replace them with positive ones that support your success.

One of the most limiting beliefs apparent today is the notion that somehow we are not capable of accomplishing our goals. Despite the best educational materials available, and despite decades of recorded knowledge about how to accomplish any task, we somehow choose to say instead, "I can't do that. I don't know how. There's no one to show me. I'm not smart enough." And on and on.

Where does this come from? For most of us, it's a matter of early childhood programming. Whether they knew it or not, our parents, grandparents, and other adult role models told us, "No, no, honey. That's too much for you to handle. Let me do that for you. Maybe next year you can try that."

We take this sense of inability into adulthood, and then it gets reinforced through workplace mistakes and other "failures." But what if you decided to say instead, "I can do this. I am capable. Other people have accomplished this. If I don't have the knowledge, there's someone out there who can teach me."

You make the shift to competence and mastery. This shift in thinking can mean the difference between a lifetime of "could haves" versus accomplishing what you really want in life.

Know that you are worthy of love

Believing you are worthy of love means that you believe I deserve to be treated well—with respect and dignity. I deserve to be cherished and adored by someone. I am worthy of an intimate and fulfilling relationship. I won't settle for less than I deserve. I will do whatever it takes to create that for myself.

There are numerous examples of people who had to break down external barriers that were preventing them from achieving their greatest goals. For example, Elvis Stojko. Being named Elvis at birth, because his parents were big fans of Elvis Presley, could be challenging enough for some people who lack confidence. However, this did not deter figure skater, Elvis Stojko. He began skating at the age of four and won his first trophy when he was six. He also studied karate, earning a black belt when he was sixteen. That would give you confidence!

Elvis Stojko's goal was to compete at the highest level, ultimately dreaming of being world champion and competing in the Olympic games. He incorporated his martial arts into his on-ice performances making him stand out compared to most of his competitors. However, in the 1980's and 90's, the world of figure skating was not as cutting edge when it came to the judges who assessed the scores at the end of a performance. Many of these experts much preferred the traditional style, which for men, often meant flowing costumes, whereas, Elvis would appear wearing a martial arts type of costume. As a result, his scores were often low despite delivering a great performance. And not just because of what he wore. His choreography was also untraditional, as well as the music he chose that accompanied his routines.

Despite being encouraged to conform, Elvis chose to be different. He went on to win back-to-back World Championships in 1994–'95 and a silver medal at the Winter Olympics in Negano, Japan, despite having to perform with a serious groin injury. When asked what the biggest reason for his success was, he paused and simply replied, "I believe in myself; yes that's it. I just believe in myself."

The message is clear. Believe in your own capability and your confidence will produce results that will astonish all of those non-believers!

What to Do If You
HIT A SLUMP

1. Recognize you are in one.

Take time out to rethink, re-energize, and refocus. Talk to the people who support you best—your spouse, mentors, friends, and family.

2. Remind yourself of a major accomplishment.

Select a notable victory that made you feel great. Replay it vividly in your mind. Talk about it. Look at photos, achievement plaques or thank-you letters. Keep a Success Log, a scrapbook of your most positive memories. Understand that you have talent. You've proved it before, and you can do so again.

"No, business is booming; we just make the signs."

3. Get back to basics.

One of the main reasons for a stoppage in results is that you're not practicing the fundamentals. Do a mini reality check. Are you doing the easy things instead of activities that guarantee you results? Take a break if you're physically or mentally drained. Recapture your energy before you start up again. Understand that you can work your way out of it. Life is full of cycles. They don't last forever, so take it one day at a time. Remind yourself, "This too will pass." Gradually the sun will start shining again.

As we stated before, famous adventurer and explorer John Goddard is one of the world's greatest goalsetters. He has accomplished more in his own lifetime than twenty people would have achieved collectively. When questioned about how he overcomes roadblocks, he replied, "When I get stuck, I restart myself by focusing on one goal I can finish in the next seven days—something simple. I don't think about anything else and that usually starts my momentum again."

JACK:
Another challenging situation is when your confidence hits rock bottom. Maybe you've lost your job, the bank foreclosed on your house, or you've gone bankrupt. Then what? To boost your confidence, start by looking back over your life and write down everything you ever did that was a success. Begin with: learned to walk, graduated first grade, learned to ride a bicycle, learned to ride a motorcycle, learned to drive a car, got my driver's license, graduated from high school, survived Mrs. Jones' biology class, graduated from college, became a sergeant in the Marine Corps, whatever it is. Realize you've had many, many successes.

Then go back and look at all the bad things that happened to you and realize you survived every single one of them.

Every single thing that you thought was catastrophic, the end of the world, and you're still here. Realize, "If I survived that, I can survive this."

To create a positive daily habit, at the end of each day take a couple of minutes to write down what you've accomplished. Most people will write down what they didn't accomplish and they'll feel bad about it. "I didn't get to that, I didn't get to that." Focusing on your daily accomplishments creates positive mental stepping stones that pave the way for hitting your bigger targets.

WHEN YOU THINK YOU CAN'T . . .

Revisit some of your greatest achievements

Insights

When you are inspired to do something special you receive a surge of confidence. All that's happening is your natural dopamine level in the brain is increased, which translates into a higher energy level.

So the key questions to ask yourself are:

- What will inspire me most in the next few months or next few years?

- What will ignite that "fire in the belly" feeling that maybe has been lying dormant for a while?

- What fired me up in the past?

- Was it the thought of closing the biggest sale I've ever made?

- Was it an incredible service I provided unexpectedly to a client, a personal friend or family member?

Look for clues that create inspiration. We've all been inspired at one time or another. Think bigger! It's hard to stay motivated if you are just setting the same old goals every quarter. After a while this may de-motivate you. Then you start procrastinating and playing all the denial games that eventually lead to a serious loss of confidence.

One other comment; everyone has their confidence dented at one time or another. In the business world that's part of the game. Everyone experiences deals that collapse, cash flow shortages, team members quitting at the worst time and clients who jump to your competition despite your best efforts.

This is called the real world! You need a thick skin to play in this game. So, suck it up, get back on your feet and start swinging again! Learn from your mistakes. Knowing you'll be smarter the next time pushes you to a higher level on the confidence scale.

One of the best confidence boosters, especially when a crisis occurs, is to first put the event into perspective. Often we mentally expand our disasters, when in reality they are pretty small stuff compared to the big picture of life.

As we mentioned in the last chapter, make sure you surround yourself with a few great people, whose experience can haul you out of the muck when needed. The next chapter is perfect for capitalizing on your newly found confidence. You'll learn numerous ways to ask for what you want—and get it!

"IF YOU HEAR A VOICE WITHIN YOU SAY,
'YOU CANNOT PAINT,' THEN BY
ALL MEANS PAINT AND THAT VOICE
WILL BE SILENCED."

—Vincent van Gogh

ACTION STEPS

Resolving Unfinished Business

RESOLVING UNFINISHED BUSINESS

Make a list of the issues that you want resolved. Write down at least three. Then write down a specific way to resolve each one. What's your action plan? Define it clearly. Finally, decide on the date you are going to have this completed. Then get started.

1. _____

2. _____

3. _____

4. _____

5. _____

Specific benefit for resolving this unfinished business.

Describe how you will feel.

1. _____
2. _____
3. _____
4. _____
5. _____

Action plan for closure. What specifically are you going to do?

1. _____
2. _____
3. _____
4. _____
5. _____

Date for completion.

1. _____
2. _____
3. _____
4. _____
5. _____

Step into your fear!

Review the list of common fears on pages 160-161. Select one fear that holds you back. Choose one or more of the strategic options provided to eliminate this fear.

My fear is:

_____

_____

I will take action as follows:

_____

_____

I will start this process on _____ (date)
and follow through consistently until my
fear has been conquered.

JUST DO IT!

LIVING AND WORKING ON PURPOSE

TAKING DECISIVE ACTION

CONSISTENT PERSISTENCE

ASK FOR WHAT YOU WANT

THE CONFIDENCE FACTOR

BUILDING EXCELLENT RELATIONSHIPS

OVERCOMING SETBACKS

DO YOU SEE THE BIG PICTURE?

IT'S NOT HOCUS-POCUS, IT'S ALL ABOUT FOCUS

YOUR HABITS WILL DETERMINE YOUR FUTURE

We're confident you'll finish the last four—go for it!

Ask For What You Want

"ASKING IS THE BEGINNING OF RECEIVING.
MAKE SURE YOU DON'T GO TO THE
'OCEAN' WITH A TEASPOON. AT LEAST TAKE A
BUCKET SO THE KIDS WON'T LAUGH AT YOU."

—Jim Rohn

It was June, 2006.
Lisa Petrilli, the CEO of C-Level Strategies Inc., was on home-based dialysis because both of her kidneys had stopped working the previous summer. Every night at around 9 PM she would go to her bedroom for the night, hook herself up to a dialysis machine via a tube in her stomach, and stay there until 6 AM. Every night.

When it had become evident that her kidneys were failing, Lisa's family started the process of getting checked to see who could donate a kidney to her. Lisa's Dad had always said if either of his two daughters needed a kidney he would give his up in a heartbeat. Unfortunately for Lisa, he turned out to be the wrong blood type. After this devastating news, the rest of the family was also ruled out for genetic reasons. Lisa had ten friends who stepped up to help. The thought of this alone was staggering for Lisa, that ten people who were not related to her were willing to donate a kidney. One even got all the way to the end of the testing, at which point they found a kidney stone. The rest were all ruled out, too.

Lisa was beside herself. She knew that being on dialysis was extremely hard on her body and that the sooner a transplant was available, the better the outcome she would have. At the time, the waiting period for a kidney in Chicago, where she lived, was six years. That was a long time to wait—and she knew that some people died while waiting.

Lisa was terrified. She was already a year into dialysis. It was at that point she knew there was only one option, an option she was horribly uncomfortable with. Yet she also knew it was her only hope for a healthy life and the brilliant future she had visualized for herself.

She would ask total strangers if they'd give her a kidney. Can you imagine a more difficult question to ask? Lisa plucked up her courage and wrote a letter in her church bulletin asking fellow parishioners to consider giving her their kidney. No one responded. One Sunday later, Lisa received a call from a woman named Rose. She said she had been driving to church that morning and realized she had the bulletin from the previous week still in her car, unread. She had been about to throw it away when she decided to flip through it just to make sure she didn't "miss anything important." She said. "I have Type O blood, and if I am a match, you are more than welcome to have my kidney—I only need one."

That's really how it happened. On March 27, 2007, Rose donated her kidney and forged a bond between her and Lisa that will never be broken. Rose, originally from Ireland, also had an interesting situation of her own. The night before she met Lisa for the first time, Rose had another first, a date with a man called Gary. She told him that she was donating her kidney to a stranger she had just met, literally fifteen hours earlier. He supported her decision. Something must have clicked, because they were soon married and Lisa had the enormous pleasure of being a guest at their wedding. As Lisa says, "That was a very poignant 24 hour period in our lives when all of our paths crossed for the first time."

The doctors told Lisa that Rose's kidney was particularly large in respect to her own. A petite five-foot-tall Lisa, who describes herself as "100 percent Italian," is happy that she now has a little bit of Irish in her! To reinforce this, Rose sent her a St. Patrick's Day card on the one-year anniversary of her transplant.

People genuinely in their heart of hearts want to help other people. You should never doubt this. No matter what you need help with in business or how vulnerable it makes you feel, just ask for help! Normally, people give first in order to receive. Lisa Petrilli asked for the ultimate favor without ever having given anything first. And the answer she received was "Yes, absolutely."

JUST ASK. Think about that. Someone might actually say "yes" to your critical need and it might change your life. Lisa's company—www.LisaPetrilli.com—specializes in empowering business executives to create clear, compelling visions for their organizations and to bring these visions to fruition through four strategic areas, namely, Leadership, Marketing, Business Development and Social Media. Lisa has no fear about asking for new business. She says, "Once you have asked a stranger for a kidney and received a 'yes' in return, you are never afraid to ask for anything ever again."

Ask and
RECEIVE

It's been around for a long, long time, this gift called asking. In fact, one of life's fundamental truths states, "Ask and you shall receive." Isn't that simple? Of course it is. If you are a parent, you will know that kids are the masters when it comes to persistent asking. Their formula is usually to ask until they get what they want. As adults, we seem to lose our ability to ask. We come up with all sorts of excuses and reasons to avoid any possibility of rejection. Kids haven't been programmed like that. They really believe they can have anything they ask for, whether it's a fifty-foot swimming pool or a chocolate ice cream cone.

Here's what you need to understand: The world responds to those who ask—Lisa Petrilli proved that was true. If you are not moving closer to what you want, you probably aren't doing enough asking. Fortunately, to create future abundance there are many ways to ask. In the next few pages you will learn a variety of asking strategies that will guarantee you tremendous success. These are powerful for business as well as your own personal life.

Here's a useful acronym to remind you about asking:

ALWAYS

SEEKING

KNOWLEDGE

Some people say knowledge is power. Not true! The use of knowledge is power. That's something to imprint in your mind forever. When you ask, you can receive all sorts of information, ideas, strategies, names of people with influence and, yes, even money. There are many good reasons to ask, and the rewards are substantial. So why do people stumble when they have an opportunity to ask? Essentially there are three reasons.

1. They have a belief system that says it's not right to ask.

2. They lack confidence.

3. They fear rejection.

(For an in-depth look at how to overcome personal barriers to asking, read *The Aladdin Factor*. See Resource Guide.)

Old, deep-seated belief systems can paralyze you. The Bible says, "Ask and you shall receive, seek and you shall find, knock and it shall be opened unto you." That comes from a pretty high authority, one that has far more power than some outdated belief system you may have inherited years ago as a child. If this describes you, then you'll need to do some analysis of your limiting belief systems. Get help. Talk to a trusted friend, adviser or counselor. Work through it. Realize there are other ways to view life and circumstances. Make a change in how you see things and what you really value. Let go of all that old stuff. It's clogging up your future and strangling your ability to ask.

Remember the second reason? Yes, it's that self-defeating old confidence trait we discussed in the last chapter. Lack of confidence will definitely stunt your desire to ask. Again, it's all about breaking old barriers. Trust yourself. Take a step forward. Ask anyway. The worst you'll hear is "No," which brings up the third reason—rejection. When you get a negative response, are you any worse off? Not really, unless you take it personally— which is the number one reason people fear rejection. Some people can't handle their emotions, even though the word "no" was never intended as a personal put-down.

So how do you rate in the asking stakes? Are any of these three negative forces playing havoc with your opportunity to get ahead? If they are, this is where you must start.

It's called taking the leap of faith. And that means releasing old beliefs, feeling good about yourself and understanding that life isn't perfect—it's normal to experience a lot of roadblocks along the way.

© Randy Glasbergen
www.glasbergen.com

"Whenever something goes wrong,
the first question we must ask ourselves is,
'Can this problem be fixed with duct tape?'"

Seven Ways to Boost
Your Business,
SIMPLY BY ASKING

Here are seven big ways to ensure that your business becomes more profitable. Do these, and your revenues will soar. To assist you with this, do the Action Steps called Seven Ways to Boost Your Business.

1. Ask for information.

To win potential new clients, you first need to know what their current challenges are, what they want to accomplish and how they plan to do it. Only then can you proceed to demonstrate the advantages of your unique product or service. It's amazing how so many people get this simple process screwed up. Salespeople are notorious for ignoring this essential part of the presentation. They often have dollar signs in their eyes, illustrating that their main focus is on lightening your wallet.

We call them dinosaurs. Here's a better way: First, suspend your own self-interest. This is critical. Focus on sincerely helping the person with whom you are meeting. Ask questions, starting with the words *who, why, what, where, when* and *how*, to obtain all the information you need. This is called the discovery process. Trial lawyers are experts at this. In discovery, they are allowed to ask virtually any question that will help them prepare their case. They don't rely on guesswork. Only when they are armed with the facts of the case can they make a compelling defense or prosecution in court.

It's the same in business. Only when you truly understand and appreciate the needs of the people you meet can you offer a solution. And if everything fits, the solution for them will be your product or service.

There are two important questions to ask in the discovery process. First, "What is your single biggest challenge at this time?" We have found this question is a great way to develop rapport. Here's the key: You must show genuine interest when you ask. If you sound like a cliché out of some ancient sales manual, you will experience resistance. When the person answers, listen carefully and ask another question, one that will give you more information. Repeat this process until you have explored this topic as fully as you need to. We call it peeling the onion. Each time you ask a new question, you peel away another layer. Removing more layers eventually leads you to the core of the issue. Often that's where the most important information lies, but it takes skillful questioning to uncover it. A good marriage counselor or psychotherapist uses the same technique to discover what lies behind a dysfunctional relationship, or acute depression. So practice asking simple, direct questions. Be attentive. Listen well, and learn to read between the lines. Remember, the real issues are usually below the surface.

The second important question to open up the conversation is, "What are some of your most important goals and objectives in the next few years?" If you think people won't answer a question like that, think again. If you have developed good rapport in the first ten minutes, suspended your desire to make a sale, and demonstrated a sincere interest in their business, people will tell you a lot more than you think.

One other tip when you are asking for information. Don't interrogate people with a constant barrage of bottom-line questions. In between your questions make a few comments, share an idea or offer a helpful suggestion. Relate to what the other person is saying, and then gently ask your next question. The more you can relate, the more comfortable and relaxed your prospect will become. This develops that magic ingredient called trust. When you establish trust, the door of opportunity swings wide open and you are welcomed in with open arms.

Eventually this leads to big checks. You can also practice this type of asking in your personal life, with family and friends. The rewards are equally substantial.

BEN WICKS AND COMPANY reprinted by permission from Canadian Speakers, & Writers Ltd.

BEN WICKS

"You hit him up for a million bucks. I'll ask him for five bucks and he'll think he's getting a deal."

JACK AND MARK:
A friend of ours, Marilyn Kriegel, told us the following story about her son Otis. He and his girlfriend had returned to San Francisco from college for the summer break. They both wanted to get a job for the summer. The difference in their approaches demonstrates the power of asking. The girl began to prepare her résumé. She spent the next two days on her computer getting ready to ask. Otis simply got on the phone and started calling people to find out if they

had any job openings. Two days later she had a half-written resumé. Otis had six serious job possibilities, one of which turned into a summer job.

Source: *The Aladdin Factor*

2. Ask for business.

Here's an amazing statistic: After doing a complete presentation about the benefits of their product or service, more than 60 percent of the time salespeople never ask for the order. That's a bad habit, one that could ultimately put you on the business scrap heap.

As we said earlier, if you need help with this, kids are your best role models. Here's more proof: We're playing golf on a hot, sunny July afternoon. The tee-off area at the sixth hole is close to a perimeter fence. On the other side of the wire mesh a six-year-old girl is sitting at a small wooden table. On the table are two big plastic jugs, one filled with iced tea and the other with lemonade. As our foursome waits for the players ahead to finish the hole, the little girl asks, "Would you like a nice cool drink while you're waiting?" She stands there holding a plastic cup in one hand and wearing a great big smile. Her name is Melanie.

It's hot and we're all thirsty, so we walk over to the fence. "Would you prefer iced tea or lemonade?" she asks. After we make our selections, she pours the drinks, holds out her hand and says, "That's fifty-five cents each, please." We pass four one-dollar bills through the wire mesh. When she has the cash carefully tucked away in a little money pouch, she passes the drinks through a hole in the fence and says, "Thank you very much, have a nice day." None of us receives any change! And who's going to complain? After all, she's worth the 45 percent tip with a presentation like that.

If you want the business, you must always ASK

How often do you think she asks? You're right. Every time someone shows up at the sixth tee. This little entrepreneur didn't have a ten-week sales training course—she did it naturally. Consider her brilliant strategy—a lesson in business we can all benefit from. First, she picked an excellent location. She also provided a valuable service on a hot day. "Would you prefer iced tea or lemonade?" proves she knew the importance of choice. And her confidence factor was so high that she felt it wasn't necessary to give change. We figured out that Melanie was pulling in sixty dollars a day at least. She definitely had a goal, maybe a new bike or the latest phone! At this rate she'll probably be delivering sales seminars one day.

Like Melanie, you must always ask a closing question to secure the business. Don't waffle, or talk around it, or even worse, wait for your prospect to ask you. Here are a few examples that have worked well for us.

"Would you like to give it a try?" This is a no-pressure, non-threatening type of question. If you have given an effective presentation loaded with value and benefits, most people will think, "What have I got to lose? I might as well try it." When selling our coaching programs and seminars, we ask directly, "Would you like to attend the next program?" The late Barney Zick, a champion sales consultant, used to add a touch of humor. He'd suggest if you're really stuck, just say, "Do you wanna buy one?" The point is, just ask. Also, note that your closing question is designed to produce a "Yes" or "No" answer, unlike your earlier questions in the discovery process, where you simply want more information. So refine your asking process and start practicing. Smoke will rise!

3. Ask for written endorsements.

Well-written, results-oriented testimonials from highly respected people are powerful. They solidify the quality of your work and leverage you as a person who has integrity, is trustworthy and who gets the job done on time.

Here's what's fascinating—most people in business don't do this. That gives you a great opportunity to jump ahead of your competition. All you need to do is ask. When is the best time? Right after you have provided excellent service, completed a major project under budget, gone the extra mile to help out, or any other time you've made your customer really happy. Under these circumstances, people will be glad to praise your efforts. Here's how to do it:

Simply ask if your customer would be willing to give you a testimonial about the value of your product or service, plus any other helpful comments. To make it easy, we suggest that you ask a few questions on the phone, and take good notes. Ask your client to clearly describe the benefits. Probe for specific results that were achieved because of your work.

For example, a sales trainer who has just completed a three-month program with the entire sales organization of a rapidly growing company could ask, "What results have you noticed in the last sixty days?" The sales manager might reply, "Since you shared your ideas with us, our total sales volume has jumped 35 percent compared to the previous few months."

This is an excellent, specific, measurable result. Stay away from general statements like, "It was a very good program—everyone really enjoyed it." This type of statement has little impact on the reader. But if you have a sales team that needs help and you read about a 35 percent increase in sales, you're more likely to think, "That's what we're looking for. If it works for them, it could work for us, too—how do I contact this successful sales trainer?"

When you have finished your mini interview on the phone, offer to write the testimonial yourself. This will save your client's time. This is important for two reasons. First, it removes any pressure from your client. He or she may not be very skilled at writing powerful testimonials, and it's time-consuming. Second, you have an opportunity to craft the wording in a way that produces maximum impact. If you are not great at writing, hire a professional—it's well worth it. When you have completed this, email or text the testimonial back to your client for approval. Then have it typed on their letterhead and signed.

Make a habit of collecting great testimonials. If you have a lot of customers and prospects visiting your office, consider having a plasma screen in a very visible position using a continuous loop to showcase your testimonials. Use photos and large fonts for clarity and impact. Otherwise, simply put them in a three-ring binder and leave it on a coffee table in the reception area of your office, or frame the best ones and hang them on a wall where everyone can read them. In the binder, highlight the most important comments. All of your promotional literature should have at least three excellent, well-written testimonials prominently featured.

Another good option is to take the most powerful sentences from ten different testimonials and place these on one page along with the names of your clients. Even better, include a small head-and-shoulders photograph of each client. If your product is easy to photograph, like a car or furniture, create an action photograph. For example, your new customer sitting in the car or showing off their beautiful dining room table.

Technology today has shifted to video endorsements. We like to carry a Flipcam, a pocketsized mini-video recorder that is easy to use and inexpensive. Smartphones of course, have video capability, too, which makes on-the-spot endorsements easy to obtain. You can then download these to your website, or include them as part of your sales presentation. Use the same questioning process as outlined earlier. Make your subject as relaxed as possible. You want a sincere, authentic message delivered with good eye contact. You can edit this later. Make sure you take enough time to obtain a few memorable comments.

With this technology you can instantly transfer powerful high definition information to prospects anywhere in the world. Compare that to ten years ago. Imagine what the next ten years will provide—maybe all you've got to do is think what you want to say and it's automatically imprinted on any device you want—that would really be awesome!

ENLIST HIGHLY CREDIBLE PEOPLE

If you have a few comments from local well-known people, chances are, your prospects will recognize them and be suitably impressed.

Here's another important aspect of written endorsements: Include a few people who are peers in your industry. The more established they are, the better. For example, the first few pages of this book contain comments from superstars in the training industry and top business achievers. Didn't they influence you just a little?

You can also group your testimonials into specific categories. If your product or service has several benefits, place each of these under separate headings such as excellent service, price, quality, product knowledge and on-time delivery. If a prospect is concerned about one area in particular, you can show several testimonials that prove you are wonderful in that capacity.

These are simple strategies that will bring you a lot more business. So take advantage, and from now on make a commitment to ask for high-impact testimonials. It's a habit that will produce big dividends.

4. Ask for top-quality referrals.

Just about everyone in business knows the importance of referrals. Simply put, it's the easiest, least-expensive way of ensuring your growth and success in the marketplace. However, here's the reality: In our experience, only one out of ten companies has a system for gathering referrals. How do you explain that?

Well, it's the same old story—bad habits, plus that recurring theme you've been reading about—fear of rejection. In Chapter 5, Building Excellent Relationships, we talked about the importance of developing core clients. These are the people who will gladly give you referrals because you treat them so well. So why aren't you asking all of them for referrals? Maybe you don't believe the benefits yet. Here's an example that will persuade you to think again:

Helen is an expert financial planner. In fact, she is consistently in the top 5 percent of the two thousand representatives who make up her company's sales team. Over the years, Helen has built a foundation of core clients. Her target market is people in the fifty- to sixty-year-old age group who have at least two hundred thousand dollars in their investment portfolios. Here's one way she boosted her business recently: She invited her core clients to attend a Saturday morning breakfast at a nearby hotel. The invitation informed them that they would hear some important information about new government regulations, which could affect their future prosperity. Included in the invitation was a request for each core client to bring three or four friends who were similarly qualified.

The result? A total of ninety-two people showed up for breakfast, many of whom were guests. The breakfast cost twelve dollars per person, which Helen was happy to pay. After her forty-five-minute talk, many of the guests requested more information. This turned into ten new clients, and twenty-two thousand dollars in commissions for Helen. Not a bad morning's work!

As all top businesspeople know, asking for qualified referrals is an important part of an overall marketing strategy. It's a habit that will dramatically increase your income. Like any other habit, it requires that you do it often. Then eventually it becomes easy.

Obtaining good referrals is not limited to your core clients, although they provide the distinct advantage of opening doors for you that otherwise might remain closed. Opportunities exist every day. When you meet a new prospect who doesn't need or want your product or service, you can still ask if he might know someone who does. What have you got to lose? The worst thing that can happen is that he may say "No." You really aren't any worse off. And often he'll say, "As a matter of fact, I do know someone who might be interested in this."

By the way, make sure you describe in detail what your definition of a good prospect is. The last thing you want is a bunch of names that are unsuitable. This will only waste your time as well as theirs. When someone gives you a referral, always double-check. Ask questions about the person until you are confident that they really do qualify.

Another smart thing our friend Barney Zick used to do is ask for referrals up front. In fact, consider making asking for referrals a condition of every sale. Most people never do this, so you have a wonderful opportunity to capitalize on their oversight. For example, you might say, "One reason we can offer you such a great price is that we also ask for three excellent referrals. All we ask is, if you are completely satisfied with our work, that you provide those referrals when our work is finished. This reduces our marketing budget significantly, allowing us to pass the savings on to you.

At this point you can reinforce your comments by sharing wonderful testimonials from other happy customers. Here's another way Barney asked: "Would you please introduce me to a few people of equal quality to you?" In this way you extend a genuine compliment, and that makes your client feel good.

A question we are often asked is, "Should I pay people for giving me referrals?" This is entirely up to you, although most people, especially your core clients, will be happy to refer you without an inducement. On the other hand, if a referral fee, say 10 percent, will stimulate someone to provide good leads every month, then do it.

You can also develop creative ways of saying "Thank you" to consistent referral givers. Find out what they like and surprise them with an unexpected gift. This could be a couple of movie passes, a unique coffee mug (with your logo on it), a specialty foods basket or a dinner for two at their favorite restaurant. Recognition of their help is more important than the size of the gift. And if their referrals lead to a substantial increase in revenue, you can upgrade the reward accordingly.

Another way to ensure that you receive referrals is to give your own clients referrals first. Also, consider offering a free consultation or trial offer in return for some good references. This works well when you are just launching a new venture, or don't know a lot of people in the marketplace.

As you can see, there are many opportunities for you to create new business by linking yourself to core clients, and others who are well-connected to people you'd like to meet. Make an effort to do something different compared to your normal networking procedures. Plan to talk to a higher caliber of client or ask for referrals more often to increase your business. Remember, continually harvesting excellent referrals can make you wealthy. One last point: Use the word "introductions" instead of referrals. It's less intimidating and is more accurate. The first step is to introduce yourself to the prospect. Some people may have had a negative experience because a pushy salesperson pressured them into giving referrals.

5. Ask for more business.

Many people lose thousands of dollars in sales every year because they have nothing more to offer after the initial sale. Look for other products or services to add to your portfolio. Also, develop a system to determine when your clients will require more of your own product or service. People buy in cycles, and you need to know when those cycles are most likely to occur. The simplest way to determine this is to ask your customers when you should contact them to reorder.

It's easier to sell your existing clients more of what you have than it is to go out looking for new clients.

LES:

Peter Thomson, one of the leading business and personal growth strategists in the United Kingdom, shared with me a very simple but effective tool for increasing sales. He calls it The Magic Matrix. I encourage you to practice this if you want bigger profits. Here's how it works.

The matrix is a grid with a list of your clients on the left vertical axis. Along the top of the grid, the horizontal axis, make a list of all the products and services you provide. Then for each client place an "x" in every box on the grid for the specific products and services they have purchased from you. It's useful to note the dates of their last purchase for each item as well.

Then look at all the empty boxes on your grid. These are opportunities to sell some of your other products and services. Peter says many salespeople have favorite products and services they like to focus on during their presentation, but they often neglect to make their prospect or client aware that there are other products and services available, too. In other words, they don't tell the whole story even months after the initial sale. Big mistake! One of Peter's clients increased their annual sales by fifty percent when the sales manager used this tool to reinvigorate his sales team.

Remember this: Business grinds to a halt when you stop asking. When you consistently ask for more business, you rapidly gain momentum.

Many years ago McDonald's, the hamburger people, came up with a unique way to ask for more. They trained their staff to ask one more question when someone ordered a hamburger and a drink. This single question added more than twenty million dollars to their bottom line. The question was, "Would you like fries with that?" Obviously a lot of people said, "Sure, why not."

Here's what's worth noting: How often do they ask that question? Every single time! This requires good communication, and training all staff to be alert with each customer. It obviously pays big dividends.

This is commonly known as the "up sell." In the car industry, once you've purchased a new vehicle, you will probably be asked to buy an extended warranty for a few hundred dollars more, or a perma-coat finish that will give you years of protection from rust and stone chips.

What else could you be asking for when you do business? Adding one more question at the end of the sale could significantly increase your income. Remember: If you don't ask, someone else will!

6. Ask to renegotiate.

Regular business activities include negotiation and the opportunity to renegotiate. Many people get stuck because they aren't very good at this. It's another form of asking that can save you a lot of time and money.

For example, if the mortgage on your home is coming up for renewal and the interest rate is currently at 5 percent, you can say, "That's a pretty good rate; I'll just sign on for another three years." But what if you met with your banker and said, "I'm looking at my renewal options. There are other banks who would like my business. I'd be happy to stay with you if you can give me a 4.5 percent rate." You'd be surprised how often the bank will agree to this, because they know the competition is fierce for this type of lending. That extra discount can save you a significant amount of money, and it only took one question to secure it.

Other opportunities to renegotiate include stretching payments over a longer period of time. If you have a cash-flow crunch, an extra thirty days at no interest (you might as well ask for that, too) can help stabilize your finances.

All sorts of contracts can be renegotiated simply by asking. As long as you do it ethically and in the spirit of win-win, you can enjoy a lot of flexibility. Nothing is ever cast in stone. If your situation requires change, ask for it.

LES:
One morning I was flying to another city to conduct a Power of Focus workshop for a group of entrepreneurs. The biggest snowstorm of the year had delayed my departure by more than an hour. By the time we were ready to land at the international airport on the outskirts of the city it was 8:30 AM. My workshop started at 9:30 AM. The captain then informed us we couldn't land because of fog, so we would continue on to the municipal airport downtown. I thought, "Great, that's closer to where I want to go," and started preparing to disembark. Upon landing, the captain announced, "We have no baggage-handling facilities here so we are going to refuel, wait until the fog lifts at the international airport and fly back there." Then he added, "Until the fog lifts I guess you are trapped in the aircraft." Interesting choice of words!

This provided me with another great opportunity to ask. I summoned the flight attendant and explained that I only had carry-on luggage, and that my meeting was due to start in twenty-five minutes. She agreed to ask the captain if he would make an exception and allow me to leave the plane. She came back smiling a few minutes later, opened the door and lowered the stairway. Until then no one on the plane had moved. As I glanced back, several other businesspeople were making similar requests. It never occurred to them that to change their predicament they just had to ask.

7. Ask for feedback.

This is another important component of asking that is often overlooked. How do you really know if your product or service is meeting the needs of your customer? Ask them, "How are we doing? What can we do to improve our service to you? Tell us what you like about our products and what you don't like." Set up regular customer surveys that ask good questions, and include the tough questions. Consider a monthly focus group where you can meet your customers face-to-face. Buy them lunch and ask them lots of questions. It's a great way to fine-tune your business.

If you supervise a team of people or run a large organization, ask the people you work with for ideas. They are often the most knowledgeable when it comes to practical, everyday activities that make the business run smoothly. Also talk to your suppliers. There may be ways to improve efficiency with better distribution, or to reduce costs using just-in-time inventory policies. No matter what type of industry you work in, you are surrounded by people who can give you valuable feedback. All you need to do is ask. As we mentioned earlier, there is a valuable workshop at the end of this chapter that will help you create an action plan to implement these seven ways to ask.

DILBERT *reprinted by permission of United Feature Syndicate, Inc.*

How to ASK

Some people don't enjoy the fruits of asking because they don't ask effectively. If you use vague, unspecific language you will not be understood. Here are five ways to ensure that your asking gets results.

1. Ask clearly.

Be precise. Think clearly about your request. Take time to prepare. Design words that have the greatest impact. This is extremely important. Words are powerful, so choose them carefully. Being incoherent won't serve you well. If you need to, find people who are great at asking, and pick their brains. Ask for help.

> "ADULTS ARE ALWAYS ASKING KIDS
> WHAT THEY WANT TO BE WHEN THEY GROW UP,
> BECAUSE THEY ARE LOOKING FOR IDEAS."
>
> —Paula Poundstone

2. Ask with confidence.

People who ask confidently get more out of life than those who are hesitant and uncertain. Now that you've figured out what you want to ask for, do it with certainty, boldness and confidence. This does not mean being brash, arrogant or conceited. Confidence can be a quiet strength, but to the people you are asking, it's visible. The only negative thing that can happen is that your request may be denied. Does this put you in a worse position than before? Of course not. It just means that this particular route to getting results is closed.

So look for another one.

3. Ask consistently.

Some people fold up their tent after making one timid request. They quit too soon. If you want to unearth the true riches in life, you'll need to do a lot of asking. Treat it like a game; keep on asking until you find the answers. Ask consistently. In sales, there are usually four or five "No's" before you get a "Yes." The top producers understand this. It's normal. And when you find a way to ask that works, keep on doing it. And if you have a dream to fulfill, don't put it on hold—start asking.

JACK:
To be successful, you have to take risks, and one of the risks is the willingness to risk rejection. Here's an email I received from Donna Hutcherson, who heard me speak at her company's convention in Scottsdale, Arizona.

"My husband Dale and I heard you at the Walsworth convention in early January—Dale came as one of the spouses. He was particularly impressed by your mention of not having anything to lose by asking. After hearing you speak, he decided to go for one of his lifetime goals (and heart's desire)—a head football coaching position. He applied for four openings within my sales territory and Sebring High School called him back the next day, encouraging him to fill out the application online. He did so right away and could hardly sleep that night. After two interviews he was chosen over sixty one other applicants. Today Dale accepted the position as head football coach at Sebring High School in Sebring, Florida."

Here is an excerpt from another email I received from Donna this past summer:

"Taking over a program that had back-to-back seasons with one win and nine losses (and a reputation for giving up), Dale led the team to a winning record (with four "come-from-behind" wins in the last three minutes), a county championship, and only the third playoff in the seventy eight year history of the school. He was also named County Coach of the Year and Sports Story of the Year. Most important is that he changed the lives of the many players, staff and students with whom he worked."

Source: *The Success Principles*

4. Ask creatively.

In this age of intense global competition, your asking may get lost in the crowd, unheard by the decision makers you are hoping to reach. There's a simple way around this. In his book, *Don't Worry, Make Money*, bestselling author Richard Carlson described the technique as "purple snowflakes." This is a strategy to help you stand out in the crowd. For example, if you want someone's attention don't just send an ordinary request. Use your creativity to dream up a high-impact introduction. Here's a good example from *The Best of Bits and Pieces*:

The chief buyer for a thriving company was particularly inaccessible to salespeople. You didn't call him, he called you. On several occasions when salespeople managed to get into his office, they were summarily tossed out.

One saleswoman finally broke through his defenses. She sent him a homing pigeon with her card attached to one leg. On the card she had written, "If you want to know more about our product, just throw our representative out the window!"

This is a good example of a "purple snowflake." What could you do to create a powerful impact with your most important prospects? Make it fun. Brainstorm with your team. Schedule time every month for "purple snowflaking," and don't be surprised when those impenetrable doors swing wide open and welcome you in.

5. Ask sincerely.

When you really need help, people will respond. Sincerity requires being real. It means dropping the image facade and showing a willingness to be vulnerable. Tell it the way it is, lumps and all. Don't worry if your presentation isn't perfect; ask from your heart. Keep it simple and people will open up to you.

Also, your request will be favored if you can clearly show that you have already put in a lot of effort. For example, if a charitable youth organization needed only $50 to achieve its target of $1,000, and the youngsters demonstrated all the things they had done to earn the first $950—car washes, bake sales, garbage clean-ups and bottle drives—you might donate the remainder, especially if they had a specific deadline, and there were only a few hours left.

When you've exhausted all avenues to get what you want, people are more likely to give you a helping hand when you ask for support. Those who ask for a free ride all the time will rarely succeed.

THERE ARE MANY WAYS TO ASK

Use All Of Them!

Insights

You have just feasted on a smorgasbord of asking strategies that can dramatically improve any area of your life. We have all proved this over and over again in our own businesses. Relentless asking got *Chicken Soup for the Soul* a publisher. Asking for business has created many other multimillion dollar opportunities and allowed us to meet and work with some of the most dynamic, innovative and inspiring people in the world. Sometimes we shake our heads in amazement at this incredible journey the habit of asking has provided.

Now, you do the same. Commit to more asking every week and you'll enjoy a unique advantage, because most people in business perform low on the asking scale. Here's some eye opening proof from research done by Herbert True, a marketing specialist at Notre Dame University. He found that:

- 44 percent of all salespeople quit trying after the first call

- 24 percent quit after the second call

- 14 percent quit after the third call

- 12 quit trying to sell their prospect after the fourth call

This means that 94 percent of all salespeople quit after the fourth call. But 60 percent of all sales are made after the fourth call. This revealing statistic shows that 94 percent of all salespeople don't give themselves a chance at 60 percent of the prospective buyers. You may have the capacity, but you also have to have the tenacity! To be successful, you have to ask, ask, ask, ask, ask!

Well, we're down to the final three areas of focus. You're on the last lap. Congratulations for sticking with it to this point.

These final three strategies will put you into overdrive, as far as results go. It will require a big effort on your part. So, stay focused as we introduce you to consistent persistence, taking decisive action and learning to live on purpose.

"A STOCKBROKER ASKED ME TO
BUY A STOCK THAT WOULD TRIPLE ITS
VALUE EVERY YEAR. I TOLD HIM, AT MY AGE
I DON'T EVEN BUY GREEN BANANAS."

—Claude Pepper

ACTION STEPS

Asking for What You Want

To help you increase your productivity and income right away, take a few minutes to complete this Action Plan for asking. Successfully implementing these strategies can increase your revenue by at least 50 percent. This is also a great exercise to do with your sales or management team.

1. Ask for information.

What's the best single improvement you could make when asking for information?

_____

_____

_____

_____

2. Ask for business.

Is your closing question for business bringing you the level of success you want? If not, create at least two new ways of asking for business. Keep them simple and specific.

A. _____

B. _____

3. Ask for written endorsements.

Write the names of five people who can give you excellent testimonials. Set a time to call these people and follow through.

1. _____ 4. _____

2. _____ 5. _____

3. _____

4. Ask for top-quality introductions.

Outline a specific system for continually bringing new people into your business. Remember, the key word is continually—that means you do it every week.

_____

_____

_____

5. Ask for more business.

Name five clients you will approach for more business. Create a good reason for them to buy more—special offers, discounts or a new product launch.

1. _____ 4. _____

2. _____ 5. _____

3. _____

6. Ask to renegotiate.

Name one situation that you want to renegotiate in the next month. Consider interest rates, lines of credit, time off, salary, job description, etc.

_____

_____

_____

7. Ask for feedback.

List two ways you can improve your feedback from customers. Consider direct calls, customer focus groups, online questionnaires, or point-of-sale comment cards.

A. _____

_____

B. _____

_____

In addition to these seven strategies, continually check to see if there's anything you have stopped asking for.

Make a list now of three things you have stopped asking for that you would like more of.

A. _____

_____

B. _____

_____

C. _____

_____

LIVING AND WORKING ON PURPOSE

TAKING DECISIVE ACTION

CONSISTENT PERSISTENCE

ASK FOR WHAT YOU WANT

THE CONFIDENCE FACTOR

BUILDING EXCELLENT RELATIONSHIPS

OVERCOMING SETBACKS

DO YOU SEE THE BIG PICTURE?

IT'S NOT HOCUS-POCUS, IT'S ALL ABOUT FOCUS

YOUR HABITS WILL DETERMINE YOUR FUTURE

Only three strategies left—good job!

Consistent Persistence

"I WILL PERSIST UNTIL I SUCCEED.
ALWAYS I WILL TAKE ANOTHER STEP.
IF THAT IS OF NO AVAIL, I WILL TAKE ANOTHER
AND YET ANOTHER. IN TRUTH, ONE STEP AT
A TIME IS NOT TOO DIFFICULT. I KNOW
THAT SMALL STEPS REPEATED WILL
COMPLETE ANY UNDERTAKING."

—Og Mandino

If you take a close look at people who are truly successful in life, you will find one character trait in abundance.

We call it Consistent Persistence. At first glance, the words consistent and persistence may seem similar. That's true, they are. We have double-barreled them to emphasize the importance of this habit. In case you feel like skipping over this without due thought and consideration, here's an important statement to digest and store forever in the deepest recesses of your being: **You will never achieve big results in your life without consistent and persistent action.**

In this chapter, you will discover how to make consistently good choices so that your dreams and goals turn into exciting reality. You will also learn what a higher level of consistency means, and how you can implement this daily. In addition, we'll show you how to build your mental toughness so you can endure hard times and unexpected challenges when they arise.

Many organizations struggle because their leaders put up with a high level of inconsistency. Well, we have news for you. The business world today is a lot different than it was ten years ago. The performance bar has been raised to a new level. Ineptitude will not be tolerated. For example: You call a team meeting for 9 AM Monday. Each one of your twenty sales representatives is asked to attend. At 9:15 AM only fourteen people have shown up. Two more eventually stroll in at 9:25 AM and the rest never appear. And it's like that almost every week.

This lack of consistency will wreck your team unity. Usually a few prima donnas are the root cause. Sometimes they show up, sometimes they don't. It's really frustrating. In today's world the answer is simple—lock them out! That's right, at 9:00 AM sharp, lock the doors of the meeting room. The message will soon be understood: "If you want to play on our team, you must be consistent."

The Benefits of CONSISTENCY

First, to give you a taste of what we're referring to, let's look at a wonderful role model. He's known as Mr. Consistency: Cal Ripken Jr.

In case you are not a baseball fan, Cal Ripken Jr. played for the Baltimore Orioles. The reason he is a legend in the sport is his incredible consistency. On September 6, 1995, Cal played his 2,131st consecutive major league baseball game. In doing so, he broke the record of 2,130 games set by Lou Gehrig, a record that had remained unbeaten for more than fifty-six years.

Let's put this into perspective: To equal Cal Ripken Jr.'s consistency, an employee working an average eight hours a day, five days a week, would need to work eight years, one month and twenty days and never call in sick! No wonder he was called the Iron Man of Baseball. He played in every single game for more than thirteen years. (On the night he broke the record, the closest person to him in consecutive starts was Frank Thomas of the Chicago White Sox, who had played a mere 235 games.)

Ripken's ability to show up for every game translated into a remarkable list of successes. During the streak he was the winner of two Most Valuable Player awards, in 1983 and in 1991. He also played in twelve consecutive All-Star games, and hit more home runs than any other major-league shortstop. Financially he is set for life, but more than the money, he had a tremendous feeling of accomplishment.

His philosophy about work is refreshingly simple. All he ever wanted was to play baseball, preferably for Baltimore, and to do his best in every game.

This demonstrates a keen sense of responsibility and a work ethic that is all too rare today. By simply showing up consistently and playing his best, the rewards eventually materialized. And through it all, Ripken maintained a humble unassuming attitude.

It's interesting that Cal Ripken Jr. has also developed the same consistency in his family life. His wife and children are important to him, and it shows. Compare this to the weekly ritual of scandals and contract demands now rampant in the world of professional sports, perpetuated by individuals of lesser maturity and weakness of character.

One last footnote to the story and a point worth remembering. When you stand for something and do a remarkable job of it, you attract the top people and create huge rewards for yourself. On his record-breaking night, Cal Ripken Jr. was feted by world-famous celebrities, multinational corporations and even the president of the United States. He was showered with gifts and received numerous standing ovations. Imagine! All for showing up every day and doing what he loves to do.

MARK:
I am a huge admirer of Professor Muhammed Yunus. This wonderful Nobel Laureate, humanitarian, and founder of Grameen Bank—bankers to the poor—has four key disciplines he emphasizes if you want to succeed in business and in life. These are daily discipline, hard work, solid ethics and consistency. The simple implementation of these has spawned hundreds of similar micro lending business models to his own, who are helping the poorest

nations around the world. When you find something that works, keep doing it. By all means strive to improve your process, but make sure your consistency doesn't falter.

Now put yourself under the microscope for a moment. Does your discipline, work rate, ethics, and consistency show up in real terms every day? Or are you bouncing around all over the place, dabbling here and there with the opportunities of life? If you are doing pretty well, we applaud you. But let's move your abilities to another level, that rarefied atmosphere where the challenges are greater and the rewards are even more lucrative.

Embrace Your Greatest
POWER

In previous chapters we positioned all of the Action Step exercises at the end so you could focus better and take as much time as you want. That's about to change. **In fact we want you to stop right now, get mentally prepared and do the following two-part exercise before continuing. If you decide to keep on reading, you will completely miss the impact of this powerful lesson.**

Using the following worksheet, make a list of six things you absolutely have to get done in the next two months. These are activities that must be completed, for whatever reason.

They may include some of the short-term goals you established earlier. Keep your statements brief. Opposite each activity that you have to complete, write one word that describes your feelings about it.

Think of how you honestly feel when you visualize each task. To help you, here are a few examples of "feeling" words: angry, sad, happy, excited, upset, worried, frustrated, joyful, loving, thankful. These are all words that directly relate to emotions.

Choose your own word to describe how you feel about each item on your Have-To list. It is really important that you complete this exercise *immediately* to gain the most benefit. In our Power of Focus Coaching Program this has been one of the biggest breakthrough activities for our clients.

HAVE-TO'S

Things I have to do in the next two months,

i.e., no later than: _____ date: _____

FEELINGS

What word best describes your feelings about having to do these particular activities?

HAVE-TO'S	FEELINGS
1. _____	_____
2. _____	_____
3. _____	_____
4. _____	_____
5. _____	_____
6. _____	_____

Well done! Now let's review your list. Take a look at each item and, one at a time, put a line through each task. **That's right, cross it off your list.**

Here's why: You don't **have to** do any of these things. No, you really don't! Now, you may be protesting that some of these things really must be done. They can't be avoided—taxes must be paid, you say. No, you don't have to pay taxes. You may end up in jail or pay a fine, but you don't have to pay taxes. These are just the consequences if you don't pay—but you don't have to. In case you are a little confused by this, let's make a simple defining statement:

IN LIFE, THERE'S NOTHING YOU REALLY HAVE TO DO

That includes working seventy hours a week, or staying in a job, business or relationship you don't enjoy.

Now look at your list again—will your world really come to an end if you do not complete these tasks in the next two months? Of course not. You may not be happy if you don't complete them, and there may be real consequences if you don't. We understand that. The big point we are making is that **you don't have to**.

Let's switch gears for a minute. (If you are still confused, bear with us. Everything will become crystal-clear shortly.) Notice the words you selected to describe your feelings. Based on years of experience, we'd guess a lot of those words are negative, especially if the task is something you have been putting off for a while or are not looking forward to. It's normal to feel anxious, concerned, or frustrated in these situations. Take another look at the words you used. What sort of energy do these "feeling" words bring out in you—negative or positive? You're right! If the feeling is negative, you automatically create a negative energy that drains your capacity to perform at a high level.

Okay, let's move on to the second part of the exercise, using the worksheet that follows. Make a list of at least six things you want to do, or choose to do in the next two months. **Make this a different list.** What are you really looking forward to doing? Again, choose a word to describe how you feel about completing each item on your list. Review the following examples first.

To get the full benefit of this it's important that you sit down and complete this activity now.

CHOOSE-TO'S

Things I choose to do in the next two months. (e.g., plan a special anniversary, launch a new product, start guitar lessons)

i.e., no later than: _____ date: _____

FEELINGS

What word best describes your feelings about wanting to complete these activities?

CHOOSE-TO'S	FEELINGS
1. _____	_____
2. _____	_____
3. _____	_____
4. _____	_____
5. _____	_____
6. _____	_____

Now look at those feeling words. They are probably much more positive than the ones on your Have-To list. If your activities are producing positive energy, then you will have a greater capacity and desire to complete them. Isn't it better to be feeling happy and excited instead of worried and frustrated?

At this point you may be thinking, "Well, it's easy to feel good about the things I want to do, but life isn't always like that. There are a lot of things I don't like to do, but I have to do them anyway. That's just the way it is."

No, it isn't. Here's the mega-point:

EVERYTHING IN LIFE IS A CHOICE

Breathing may be the one exception!

JACK:
Recently, I chose to set a goal of doing one hundred push-ups in a row. I bought a program called *100 Push-Ups*, an iPhone app, and the book by the same title. And I started. I went from twenty push-ups to fifty pretty quickly. Then I got up to sixty-five, then seventy-five, where I plateaued. I couldn't get past that. I started having wrist problems and shoulder problems and I was backing away from it. Part of me was saying, "This is a stupid goal. What am I doing? I'm nearly sixty-seven years old." I just thought, "I don't have to do this!" Then I realized, "No, I set this as a goal." I want to be able to do this, so I had to get myself back into it and push through the pain. Then I found a guy who's actually going for a world push-up record and he taught me some exercises. Then I sought out some other people, went online, and read some more. So I'm back on it. There were a couple of weeks when I thought, "You know, I'm going to bail." Then I said, "No, I'm going to do this!" Quitting too soon is one of the main reasons why people don't achieve their goals. Sometimes you've just got to hang in there and tough it out.

Over the years I've had lots of people ask me, "How can I keep going when I don't feel like it?" My answer to that is, you've got to really figure out what is your why. The why for me is not just so I can show off my push-ups. It's to build core strength, to have something to give me focus, to keep exercising and not atrophy. To be healthy, to look sexy in

221

my clothes to my wife and be attractive, and not look at myself on stage and say, "This guy teaches success and he's thirty pounds overweight? Wow, what's that about?"

A clear picture of your big reason to succeed, plus a healthy dose of daily discipline in the form of specific action steps, is a powerful formula that will help you through self-doubt and negativity.

The man who sold the world on choosing a new direction.

Imagine if you had spent years building a cutting-edge business, using pioneering research to create a breakthrough product line, and were then dumped unceremoniously by the CEO you had personally hired two years earlier.

How would you feel?

What emotions would be coursing through your body?

What would you do?

Even worse, you then spent the next twelve years on the "outside," attempting to keep two new ventures afloat, struggling with low sales, uncertain cash flow and constantly hearing predictions of doom and gloom about your future, from experts in your industry.

Most people would not survive this fast moving downward spiral. They'd simply throw in the towel and surrender to the wisdom of the day.

Not Steve Jobs. The man whose motto became, *"Stay hungry. Stay foolish."* established a new benchmark for consistent persistence. Have you noticed, when faced with seemingly impossible odds, men and women of vision will stay focused on their ultimate goal? They will find a way to circumvent, climb over, burrow under, or simply blast through any obstacle that blocks their path.

Jobs stuck to his Big Picture vision of creating "tools" that would change the world. That often meant any naysayers on staff, including his team of engineering hot shots, would face his wrath in no uncertain terms. In short, he could be extremely difficult to work for and never liked hearing the words, "It can't be done!"

This anti-establishment characteristic showed up early in Steve Jobs' life. His attempt to go through college ended after one semester. He enjoyed hippie status in the seventies and suffered almost as many failures as successes in his turbulent career. **Did you get that?** He suffered almost as many failures as successes along the way. Please drill that into your brain! Consistent persistence requires that you stumble more than once. It strengthens your resolve to win.

> "OH NO, NOT ME, I NEVER LOST CONTROL.
> YOU'RE FACE TO FACE WITH THE
> MAN WHO SOLD THE WORLD."
>
> —David Bowie

Apple Inc. was recently proclaimed the most successful company in the world, knocking aside perennial giants such as Exxon Mobil and Microsoft.

The "tools" that Jobs and his team of skilled artisans created have engaged millions of people around the world like never before. The iPod, iTunes, iPad, and state-of-the-art Apple computers are iconic symbols of his legacy.

In his last decade on earth, Steve Jobs battled one of the world's toughest diseases, pancreatic cancer. Right up to his unfortunate passing at age fifty-six, he was still planning newer and better devices to make our lives even more enjoyable. One of his most meaningful statements that will challenge us all to keep pushing forward is this:

> "REMEMBERING YOU ARE GOING TO
> DIE IS THE BEST WAY TO AVOID THINKING
> YOU HAVE SOMETHING TO LOSE."
>
> —Steve Jobs

By now we hope you are convinced that life is all about choices. Look at the evidence surrounding you every day. Have you noticed that some people choose to lead lives of mediocrity? Sadly, some people even make the ultimate choice—they choose to take their own lives.

In contrast, others arise from the most difficult setbacks and choose to create better circumstances for themselves. And they often do it magnificently. Libraries are full of biographies and autobiographies about men and women who developed the habit of Consistent Persistence to turn their lives around. The trigger point came when they realized they could choose a different future. Steve Jobs is a great example.

Please understand this. It's vital. All of the results you are currently experiencing in your life are absolutely perfect for you. This includes your career, personal relationships and financial status. How could it be otherwise? The reason you are where you are in life is simply a result of all the choices you have made to this point. In other words, the consistency of your positive choices, or the lack of them, has given you the lifestyle you now own. When you accept total responsibility for this fact, you are well on your way to enjoying peace of mind. Many people endure a life filled with frustration because they are stuck in Have-To's.

When you say things like, "She made me angry," the truth is that you chose to be angry. You didn't have to be angry. You responded with anger instead of making a different choice.

Other popular commentaries you'll hear are, "I'm stuck in this relationship." In other words, I have to stay stuck. Or, "I hate this job, I'll never make enough money to enjoy real freedom," which really means, "I have to stay in this low-paying job forever." How sad!

HAVE-TO'S PUT YOU IN A POSITION OF PRESSURE, WHEREAS CHOOSE-TO'S PUT YOU IN A POSITION OF POWER.

CHOOSE WISELY!

When you constantly live your life in Have-To land, you put yourself in a position of pressure. This causes resistance and resentment, and drains your life of energy.

When you live each day from a position of Choose-To, you are in a position of power. You feel in charge and more in control of your life.

This takes a conscious effort to consistently think about your everyday decisions—even simple tasks like washing the dishes. Say to yourself, "I'm choosing to wash the dishes now, and I'll do the best job possible." This is much better than, "Oh no, I have to do the dishes, what a drag." If you really detest doing mundane tasks, choose now to create a lifestyle where you won't be required to do those things. Delegate them to someone else, or hire the work out.

It's also worth noting that the resistance caused by your Have-To jobs often leads to chronic procrastination, and you know how unproductive that can be. Decide now to shift your focus. Make every activity a conscious choice. No more Have-To lists. Starting today, eliminate those words from your vocabulary. Regain your power. Expand your energy and enjoy the freedom that consistent choosing adds to your life.

Here's a good example: One of our clients, a man in his early fifties, was frustrated about his inability to stop smoking. In one of our Power of Focus workshops he stood up, and in a voice filled with emotion said, "I have to quit smoking or I'm going to die, and I don't want to die yet!" He felt totally frustrated and was obviously anxious about his future.

We asked him to reframe his situation to one of choice, instead of Have-To. He came up with this very powerful statement: "Today, I choose to win the battle over smoking."

Being competitive, he decided to treat his smoking like an adversary. It was a battle, and he was going to win it. He used this affirmation every day, and within two months he quit smoking for good. By putting himself in charge through choosing to, and acting on his new choice, it was no contest. That victory spurred him on to make other lifestyle changes, including a regular exercise program and better eating habits. As you can see, consciously making better choices creates an exciting chain of events.

When you consistently make better choices you create better habits. These better habits produce better character. When you have better character you add more value to the world. When you become more valuable you attract bigger and better opportunities. This allows you to make more of a contribution in your life. This in turn leads to bigger and better achievements. People who have figured this out stand out in society as people of strength, vision and commitment.

Another of our clients, a sprightly seventy-three-year-old lady, was given the Have-To list in one of our workshops. When confronted with this, she folded her arms and in a loud voice declared, "I don't have to do anything!" She simply refused to participate. We later found out that she had a long history of building successful enterprises and had obviously learned this important lesson many years ago.

Remember, your dominant thoughts usually win out when it comes to everyday decisions. Make sure your conscious choices are moving you closer to the completion of your most important goals. It's also important to understand that choosing not to do something is a valid position. If someone asks you to join a committee that will require you to give up two evenings every week, you can always decline if it's not in your best interest. Choosing to say "No" is often the best strategy to keep your life well-balanced, and in control.

Now, here are a few more choices for you to consider:

1. I choose not to watch TV or play video games for three hours every night.

Instead, I choose to invest one hour learning more about my business, financial independence, public speaking or any number of other interesting activities that will broaden my knowledge and awareness.

2. I choose not to waste my time reading sensationalist newspapers and trashy magazines every day.

Instead, I choose to start my day reading something inspirational, like a *Chicken Soup for the Soul* book, an inspiring autobiography or a spiritually uplifting message. By the way, we're not suggesting you stop reading relevant newspapers or websites. In business it's important to keep up with current events. Just avoid the tabloid nonsense.

3. I choose not to become a workaholic.

Instead, I choose to schedule personal time off every week with my family and friends, as well as special time for myself, to be enjoyed guilt free.

Are you starting to get the picture? Do you see how powerful you can become by owning your choices every day? From now on, when the words, "I have to" jump into your head, yell,

"Cancel, cancel—I choose not to suffer any more Have-To's in my life." It's exhilarating. In the early stages you will need to be on guard at the doorstep of your mind to prevent those nasty little Have-To's from sneaking inside. Be absolutely ruthless in this respect. Stamp them out persistently until your new Choose-To habit is firmly entrenched.

> "IF I'M EVER ON A LIFE-SUPPORT SYSTEM
> I CHOOSE TO BE UNPLUGGED, BUT NOT UNTIL
> I'M DOWN TO A SIZE EIGHT!"
>
> —Henriette Montel

The Double-A
FORMULA

Now that we've sorted out the importance of choices, get ready for one of the single-most-important strategies you will find in this entire book. You'll need total consciousness to fully grasp this one. If you need to stretch, or take a quick energy break, do it now so you'll be alert. Here's our guarantee: If you adopt 100 percent of what you learn in the rest of this chapter, your business and personal life will leap to a whole new level of performance. In our experience very few people utilize this strategy consistently. As a result, their lives are like a roller coaster, often having more downs than ups.

The Double-A formula is all about you. It stands for: **Agreements and Accountability**.

Here's a personal story to introduce this all-important formula, and to illustrate our point:

LES:
Very early in my career I was selling seminar packages to sales teams and business owners. My cash flow was tight and every sale was important.

One morning I did a presentation to a group of six people plus the company owner. They sold vending machines. My presentation went over well and the owner was excited about the benefits his team would enjoy from the business experts I had on my training program.

I also explained to the owner after he had agreed to have his entire team participate, that he would receive a 20 percent group discount for having five or more people signed up. We shook hands and I told him he'd receive our invoice and details of the program within forty-eight hours. Again, he agreed to everything and said his team was enthused about the program. Three days later the owner telephoned to say he had received everything as promised. However, he had one request. He said, "I want a better deal than the twenty percent. I want a third off the full price."

Decision time for me! At that stage of my fledgling business, every sale counted. The thought of losing several thousand dollars after the time and energy I had invested was a major concern. On the other hand, I had signed up several businesses that were paying for ten to twenty five people to attend my program. None of those companies had asked for more than the 20 percent discount.

I wrestled with this situation overnight, before I called the owner of the small vending machine company to explain I'd be out of integrity if he received a much larger discount than the companies who were sending more people than he was. Do you know what his response was?

"Who will ever know?"

I pondered this for a moment and replied, "Well, you'll know and I will know. Sorry, no deal."

Sometimes it's tough to walk away from new business. However, I've had the benefit of excellent advice from experienced mentors, who all said, "Never put your reputation in jeopardy by creating an unfair playing field for your customers. Word of mouth travels fast. One bad experience can damage your business more than you will ever know."

Have you ever gone into an agreement thinking you knew what the deal was, and then the tables were turned unexpectedly? How did you feel when that happened? Probably upset, frustrated, angry and disappointed, maybe even blaming yourself for not being smarter. Here's the first big point we want to impress upon you: **all broken relationships can be traced back to broken agreements.**

This includes business deals, marriages, family situations, your banker, friends, partnerships and any other flawed relationship between two or more people.

Have you noticed how Western society in particular is having more difficulty keeping agreements these days? If you need proof of this, just look at the thousands of lawyers required to sort out all the messes. Fear of being sued today is stunting growth in many industries, particularly the medical profession. That's crazy. And of course the global financial meltdown in 2008–2009 can be traced directly to a whole series of broken ethical and moral agreements. Here's the good news. You have an incredible opportunity to stand out, simply by maintaining your integrity. You may be thinking, "But how do I maintain my integrity consistently?" Here's the all-important answer:

Consistently keeping your agreements is the foundation for true integrity.

Really digest that sentence. If you seriously want to live on higher ground and reap bigger rewards, your consistency will be tested frequently. Consider this: Every day you make agreements. And every day you are judged by others on the way you act after those decisions have been made. What does your scorecard for keeping agreements look like on an average day? Here's a clue: There is no such thing as a small agreement.

One of our clients made that remark, and it's a profound statement. For example, a salesperson calls and invites you to lunch tomorrow at 12:15 PM. You arrive on time and he shows up twenty-five minutes late, with no excuse and no apology. Assuming that you waited for him, how do you feel? Is this acceptable? If there is a reasonable excuse, like heavy traffic or a mini-crisis at the office, you might let it pass. But what if it happens a second or a third time? Now we have a series of broken agreements. You are always on time, but the other person is chronically late. In today's competitive marketplace this will not be tolerated.

When you break an agreement once, you will probably be given a second opportunity. When you repeatedly break agreements, your stock and value in the marketplace rapidly diminishes—people go elsewhere. When you develop the habit of consistently keeping your little agreements, the big ones will look after themselves. Make this a philosophy for how you choose to live your life. When you do, you will be blessed beyond measure. It's been that way for centuries.

Here's another example. This one's for the married men, although if you are a woman you'll probably relate to the situation. Your wife asks you to replace the burned-out lightbulb in the hall at home. You reply, "Okay, I'll do it before lunch." By supper it's still not fixed. Your wife asks again, politely but firmly. Two days later there's still no light in the hallway. Frustrated, she eventually does the job herself. You may delight in getting out of that little diversion and not think any more about it, but here's the point: If you consistently avoid doing what you say you will do, your reputation becomes tarnished. The relationship gradually deteriorates, because bigger commitments are not being kept too, and in many cases the marriage eventually collapses. If this happens you may end up with the letters DD—Duly Divorced—after your name. That's a pretty serious consequence, and one you may regret for a very long time.

In contrast, when you consistently do what you say you will do, the names attached to you are reliable and trustworthy. When you practice this every day, your rewards are numerous. They include loyal clients, increased profits, loving relationships and maybe most important, a sense of well-being in the knowledge that you are a person of high integrity. That's a badge you can be proud to wear. It will serve you very well indeed.

In remote parts of Ireland, farmers have a traditional way of sealing an agreement. After the sale of a few cattle they spit on their hands, rub them together and seal the deal with a firm handshake. Their word is their bond—and there isn't a lawyer anywhere in sight. It's that strength of character that breeds trust and respect.

There is one situation where it is okay to break your agreement. It's called Intelligent Disobedience. Let's say you have a value system that strongly believes it is wrong to physically injure anyone. One day you arrive home and hear a scream. You quietly open the door to your living room and see a man with a gun, threatening your family. It's a potentially explosive situation. You intervene by smacking the intruder with a golf club behind the knees, disarming him and defusing the situation. Now you know why it's called Intelligent Disobedience!

One other point. Remember, in normal circumstances if you have difficulty keeping an agreement, it is possible to renegotiate. Always use this option to maintain your integrity. It only takes a moment to call and say, "I'm running fifteen minutes late, is that okay with you?" When you develop the habit of being accountable for your actions, you will stand out as a unique individual. Eventually, when the book is written about your life, you will be remembered for what you did, not what you said. So be accountable for your performance. Make your actions measurable. As film director Woody Allen says, "A big part of life is just showing up!"

The Integrity
FACTOR

This is a three-part formula to help you live with the utmost integrity. It's simple and effective. We challenge you to start using it every day.

1. **When you always tell the truth, people trust you.**

2. **When you do what you say, as promised, people respect you.**

3. **When you make others feel special, people tend to like you.**

The words "as promised" in part two are significant. Use these in your regular correspondence. It will reinforce the fact that you really do follow through. If a client requests you to email specific information within the next twenty-four hours, always start the correspondence with, "As promised." For example, "As promised, here is the quote you requested yesterday." When you do this, it is a subtle reminder that you really do keep your commitments, as you promised you would.

Do you remember the Three Big Questions we referred to in Chapter 5, Building Excellent Relationships? Do you like them? Do you trust them? Do you respect them? The Integrity Factor couples these with the principles of being accountable and keeping your agreements. It's a powerful formula. Learn to live it. Decide now to set a new standard in the way you operate every day. It will put you in the top 3 percent of achievers. You'll attract more opportunities than you ever thought possible. When you practice the Integrity Factor, your clients will be more than happy to refer you. And that goes straight to improving the bottom line.

Insights

In the long run, consistent persistence is a choice. You don't "have to" keep hanging in there, fighting battles in business or at home. You don't "have to" stay the course to be healthy or wealthy. You don't "have to" clench your teeth and pick yourself up when you've suffered a setback. Your alternative choice is to just throw in the towel and quit. And sometimes that's a valid choice if consistent persistence becomes life threatening or the sacrifice is too great. For example, is saving your business more important than saving your marriage and having your family broken apart? Only you can make a decision like that.

We love to quote our friend and mentor, Jim Rohn. He really was a master when it came to clarity and making better choices. When someone was tempted to quit on their goals, Jim would ask four simple questions. Consider your own answers as you read through them.

1. Why?
Why bother? Why work that hard? Why do so much? Why push yourself? Why keep going? Why? Good question!

2. Why not?
Why not become all you can be? Why not test your capacity? Why not be successful? Why not enjoy the full abundance of what life has to offer. Why not?

3. Why not you?

Why not you, enjoying a wonderful lifestyle? Thousands of others are doing it. Why not you, seeing the world and visiting exotic locations? Why not you, enjoying the freedom of financial independence? Why not you, living in a beautiful home? Why not you, making a difference and being the catalyst for helping people in need? Why not you, living a life of integrity while others flounder? Why not you, fulfilling your dreams? Why not You?

And finally . . .

4. Why not now?

Why wait? Why hold back? Start the process right away and keep going. Yesterday can never be recovered, today is quickly disappearing but tomorrow is ready and waiting for you to focus and follow through. There is no better time. Soon, the years will fly by and your memories will either exhilarate you or exasperate you. It's your choice!

The next chapter, Taking Decisive Action, will help that adrenaline to start pumping and guide you into successful focused action.

> "LET ME TELL YOU THE SECRET THAT
> HAS LED ME TO MY GOALS: MY STRENGTH
> LIES SOLELY IN MY TENACITY."
>
> —Louis Pasteur

ACTION STEPS

The Integrity
Factor

Answer these questions honestly. They will help you plot a new course of action. They will also clearly demonstrate your current level of integrity and accountability.

1. In what areas of my life do I not consistently keep agreements?

_____

_____

_____

2. What will this cost me if I don't change? Consider the long-term consequences.

_____

_____

_____

3. What specifically do I need to change to enjoy The Integrity Factor lifestyle?

_____

_____

_____

4. What specific rewards and benefits will I receive by making these adjustments?

_____

_____

_____

Understanding the importance of integrity in your life is one thing; living it is an entirely different challenge. The next chapter will show you how.

LIVING AND WORKING ON PURPOSE

TAKING DECISIVE ACTION

CONSISTENT PERSISTENCE

ASK FOR WHAT YOU WANT

THE CONFIDENCE FACTOR

BUILDING EXCELLENT RELATIONSHIPS

OVERCOMING SETBACKS

DO YOU SEE THE BIG PICTURE?

IT'S NOT HOCUS-POCUS, IT'S ALL ABOUT FOCUS

YOUR HABITS WILL DETERMINE YOUR FUTURE

You're in the home stretch...
persistence will pull you through.

Taking Decisive Action

"THOSE WHO EXPECT MOMENTS OF CHANGE
TO BE COMFORTABLE AND FREE OF CONFLICT,
HAVE NOT LEARNED THEIR HISTORY."

—John Wallach Scott

Are you in the habit of putting things off?

For example, you need to complete a report by the end of the month, but instead of planning to do it in three simple stages, you leave everything until the last couple of days and it becomes a panic. Other people get pulled into your mess, creating even more turmoil and anxiety. Somehow you manage to get it done, vowing, "Never again—that's the last time I'm letting things go like that —it's not worth the stress." But you do repeat the same behavior again and again, don't you? Why? Because it's your habit. Go on, admit it, you're a procrastinator.

If it's any comfort, you're not the only one. Just about everyone procrastinates. Sometimes that's good, but mostly it's an insidious, chronic malaise that will cripple your future.

In this chapter we'll help you get rid of this nasty habit once and for all. Of all the strategies we've discussed,

Taking Decisive Action is easy to measure. It's black and white. You won't be able to hide from the consequences with this one. It separates the weak from the strong, the timid from the courageous, and the endless talkers from the doers.

Decisiveness is your greatest ally as you chart your path through life. Procrastination is a thief, waiting in disguise to rob you of your hopes and dreams.

If you want proof, take a closer look.

There is another word hidden inside the word procrastinate that will alert you to the perils of not taking action. Can you see it?

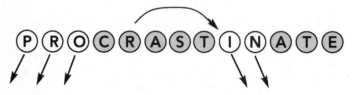

What a cunning word *procrastinate* is. It disguises the real word, *castrate*, which also means to impoverish or render ineffective. Do you get the picture? When you procrastinate, you are actually impoverishing your future, cutting it off. "Y-E-E-A-A-O-W-W . . . that's painful!" You're right, it's very painful. From now on, every time you go into procrastination mode, sear this painful image of castration into your mind so that it shocks you into action.

Ed Foreman, president of Dallas-based Executive Development Systems, is a man who enjoys taking action. At the age of twenty-six he had already made his first million. He then went on to create many successful businesses including oil and gas, ready-made cement, sand and gravel, and cattle ranching.

Ed even found time to get elected to the United States Congress on two different occasions, from two different states—Texas and New Mexico—the only person to do so in the twentieth century.

Now he spends most of his time sharing positive action strategies with corporate executives from all over the world. He has a contagious energy and enthusiasm for life, and no time for people who sit back whining and complaining about what they don't have. He calls their malaise the Someday Syndrome. It was written especially for procrastinators, and is also known as the Procrastinator's Creed.

"SOMEDAY WHEN I GROW UP,
FINISH SCHOOL AND GET A JOB, I'LL START
LIVING MY LIFE THE WAY I WANT. . . .
SOMEDAY AFTER THE MORTGAGE IS PAID OFF,
THE FINANCES ARE ON TRACK AND THE
KIDS ARE GROWN UP, I'LL DRIVE THAT NEW CAR
AND TAKE EXCITING TRIPS ABROAD. . . .
SOMEDAY, NOW THAT I'M ABOUT TO RETIRE,
I'LL BUY THAT BEAUTIFUL MOTOR HOME AND
TRAVEL ACROSS THIS GREAT COUNTRY, AND
SEE ALL THERE IS TO SEE. . . . SOMEDAY."

—Ed Foreman

One day, after a lifetime of someday-thinking and someday-regrets, these procrastinators come to the end of their lives. The one sentence that fills their thoughts as they prepare to pass on is, "If only I'd done the things I really wanted to do, my life would have been so different." They sadly reflect on all the missed opportunities. "If only I'd invested 10 percent of my income every month." "If only I'd taken care of my health." "If only I'd bought that one-hundred-dollar stock when it was selling for a dollar." "If only I'd taken a chance and started my own business." Alas, now it's too late. And another procrastinator makes his or her exit, consumed with feelings of remorse, guilt and a lack of fulfillment.

Beware, dear reader, the Someday Syndrome is a fatal trap. Life is too short not to enjoy it to the fullest. Indecision and uncertainty will confine you to a world of "if only." That's not what you want, is it? Okay, so let's put together a powerful plan of attack that will guarantee you a life full of positive action and unique memorable experiences.

"You've got pussyfooting from 10 to 11, shilly-shallying until 12, then hemming and hawing the rest of the afternoon."

LES:

More than once I've been accused of being a procrastinator, notably by my loving wife, Fran. As this chapter is all about taking decisive action, an update is definitely in order. Simply put, I've improved! However, I'm not cured. In fact, I've discovered a very important insight. Everyone has a distinct process when it comes to getting things done. For me, the breakthrough realization was centered on new ideas. I believe another mentor of mine, Dan Sullivan, first planted this seed in my mind.

Here's how it works for me. When a new idea for my business pops into my head, which happens often, I immediately scribble a few initial thoughts on paper. Then I leave it for a couple of days. When I revisit my notes, one of two things happens.

I crumple the paper up and say "Rubbish, what was I thinking?" and put it out of my head for good.

The second scenario is, I start massaging the idea.

If the energy starts to flow, I usually end up with two or three pages of notes and a specific plan of action. With really good ideas, I experience a surge of adrenaline. Then I just leave the idea to marinate. This step in my unique process can last up to a year. Now, having done this several times in the last few years, I know this incubation stage is very important. This is not procrastination. Eventually an opportunity comes along and I notice there is a very good correlation with my idea. What triggers this is the arrival of a new business relationship, someone who has a big dream and needs help. And my new idea seems to be a perfect match. Then the magic happens. There is a combustible energy force that ignites the idea and I roar into action with all guns blazing! By the way, I don't always end up with a major victory in these situations, but more often than not I jump to another level of accomplishment.

Please note: This is *my* process. You must figure out your own unique way of making things happen. Track each step of your process and use it to help you along, especially when you come to a fork in the road regarding your future. And make sure you clarify the difference between numbing procrastination—a very bad habit—and a well-defined process that leads ultimately to significant rewards.

4 Good REASONS You Procrastinate

First we'll take a look at why people procrastinate. Then we'll show you how to get this annoying monkey off your back. If you are not a procrastinator, please read the rest of this chapter anyway, just in case you get the urge later. You'll learn some excellent techniques that will make you even more decisive than you are now.

There are four good reasons you may be procrastinating:

1. You're bored.
It's a fact of life. We all feel less than enthusiastic from time to time. Sometimes our work becomes routine and we end up just going through the motions. As we mentioned earlier, entrepreneurs are famous for this. After the initial thrill of launching a new business wears off, they need a new challenge, something that keeps the juices flowing.

How do you combat inertia? Here are a few suggestions: First, recognize that you are bored. Be conscious of your feelings, your falling energy levels and your lack of desire to finish projects. You may feel tired and yet not be doing much physical activity. (If you are unusually tired, check things out with your doctor. There might be a medical reason for your lethargy or sluggishness.)

Ask yourself a few questions and be totally honest with your answers. Am I bored with what I'm doing? (The answer to that is "Yes" or "No.") Why am I bored? What would give me a lot more energy?

Successful entrepreneurs maintain their excitement by constantly going after new projects and bigger opportunities. They keep raising their level of expectation and are never satisfied with routine business that requires no challenge or ingenuity. They thrive on taking new risks and the possibility that they might hit a massive home run. And the uncertainty makes it even more appealing!

One way to get your energy flowing again is to think about creating bigger deals and what it would take to produce that kind of revenue. There are two possibilities. You could sell more of your product or service to your existing clients. Or you could go fishing for bigger clients. Imagine closing deals two or three times larger than any you've ever had before. Start expanding your vision.

This of course requires a whole new set of contacts and connections. You also need to be more creative and innovative. Creativity produces energy, and innovation starts the adrenaline pumping. Suddenly you are developing much bigger goals and a new excitement starts to permeate the office.

Be careful, this can be extremely contagious! Pretty soon everyone on your team is charging forward with a whole new set of incentives and initiatives. Suddenly life is fun again and you are on a roll. Good-bye boredom, hello bigger targets and even bigger rewards.

2. You are overwhelmed with work.

Often people procrastinate because they let things pile up, instead of handling one task at a time and taking each task to completion. This may start with one little thing that doesn't get done because the time wasn't right, or you just didn't feel like doing it.

Then something else comes along, and you postpone that, too. Now you have two things to do. Individually, neither one seems too big to accomplish, but together they create resistance. You end up postponing them both. After a while a growing list of half a dozen items has been put off and procrastination has reared its ugly head. It begins controlling you. Soon there are so many things to do you feel overwhelmed at the thought of even starting, so you don't. If this describes you, take heart. There are ways to help you break through the roadblocks. We'll show you how before the end of this chapter.

3. You are doing work you don't really enjoy.

There are two sides to this dilemma. First, all of us are required to do certain things we don't enjoy. That's one of the rules of the game if you want to become more successful. You may not like it but that's the way it is. For example, you may not like to do mundane things like paperwork or book-keeping, but it's hard to completely avoid these tasks even if you are a really good delegator. Our friend Ed Foreman did some major research on this issue. Here's what he found: Successful people do the things that unsuccessful people don't like to do. They don't enjoy doing some of these things either, but they go ahead and do them anyway. This is a fundamental point, one that you need to fully understand.

The other side of the coin is that you may be stuck in a mediocre job or career that doesn't allow you to use your greatest abilities. If that's true, then look for an opportunity to expand your talents. Life is too short to be stuck in work you don't enjoy. Most of the time the type of work you do should stimulate you and give you energy. Why stay in something that drains your energy and is not fulfilling?

Many people don't shift because they have a need for security, or the thought of doing something different scares them. Change is out of their comfort zone and is intimidating. Well, here's the reality: The biggest rewards in life are found outside your comfort zone. Live with it. Fear and risk are prerequisites if you want to enjoy a life of success and adventure.

4. You are easily distracted, or just downright lazy!

There's not much to talk about here. Let's be blunt. If you avoid taking action because you'd rather put your feet up every night and watch movie reruns on TV, there's little chance you'll be enjoying an abundant lifestyle any time soon. The bottom line? Success takes effort and consistent, focused activity. Laziness is not part of the equation. It's a banned substance.

Active
DECISION-MAKING

Generally speaking, lack of motivation is usually at the root of your procrastination. It's easier to put things off than it is to act decisively. Being conscious that you are going into a downward spiral of inactivity is important. When you are aware of this, have a little chat with yourself and focus on finding a way to work things out.

There are primarily two ways to motivate yourself: You can fear the consequences of not taking action; or you can get excited about the rewards and benefits of being proactive.

You must keep these two pictures front and center, one negative and one positive. Ask yourself, "What do I really want—a future where I'm always struggling to make ends meet, or a lifestyle of prosperity, joy and fulfillment?" The more vivid these two pictures are, the more decisive you will become. Don't allow yourself to be lulled into a false sense of security. When you hear that destructive little voice whispering inside your head, "Leave it until tomorrow, next week, next month or next year," immediately flash those two pictures on your mental video screen. What's the picture look like if you don't get started? Do you want to look back on your life with a big list of If Only's? Of course not! Clearly understand this and feel the pain of your castration. (No, that's not a misprint!)

Now flip the switch and take a look at the other picture. This time see all of the rewards and benefits that happened just because you took action and didn't hold back. Feast on this picture. Imprint it into your mind. Sense the feeling of accomplishment. Feel good about challenging yourself to a higher level of performance. Here's a fantastic example of what we're talking about.

MARK:

One of the best action takers I've met is a young man named Cameron Johnson. Before he was twenty-one years old he had started twelve businesses, all of them on the Internet. I'll let him tell his amazing story.

"I started my first business when I was nine years old. It was a small printing company called, Cheers & Tears Printing Company, and I printed greeting cards, stationery, anything that I could print with my computer and printer. I ran that business for several years.

"I got my first checking account when I was ten years old. My parents tried to help teach me the importance of saving money and financial literacy. And when I was twelve years old, I started selling Beanie Babies over the Internet. That year, for my thirteenth birthday, I made 50,000 dollars' profit selling Beanie Babies through a website that I started and also on eBay and everywhere else that I could sell them. I became one of the biggest online retailers of Beanie Babies. My website, Beanie Wholesale, would sell to hundreds of retailers across the country and consumers around the world.

"At our peak, I was shipping forty orders a day and I was stocking five thousand Beanie Babies in a closet in my parents' basement (I paid seventy-five dollars a month rent to use it). And every day after school I would come home and get all of the orders from the night before. Before I'd go to bed, I would fulfill all of the orders and box them all up, print the labels, and have all of the invoices done. That was my business when I was twelve and thirteen.

"When I was fifteen, I started an online advertising company called surfingprizes.com, which provided scrolling advertisements across the top of users' web browser windows. I launched this with two other teenagers. We partnered with a few other online advertising companies as well and were placing fifteen million ads per day in just our first six months of operation. We had 200,000 customers and were generating $15,000 per day. We were receiving checks between $300,000 and $400,000 per month from our share of the total revenue.

"When I was seventeen, I owned an Internet company called Emazing Sites. We were a holding company for several large Web properties, one called InternetProfiles. com. I had my hands in a lot of different businesses. At the time we had a web design firm where we would design websites for different companies. I ran that for several years until ultimately I closed it.

"Then I went off to college at Virginia Tech. I started a company my first semester there called Certificate Swap. Eighty percent of Americans either buy or receive a gift card; my idea was to have an outlet where you can get rid of the gift card you don't want. CertificateSwap.com enabled people to come onto our website and list their gift card for sale. Say you had a card with a one-hundred-dollar value; you would list it for sale for eighty-five dollars. Someone else is happy to buy that one-hundred-dollar certificate for eighty-five dollars and you're happy to get eighty-five dollars in cash that you can spend anywhere. So we just connected buyers and sellers, much like eBay. I left college and raised venture capital for that company and ultimately turned down a ten-million-dollar venture capital offer because of some of the contingencies. I moved on and my partner and I sold the business and we made a really nice return in just several months of operation. That was my business when I was nineteen. There were several others, too.

"The beauty of IT is that it lets all of us compete on an equal platform. Think about where we would be without the cell phone. Think about how much that has fast-tracked business. Think about what email has done. Think about the way you can now virtualize your company and you can have an 800 number and that 800 number can ring into voicemail and those voicemails can be sent to you on email. This is how I operate. I have an 800 number for my office and voicemails come straight to my computer as an email file, as a sound file, so I can be on the beach in Cancun listening to my voicemail, running my business and I don't need to be paying an office building. I don't need to have manufacturing. I don't need to have anything.

"Anytime I would come up with an idea for the Internet I would write it down and then later I would do research on that idea to see if (1) that idea already exists (2) if it doesn't exist how can I create it and bring it to market and monetize it?

"And if it does already exist, is that company making money? **Just because it already exists, that shouldn't discourage you from your idea. _Competition is a beautiful thing._** So if something already exists, that's actually validation for your idea. That means you're actually on to something and then maybe there's a way you can make it better or cheaper or faster or easier.

"Many of these Internet companies might have big revenues or they might have millions of users but they don't actually make a profit. All of my businesses were profitable but that was because they were much smaller. I always believed in starting small. I always believed in investing my own money, not taking on outside investments and starting with literally, sometimes fifty dollars, sometimes five hundred dollars, never more than several thousand dollars to start any of my businesses. So it's something that can be duplicated, because even though I did raise money and was offered venture capital for one of my companies, I turned it down.

"I've never taken on millions of dollars nor taken on any loans. I've never taken on any debt and I've always started small. Everything has been a stepping stone; every business has just been a little bit bigger than the previous business and I think that's what helped me be successful. And even though I'm twenty-four today, my success didn't happen overnight. I've been doing this for fifteen years, so the better part of my life has been dedicated to my businesses and that's why I am where I am today."

The message is clear: Whether you're working on a small project or a major goal, stick with it so you can celebrate its completion. Make sure you are not one of those frustrated individuals who goes all the way through life with the label, Does Not Complete.

To ensure that you have absolutely no excuses for being indecisive, we are now going to reveal a simple proven formula that will help you resolve any future situation that requires you to take action.

The TA-DA FORMULA

This will help you stay alert as you head into the uncharted waters of the future. Before you make any major decisions, we highly recommend that you use this acronym to guide you as outlined below. You can even use it on a daily basis to help you stay focused. If you are uncertain about a decision, just say "TA-DA" out loud to trigger your good habit. This works!

1. Think.

As we discussed earlier, time for reflection is essential. Reflective thinking allows you to pause so you can consider all of your options. "Will this help me accomplish my major goals more effectively?" "Why do I want to do this?" "What specific benefit will I gain from taking this course of action?" "What is the downside if it doesn't work?" "How much time will this really take?" The more conscious you are when going into a major decision, the less likely you are to screw things up. Take time to think. Like an airline pilot, create a foolproof checklist to guide you every time.

2. Ask.

Ask good focusing questions. Find out everything you need to know to make an intelligent, informed decision. Ask other people, your mentors or people who have specific knowledge and experience in this area. The more important the decision, the more time you should take to check everything out. This doesn't mean analyze it to death. Only when you have gathered sufficient information from a variety of sources are you ready for the next step in the formula.

3. Decide.

Make a pros and cons list. Write down the negative consequences if you don't make a decision. Compare these with the positive benefits of moving forward.

Then make a firm decision about what you are going to do. Making the decision is half the battle. Chronic procrastinators lead lives of discontent because they won't make the decision to go forward. After awhile, sitting on the fence becomes very uncomfortable. If you're not careful, you'll stay stuck, unable to get off.

4. Act.

Now that you have done some reflective thinking, asked around for more information and finally made your decision, it's time to act. This is the most important part of the TA-DA formula. Many people live their lives in ready-steady mode, instead of ready steady GO! You must go. Kickstart yourself into focused action. Just take the first step. Gradually you will build momentum. Like the proverbial snowball rolling downhill, you won't be able to stop after you make that early push. Remember, the big rewards in life only materialize when you start doing.

> JACK:
> As a visionary, I can spot opportunities and solutions before many others would.
> I don't know if it's a trained talent or a gift but I've always been able to walk into any organization or any company and see ways to improve it. I remember working in a General Electric plant when I was in college and seeing ten ways to improve the assembly line. But I think the main thing is to ask yourself the right questions. The quality of the question you ask determines the quality of the results and the quality of your awareness. To do this, continually ask, "How could this be improved?
> One of the great questions I learned many years ago was, for every situation I find myself in to ask, **"What's the opportunity that exists in this situation?"** It could be an opportunity to grow or develop patience. It could be an

opportunity to develop perseverance or an opportunity to provide a service that's needed at that moment in time. Be alert to the trends and where they're going. Pay attention and you'll discover new opportunities.

Someone once asked me, "How did you get the idea for *Chicken Soup*?" It wasn't really my idea. It came to me when people kept asking, "Is that story in a book anywhere?" All I did was pay attention to the fact that people wanted those stories in a book. Basically, it's a matter of just being aware and constantly living in the questions.

DILBERT *reprinted by permission of United Feature Syndicate, Inc.*

Let's Talk About
MONEY

Hitting your financial targets with certainty every year is obviously very important, especially if you live in a society where the price of almost everything keeps going up. If you have a growing family that includes teenagers, you'll know what we mean!

The recent turbulence in financial markets around the world requires even more prudence to ensure future prosperity.

A complete in-depth analysis of money and investment strategies is way beyond the scope of this book. We thought it would be a good idea to share some basic essentials from our perspective. It's all part of your education in the field of taking decisive action.

What does money mean to you?

Everyone forms beliefs about money. Contrary to what some people think, money is not the root of all evil. If that were true, just about every nonprofit organization, charity and church would cease to exist. However, the total love of money to the exclusion of everything else causes all sorts of anxiety.

There are basically three things in life that can ruin you:

1. Power—observe the dictators and megalomaniacs of this world.

2. Sex—usually with too many people, the number-one example being politicians and celebrities.

3. Greed—the unhealthy pursuit of too much money often at the cost of someone else. Think merchant bankers, dictatorial governments, and the victims of the sub-prime mortgage fiasco.

To understand how you really feel about money, ask yourself a few simple questions. For example: Is it okay to have a lot of money? What money habits have shown up in my life so far? Do I joyfully earn and accumulate money, or do I sabotage myself when things go well unexpectedly?

We've included an excellent Money Quiz at the end of this chapter that will help you identify your financial realities. Make sure you complete it.

Here are a few other thoughts about belief systems around money. Some people were brought up in a very thrifty environment, so penny-pinching was a natural way of life. Others were told by parents and various authority figures that money was "dirty." Did you ever hear this one? "Don't put that money in your mouth, it's dirty!"

Some people were more fortunate and were brought up in an environment where a good work ethic was valued and money was spent and invested wisely. There was also an element of fun without being too frugal.

Money flows to those who attract it.

In our opinion, money is simply a reward for services rendered. If you provide excellent service and create significant value for the people around you, the money will show up. Therefore, to attract more money, you must be attractive, in the sense that people will want and prefer your products or service over those of your competitor. The bottom line is always to focus on creating more value. Do whatever it takes to make whatever you offer in the marketplace the absolute best. The story of Apple Inc. mentioned in an earlier chapter is a great example of this mind-set.

If you are struggling financially or would like to significantly boost your net worth, understand this: Your money habits are primarily the cause of your current financial status. So if you've never been in the habit of saving or investing, you may be experiencing some consequences right now. If you constantly spend more than you earn, you will definitely experience major consequences at some point. People who earn $50,000 per year have $50,000 habits. People who earn $500,000 have $500,000 habits. And that's an absolute take-it-to-the-bank fact.

To change your habits you must first accept your present financial reality. Denying the obvious won't work! The next step, if you want to be financially independent, is to make it a study. Do your homework. Learn how money flows, how it expands and grows and most of all, who is really good at attracting it.

Undoubtedly there are people in your neighborhood or city who have earned a lot of money. Find out how they did it. Be creative. Be courageous. Be so bold as to set up an appointment to meet with them. In addition, you must have a brilliant financial coach or team of advisers to help and support you. Ask around. Find out who is the best. Again, do your homework. Focus. Most people won't make this type of effort. It's a lot easier to sit in front of the TV every night instead of creating a strong financial future that their families would relish when they want to relax in their senior years.

Basic rules for creating wealth.

We are now going to introduce you to two wealthy veterans—Sir John Templeton and Art Linkletter—and share their specific Top-10 lists on how they created unlimited prosperity. We selected these individuals because of their integrity and ability to accumulate money. You may be surprised at the simplicity of their findings. Study each one carefully. Their insights can shave years off your wealth curve.

First, Sir John Templeton. The founder of the Templeton Group, Sir John Templeton was a legendary mutual fund manager. His genius for financial management created wealth for thousands of investors all around the world. The following ten principles are the heart and soul of his incredible success.

1. To achieve success, be neither an optimist nor a pessimist, but a realist with a hopeful nature.

2. Count your blessings to enrich yourself and your neighbors, first spiritually, and then financially.

3. Debt, whether personal or collective, should not keep you from investing in your future. Strive to be debt free.

4. Invest in many different places—there is definitely safety in numbers.

5. Your money should do far more than simply reproduce itself.

6. Remember that patience is a virtue.

7. If you want to prosper, investigate before you invest.

8. Never forget: The secret of creating riches for oneself is to create them for others.

9. Looking out for Number One doesn't make you Number One.

10. Make success with a single word—Love.

Source: *Ten Golden Rules for Financial Success*

Art Linkletter was probably best known as an entertainer and show business personality. As a baby, he was abandoned and then adopted by a church minister, in the small community of Moose Jaw, Saskatchewan, Canada. His famous show, *House Party* on CBS, was one of the longest-running programs on television. Art Linkletter was also a very astute businessman with direct involvement in dozens of successful enterprises. Here are Art's most important insights for creating wealth and success.

1. I'm going to do the work I enjoy. You only live once, so do what you love.

2. There will always be difficulties, failures and challenges along the way.

3. The margin between mediocrity and success is very small when related to time and effort, over and above what is expected.

4. I will use pull whenever I can to open the doors to opportunity, but I will make sure to work when the door is opened for me.

5. I will recognize and be alert to my own weaknesses, and find people who excel in the things where I falter.

6. I will consider an opportunity to advance more important than the immediate money and fringe benefits of the situation.

7. I will always stretch my abilities and goals a little further than my comfort zone, within reason.

8. I will learn from my failures and then put them behind me.

9. I will follow the Golden Rule. I will not do a deal where someone else is short-changed, cheated or taken advantage of.

10. I will use other people's money provided I feel certain the money itself can grow at a faster rate than the interest charges. I will not be greedy.

To wrap this up, we'll throw our hats into the ring as well. These are the most important strategies we focus on.

JACK:
- Do what you love with passion and excellence and the money will follow.
- Read all you can, attend seminars, listen to instructive audios and videos. Put what you learn into action.
- Make a study of the universal laws of success, prosperity and abundance.
- Tithe a percentage of your income to your church and favorite charities.
- Always strive for constant and never-ending improvement in everything you do.

MARK:

- Make the decision to be financially independent and your subconscious will make a provision. Write it into a plan, "I will earn . . ."
- Create an affirmation for your Smartphone, iPad, or screensaver, that says, "I am so happy I am . . ." (On schedule to be a millionaire; growing 50 percent annually; meeting one new prospect or client per day; selling X amount of Y daily; or whatever your particular goal is.) Read this at breakfast, lunch, dinner and just prior to sleep, so you become one with the idea, and eventually it will become reality.
- Love your job or right livelihood, and let it love you. I love speaking, writing, creating, thinking, promoting and marketing, and because I love it, it thrives.
- Create a dream team of like-minded colleagues who will help you make your hopes come true.
- Serve greatly with love and a happy heart.

LES:

- Focus on what you do best. Strive to be the authority figure in your field of expertise. My talents are coaching, writing, speaking and creating self-awareness products and programs.
- Look for specific opportunities that will complement and expand your greatest strengths. I created *The Power of Focus* Coaching Program for entrepreneurs and leaders because I relate easily to their challenges.
- Invest first in your own business. Stay away from deals and industries you know little about. That's why Warren Buffet has done so well.
- Surround yourself with brilliant financial mentors as previously suggested. Who you know is at least as important as what you know.

- Develop and maintain simple financial habits. Invest 10 percent of your income every month. Do not consume more than you earn. Know where your money goes. Strive to be debt-free. Be a good steward of the resources you have been privileged to receive.

GOD GIVES EVERY BIRD ITS FOOD

But He Does Not Throw It Into The Nest!

MAKE WEALTH A STUDY

To help you further, here's a list of great books about money and wealth creation. Set a goal to read all of them. There are literally hundreds of books on this subject. Make these a first step in your quest for financial wisdom.

1. *The Richest Man in Babylon* by George S. Clason, (Penguin Books, 1989).

2. *The Wealthy Barber Returns** by David Chilton (Financial Awareness Corporation, 2011).

3. *The Millionaire Next Door* by Thomas J. Stanley and William D. Danko (Longstreet Press, Inc., 1996).

4. *Ten Golden Rules for Financial Success* by Gary Moore (Zondervan Publishing House, 1996).

---

* *written for the Canadian market but contains excellent information for a broader audience.*

5. *The One Minute Millionaire* by Mark Victor Hansen and Robert Allen (Harmony books, 2002).

6. *Think and Grow Rich* by Napoleon Hill (Fawcett Crest Books/CBS Inc., 1960).

7. *Rich Dad, Poor Dad* by Robert T. Kiyosaki with Sharon L. Lechter (Techpress Inc., 1997).

8. *The Greatest Salesman in the World* by Og Mandino (Free Press, 2011).

9. *Crush It* by Gary Vaynerchuk (Harper Studio, 2009).

10. *Allowances, Dollars and Sense: A proven system for teaching your kids about money* by Paul Lermitte (McGraw-Hill Ryerson Ltd, 1999).

11. *The Success Principles* by Jack Canfield (Harper Collins, 2005).

12. *Get Rich Click!* by Marc Ostrofsky (Razor Media Group, 2011).

Now you have the tools for taking decisive action in your financial affairs. Our last word on this? Take the necessary steps now. When it comes to money, time is of the essence.

Insights

Well, now you know for sure that procrastinators are not successful decision makers! Great leaders are indviduals who make numerous decisions every day.

So, to wrap this chapter up, we thought it would be useful to share a list of Leadership Essentials with you. If you are in a leadership role or aspiring to be, as you read each of these statements below, place a checkmark against any that are missing from your current skill set. This will provide an excellent platform for you to expand your leadership ability. And by now, of course, you know what to do—**make a decision to take action!**

- EXCELLENT COMMUNICATORS: The best leaders are excellent communicators. They know how to share their vision with passion and clarity.

- SKILLFUL DIRECTION: Leaders provide skillful direction and ongoing support to ensure each project moves forward on time and on budget.

- POTENT MIX OF SKILLS: Leaders need a potent mix of skills including effective delegating, mentorship, inspiration, and the ability to confront issues head on. When tough decisions need to be made, they make them! In the process they may find it necessary to cajole, critique and give strong feedback.

- RECOGNITION: Leaders understand that criticism is always best delivered in private, and that praise deserves a public forum where recognition can be maximized.

- PROVIDE SUPPORT: The successful leader works closely with key individuals on the team, assessing their various personality styles and the best way to communicate.

- FOCUS ON THEIR STRENGTHS / DELEGATE WEAKNESSES: Productive leaders focus on their strengths and delegate their weaknesses. To achieve optimum performance, every person on the team must do the same.

- FOCUSED ACTION: Leaders understand the importance of focused action and 100 percent commitment. They also ensure that people have sufficient rejuvenation breaks to prevent burn out.

- BALANCE: Balance is encouraged and seen as a prerequisite for success. Constantly working eighteen hour days, seven days per week is not valued as a "badge of honor" by a truly successful leader, who may have learned this the hard way.

- EXCELLENT ROLE MODEL: A respected leader is an excellent role model for the team. He or she really walks the walk consistently. Integrity is one of their highest values.

- THE RIGHT PEOPLE: Having the right people with the right attitude creates a unique team synergy. Each person must display a strong work ethic and bring their unique talents and abilities to each project. They also know how to have fun and enjoy celebrating their victories together.

- BE THE BEST: Every member of the team must make a personal ongoing commitment to become the best they can be, professionally and personally. For example, a 10 percent increase in focus across the board, creates a significant outcome.

- YOUR TEAM IS AS GOOD AS THE WEAKEST LINK: Any team is only as good as its weakest link. One off-purpose person with a negative attitude and a less than healthy work ethic can undermine the progress of the remaining team members.

- KNOW THE RIGHT TIME TO LET GO: A good leader knows the right time to let people go in order to preserve the integrity and focus of the entire team.

As a leader, how are you doing so far?

Our final focusing strategy is all about Living and Working on Purpose. Many of our clients have said this was a life changer for them and made previously tough decision-making easy. Now you can find out for yourself.

"LEADERS MAKE DECISIONS—ALL THE TIME.
FOLLOWERS MAKE SUGGESTIONS.
MAKING SUGGESTIONS IS EASY BECAUSE IT
REQUIRES NO ACTION OR FEAR OF FAILURE.
MAKING DECISIONS IS TOUGH.
IT TAKES GUTS BECAUSE THERE IS ALWAYS
SOMETHING AT STAKE."

—Ruben Gonzales

ACTION STEPS

Eliminating Procrastination

Financial
Certainty

1. Make a list below of a few of your specific procrastination habits that cause you frustration.

Examples: being late for appointments; not returning phone calls, as promised; leaving projects to the last minute, causing turmoil. Beside your list, describe the specific consequences that result from delaying your actions. Be honest!

My Procrastination Habits: **Consequences:**

_____

_____

_____

_____

_____

2. Select one habit from your list and create Action Steps that will motivate you to put an end to the behavior.

Procrastination habit I want to eliminate:

_____

_____

_____

My Three Action Steps are:

_____

_____

_____

Now, follow through!

THE HABIT OF FINANCIAL CERTAINTY

A Money Quiz to Clarify Your Current Position.

1. What does money mean to you?

_____

_____

_____

2. Do you deserve a lot of money?　　　❏ yes　　❏ no
   Why? or Why not?

_____

_____

_____

3. Define FINANCIAL FREEDOM as it relates to you personally.

_____

_____

_____

4. Do you know how much you spend, and how much
   you earn specifically each month?　　　❏ yes　　❏ no

5. Are you consumption-oriented, or do you have a clear
   savings and investment program that takes priority?

_____

_____

_____

6. Are you in the habit of paying yourself first every month?

❑ yes ❑ no

7. Do you have a brilliant financial adviser or team of advisers?

❑ yes ❑ no

8. How much money will you require when (and if) you retire, to enjoy the lifestyle you want?

_____

_____

_____

9. What is your present shortfall, if any?

_____

_____

_____

10. Are you on track to have a healthy net worth?

This means having enough money to enjoy the quality of life you really want. To have the choice of working or not working, because you can afford it.

If you are not at this level of financial freedom yet, what do you need to change?

_____

_____

_____

_____

LIVING AND WORKING ON PURPOSE

TAKING DECISIVE ACTION

CONSISTENT PERSISTENCE

ASK FOR WHAT YOU WANT

THE CONFIDENCE FACTOR

BUILDING EXCELLENT RELATIONSHIPS

OVERCOMING SETBACKS

DO YOU SEE THE BIG PICTURE?

IT'S NOT HOCUS-POCUS, IT'S ALL ABOUT FOCUS

YOUR HABITS WILL DETERMINE YOUR FUTURE

Only one strategy left—you're almost there.

Living and Working On Purpose

"WHEN I STAND BEFORE GOD AT THE END OF MY LIFE, I HOPE THAT I WOULD NOT HAVE A SINGLE BIT OF TALENT LEFT, AND COULD SAY, I USED EVERYTHING YOU GAVE ME."

—Erma Bombeck

Every decade we have a new young adult population emerging, most of them looking for a career, a job, or about to embark on further enlightenment at college or university.

What are the hopes and dreams of these "apprentices" in the world of adult life? Looking back, we've had some interesting labels attached to various demographics.

1900—1924	G.I. Generation
1925—1945	Silent Generation
1946—1964	Baby Boomers
1965—1979	Generation X
1980—2000	Millennials/Generation Y
2001—?	New Silent Generation/Generation Z

What label are you wearing today? As Generation Y are in the spotlight right now, let's zero in on these young hopefuls. Research has shown that Generation Y professionals are able to adapt quickly to changes in technology and that they work most productively when they are passionate about a cause. What can they teach us about maintaining focus and working effectively in a very fast-moving environment?

Aaron Trenouth, age twenty-six, is a talented, outgoing young man. He's a graduate of the University of Lethbridge, a school with a reputation for producing top-notch business majors. Small class sizes and entrepreneurially minded professors are an integral part of this success formula. As a Generation Y young adult, let's take a peek at Aaron's outlook for the future in his own words.

"Regarding career, there are no guarantees today. If you want to build a career in a large company, you start at the low end and pay your dues. When the economy was booming years ago, university grads had a different viewpoint. They felt entitled to start in management with a corner office and an annual starting salary in the $80,000 range. Not anymore! I wanted to find a company that was growth oriented, had excellent opportunities for quick promotion and provided excellent training. Money isn't top of my "must-have" list. A lot of my friends feel the same way. The most important thing for me is that I'm happy—that means a happy work environment. When I looked at potential companies to work for, their reputation was important. Are they really providing value to their customers and employees? Is their business purpose driven? Are people happy working there?

"For me, being happy is waking up in the morning and not dreading going to work. And when I get home at the end of the day, I'm not stressed out; I still have plenty of energy to enjoy my evenings and do other things. I also want to be challenged. So many people seem to plateau after a few years in the job. First, they get comfortable and then they become complacent. I don't want to get stuck in a routine like that."

Like thousands of other young adults, Aaron wants a future where there is hope and opportunity and a sense of pride from the service he provides. That's not an unreasonable request. So what has he found? Aaron chose to work with Enterprise Rent-a-Car, the number-one car rental company in America, with more than six thousand locations, including international operations in Canada, The United Kingdom, Ireland and Germany.

This $9 billion powerhouse has built their business and reputation on one simple purpose—to create completely satisfied customers.

Let's see how they match up with Aaron's expectations. The top four areas for Enterprise that create value are:

1. Completely satisfied customers

2. Employee development and empowerment

3. Growth

4. Profit

To help you derive some useful ideas for your own business, here is an expanded version of these four value creators.

1. Concentrate foremost on taking the best possible care of your employees and customers. Profitability will naturally follow.

2. Don't just endeavor to make customers satisfied. Treat them so well they'll be *totally* satisfied.

3. Rather than lavish interior design, set up your place of business with customer convenience top of mind.

4. Don't forget the basic niceties—shaking hands and greeting people by name—that turn your first-time renters (or shoppers or clients) into lifetime customers.

5. Remember that repeat business is crucial, because it costs between five and six times more to gain new customers than to keep current ones.

6. View your customers as the most important people who will ever walk through your doors.

7. A total commitment to customer service must begin at the highest level of the organization.

8. Never compromise your integrity.

9. Abhor practices that are unfair to your customers, even if they are considered commonplace in your industry. While crossing the line might increase profits in the short term, such actions will prevent people from wanting to do business with you again.

10. Avoid charging customers for small services that cost you little or nothing to perform, especially with customers who do business with you on a regular basis.

11. Uncover opportunities that will serve you well over the long haul.

12. Go the extra mile to make good first impressions.

13. Surround your business with like-minded, entrepreneurial people and listen to what they have to say.

14. Be ready to act and stand tall in times of crisis, even if it means taking a temporary hit to the bottom line in order to do what is right.

Source: *Exceeding Customer Expectations*

Enterprise also puts a huge emphasis on teamwork. Their mission is to cultivate a fun and friendly workplace where teamwork rules. They do this by hiring young, smart people, training them well and promoting those who consistently create high customer satisfaction scores. These are measured every month by an independent outside agency.

As of this writing, Aaron started as a trainee manager fourteen months ago. Today, he is a station manager, overseeing two offices, a team of fifteen people and a fleet of 270 vehicles valued at seven million dollars. That's a pretty good start! Aaron enjoys the challenge of creating innovative solutions to ensure his customers are completely satisfied. As in every business that has thousands of customers, sometimes initial expectations are not met. However, before a less than happy customer leaves, the fun is to change that situation and exceed their expectation. And it works.

Full-day training sessions once a month also ensure personal and professional growth for Aaron. The prospect of working overseas is also very enticing with Enterprise expanding further into France and Spain. Aaron is fluent in French, so the chance of plateauing early in his career seems far-fetched at this point.

As you learned in Chapter 5, operating with a win-win philosophy creates incredible success. Enterprise seems to have figured out the formula. It looks like the Gen-Y's group are in alignment with win-win, too. Although money is important, at the end of the day, for them, hope springs eternal when you're happy. And doing purposeful work provides a great springboard.

"THE BEST CAREER ADVICE TO GIVE THE YOUNG IS, FIND OUT WHAT YOU LIKE DOING BEST AND GET SOMEONE ELSE TO PAY YOU FOR DOING IT."

—Katherine Whilehaen

Finding Your PURPOSE

Entire books have been written about this all-encompassing topic. We have condensed it down to the fundamentals. Please note, this is a vitally important chapter for you. In the following pages you will discover how essential it is to have a purpose for your life. We'll even help you create a clear definition. Most people don't have a clue about this. We don't want you to end up like masses of other people out there, wandering generalities who are unsure of what they are doing, and why they are doing it.

Then there are those people who come to a crossroads in their life. Somewhere between thirty-five and fifty-five years of age, the famous mid-life crisis appears. Suddenly deeper questions begin to surface like, "Is this all there is?" After some serious navel-gazing, they begin to feel a void, a sense of emptiness. Something is missing, but they can't quite put their finger on it. Gradually they come to the realization that collecting material things and paying off the mortgage isn't doing it for them anymore.

LEARNING TO LIVE ON PURPOSE

Is this scenario familiar to you? Are you wondering about a lack of purpose in your own life? The ideas in this chapter go far beyond the specific daily habits you have started working on, important though these are. At some level we all hunger for meaning in our lives. We need to feel at our core that we matter, and that we are making a difference.

Adopting a lifestyle that is on purpose provides an opportunity to enrich others, by leaving your imprint in a positive way. For example, if you have a daily philosophy of being a giver and you develop the habit of helping others with no immediate thought of personal reward, you are demonstrating the beginnings of a sense of purpose. When you are able to expand this philosophy to encompass a broader vision, your purpose will crystallize.

JACK:
One way to get closer to your purpose is to look back over your life and ask yourself, "What are the ten or fifteen times I've felt the greatest amount of joy in my life?" I interviewed a woman named Julie Laipply, who was Miss Virginia USA in the Miss USA contest. But she wasn't happy. In fact, she was miserable. Julie was studying to be a veterinarian because she loved animals. Then she realized that she loved playing with animals and taking care of them, but she didn't love biology, physiology, and biochemistry. So she stopped wanting to be a veterinarian. Then she asked herself, "When was I happiest?" She realized the time she was happiest was when she was in a leadership role and teaching leadership in high school. She was the student president. She'd go to the student leadership conferences at Ohio State when all the high schools would send two representatives. Then when she was at Ohio State she was one of the chaperones who worked with those kids while they were there. She discovered, "I'm happiest when I'm

leading." So she approached Ohio State and said, "I want to graduate with a degree in leadership." And they said, "We don't have such a thing." She asked, "Can I create an independent study and develop such a program?" They said "Yes". It took her an extra year to graduate, then five more years to get out of school. She took courses in journalism, psychology, and public speaking, and at the age of twenty-six, she was running leadership trainings in the Pentagon for the military. She was happy and fulfilled because she maintained hope and stayed true to her purpose.

The Marathon of HOPE

Here's the remarkable story of Terry Fox. When he was only eighteen years old, Terry discovered he had cancer. The diagnosis was osteosarcoma, a fast-metastasizing cancer that often strikes the legs and arms and may spread to the lungs, brain or liver. After the agony of his new reality set in, Terry basically had two choices: give up hope and wait for death, or discover something meaningful to live for. He chose the latter. The cancer meant he would lose his leg. As he lay in his hospital bed, Terry dreamed of running across Canada. That day he made a commitment to make his dream a reality. His vision was starting to take shape.

By committing his life to making a difference in the fight against cancer, he created a true purpose. The goal of his one-legged run, named the Marathon of Hope, was to raise one million dollars for cancer research. The final total he raised was $24.17 million!

Young Terry discovered a purpose so great it uplifted him physically and mentally every day. This power of purpose drove him to remarkable heights of performance. Even though he had only one healthy leg, a prosthesis attached to the stump of his other leg enabled him to run. The action was more like a hopping movement. It created the sensation of stubbing his toe with every step. Terry wore shorts while running. This of course exposed his false leg and made some people feel uncomfortable. Terry's response was, "This is me, why hide it?" Starting out on April 12, 1980, he ran the equivalent of a marathon (twenty-six miles) almost every day, covering a total of 3,339 miles in only 143 days—an amazing feat! By doing so, he provided hope for thousands of people all over the world.

This may prompt you to ask, "What am I doing with my life? What is my life's work all about? What legacy will I leave behind when my time is over?"

Important questions, don't you think?

The Challenge

Let others lead small lives,
but not you.

Let others argue over small things,
but not you.

Let others cry over small hurts,
but not you.

Let others leave their future
in someone else's hands,
but not you.

Jim Rohn

Three Key POINTS

Let's take a closer look at the key points that helped Terry Fox successfully forge his new purpose. First, we need to clear up the distinction between setting goals and having a purpose. Your purpose transcends your goals. It's the Big Picture—like an all-encompassing umbrella. Goals, on the other hand, are the steps you take along the way. Terry's purpose was to help eliminate cancer. His specific goal, however, was to raise one million dollars for cancer research by running across Canada. When you align your everyday goals with a well-defined purpose, you will enjoy peace of mind and a wonderful sense of being alive. That's a rare commodity these days.

The following three key points will help you activate your own purpose:

1. Align your purpose with your natural ability.

Terry Fox aligned his purpose with something he really enjoyed —athletics. He excelled at running, so running across the country became the natural vehicle for him to achieve his goal. We have all been gifted with natural talents. Discovering what these are is part of the game of life. Often, our work is not aligned with what we do best. Our values and our actions may be at cross purposes. It's these mixed messages that cause internal conflict and uncertainty.

2. Be determined.

Every day Terry stayed true to his purpose. Despite snow, rain and sleet, he soldiered on. In the early stages there was almost no media coverage and he sometimes felt alone and misunderstood. He overcame that by keeping his purpose in the forefront of his mind. Many people lose their direction in life because they are easily distracted or influenced by other people. Consequently they wander along bouncing from one situation to the next, like a ball in a pinball machine.

Living your purpose requires single-mindedness—a resolve to do whatever it takes. It separates the weak from the strong, the procrastinators from the truly committed. It inflames a deep passion and creates a feeling of significance. When your purpose is clear, your life will have meaning. You'll sleep at night fulfilled, instead of worrying about all the day-to-day stuff that creates stress and tension.

3. Maintain a humble attitude.

Don't allow an unhealthy ego to override your good intentions. Individuals who have the greatest and most positive impact on society are not concerned with fame and fortune. Mahatma Gandhi, Mother Teresa, and thousands of others who are not as well-known, simply got on with the work. Greed and power were not part of their formula for living on purpose.

In the later stages of his Marathon of Hope, Terry Fox attracted thousands of people in every major city. His attitude throughout was, "I'm just an average person, no better or no worse than anyone else. There are a lot of other people involved with this, and they deserve recognition too." It was this humble outlook and genuine concern for others, plus his never-give-up attitude as he battled adversity, that endeared him to millions of people. Even after the cancer spread to his lungs, he was determined to carry on. Terry never did get to finish his run. He passed away on June 28, 1981. However, the ongoing legacy he left continues to help cancer victims.

To date, more than 400 million dollars has been raised for cancer research from the annual Terry Fox Run. The event is held in at least fifty countries and more than two million people have participated. At this point you may be thinking, "That's a great story, but I really don't see myself dramatically changing the world. I'm not a celebrity. My struggle is just getting to the end of the month."

That's the very reason you are struggling—you don't get it yet. The importance of purpose, that is. If you did, you wouldn't view your life as a struggle.

As trainers, our biggest challenge is getting people to understand how critical this is to their future. Wouldn't it be nice to have a ready-made "purpose button" on the top of your head, that you could hit and your true purpose in life would immediately become clear? Obviously there's more to it than that. The remainder of this chapter will clarify how you can make this happen.

Here's the next step to making your purpose come alive.

Discovering Your PURPOSE

As we stated earlier, most people do not have a well-defined purpose. To help you figure out yours, there are some probing questions. Take your time to think through these before answering. If you are feeling stuck, or going through a major transition, consider taking a couple of days off and going to a quiet retreat where you can really think about what you want to do with your life. It's impossible to make excellent decisions when you are caught up in the busy whirl of everyday activities. You can't think on the run! If you don't have a special sanctuary of your own, there are probably a few retreats in your area. Check the Internet or your local churches for assistance.

David McNally, bestselling author of *Even Eagles Need a Push* and *The Eagle's Secret*, is the producer of a wonderful award-winning video about Terry Fox. (See Resource Guide for details.) It is truly inspiring. David is regarded as a leading authority on how to thrive in our personal and professional lives. He created the critically important ten-question exercise called Discovering and Living Your Purpose (see Action Steps). These are essential questions. So don't sell yourself short—reserve a few minutes to complete the exercise—it could lead to a major breakthrough for you. But first, finish reading the chapter. In doing so, you will develop a greater understanding of how to determine your purpose. Here are some key considerations: Your quest begins with recognizing your special skills and talents. What do you do best? What do you really enjoy doing? Chapter 2, Priority Focus, helped you to figure this out. Most people stagnate in their jobs. They end up bored, just going through the motions. It's very frustrating. Often, the reason is a lack of challenge. The work does not utilize their strengths and they end up stuck doing activities that deplete their energy, instead of being inspired by some magnificent project. Does this in any way describe you?

Purposeful work also means that you care deeply about something. You don't feel obligated to perform, rather you are passionate about it. Terry Fox was profoundly touched by younger cancer victims. It spurred him on every day, despite the hardships.

When you are living on purpose you feel that you are making a difference. And you don't need to be famous. You can make a significant impact in your own community. Another important factor is your level of enthusiasm. If you are focused only on making money, a large slice of life will pass you by.

To help you fully understand this, we had to include the following story about a young girl whose purpose was thrust upon her in a cruel way.

Ten-year-old Anna Jarmics saw the small oval-shaped metal object land in the sandbox near her brothers and sisters. She knew she had to do something. So she picked it up and decided to throw it away in the hope of protecting her siblings. She started running, suddenly tripped on the sidewalk, and as she lay there, the live hand grenade exploded, mangling both of her hands. It was 1945 in war-torn Hungary, and the grenade had been tossed onto the street from a passing Russian tank.

Anna was rushed to an army hospital three blocks away. She remained conscious. The doctors immediately amputated both of her hands just below the wrist. Times were tough and supplies were meager. She endured the traumatic procedures without anesthetic. Recovery was painful and slow. There were no rehabilitation facilities in those days. Altogether she spent six months in hospital.

Now, age seventy-six, Anna has led a purposeful life inspiring others to break through their limitations and discover what their life can become. She has never been bitter or angry about her own misfortune. In fact, she wouldn't even use the word *misfortune* in her vocabulary. What do you do when you're ten years old with no hands? Well, you go to school and you eventually learn how to pick up a pencil. Then, despite having no fingers or thumbs, you somehow learn to write. It's hard and it takes persistence, but Anna is not a quitter. She never has been.

In 1956, she moved to England, got a job cleaning offices, got married and had four children. Another major challenge came when her husband, an alcoholic, suddenly walked out on the family, emptying the bank account leaving Anna with nothing to her name. She explains, "I just kept working and raised my kids the best way I could." She then decided to immigrate to Canada.

When she arrived there, Anna wanted to drive her own car. With no hands? Impossible! Anna Jarmics doesn't use the word *impossible* in her vocabulary either. The day of her driving test she said the instructor looked more nervous than she was. All of the staff at the driving school were glued to the windows as she stepped into her vehicle. They were cheering when she returned, having passed on her first attempt.

When pursuing a job at a local hospital, she said to the skeptical human resources person, "Let me show you what I can do. I'll work two weeks for nothing, then you can start giving me a paycheck." She got the job. Anna is always looking for new challenges. She relishes change and looks at life as a series of positive opportunities. Among her long list of victories are several trophies she's won for target shooting. She garnered first, second, and third prizes for her exquisite watercolor paintings, and she is considering an exhibition in the near future. She's also an accomplished calligrapher. There have been other physical challenges along the way. While working as a security guard, Anna broke her back, requiring two major operations before she was on her feet again.

You can add determination to her list of qualities. She'll be the first to tell you she has a very definite competitive streak. And she has a can-do attitude. "I don't find anything difficult. I can do anything I want," she says.

Perhaps her crowning achievement is her twenty-eight-year love affair with the game of darts. It started innocently enough, watching a friend play at a local Legion Hall. He said, "You should play." So she did. Her very first throw was a bull's-eye and she has been winning ever since. In fact, several men refuse to play with her because she always beats them. Her many championship wins include a gold medal in darts at the Senior Olympics.

When asked what advice she would offer others, particularly those struggling with change, Anna says: "It's important to think for yourself. Buy a journal. Take time to write down your thoughts. Ask yourself questions. What bothers you most? Why? What can you do about it? Go back and read over your notes. It will give you clarity and help you make decisions."

Anna has learned to overcome her physical pain using mental strength instead of pills. She practices meditation and believes greatly in the power of prayer. "I leave it up to God. I always say, 'What will be, will be.' I'm just having fun."

Anna's latest project is speaking to new immigrants at the local YWCA. Many of these people are anxious about their future. Anna's story inspires them to let go of their fear and helps them believe that they can succeed. She says, "It's made me so happy, because I can tell somebody how to make their life better—I've succeeded in a lot of things because I wanted to. Nobody taught me how to do things. It was all my own doing. I never give up. I never did, and I never will!" Inspiring words from a very inspiring woman whose purpose is clear when you spend a few minutes with her—to be a beacon of enthusiasm for others so that their light can shine too.

Source: *The Power of Focus for Women*

"Then, once you discover what it is you are searching for, just type it into the search engine."

Statement
of
PURPOSE

Many businesses have spent large sums of money developing mission statements. This usually involves the leaders of the company. Sometimes a management consultant is hired to help with the process. The result is usually three or four paragraphs of well-meaning words and clichés. These are often made into a beautiful plaque that hangs elegantly in the main entrance of the office. Sadly, this is as far as it goes for many companies. Even sadder is the fact that, when asked, most people who work in the organization cannot repeat the mission statement. It never becomes part of the culture. All too often it is just something management dreamed up, and becomes another flavor of the month.

LES:
I had a speech to deliver to the board members of a large national food chain. I knew they had a mission statement and were upgrading it. So I randomly called several of their stores and asked the person who answered the phone, "Can you tell me what your company mission statement is, please?" Not one person was able to answer the question. One manager responded, "I think we have a copy of it somewhere. I'd need to check my filing cabinet." So much for living your mission!

If you own a business or are a key decision-maker, consider these suggestions: First, change the phrase "Mission Statement" to "Our Purpose." Generally speaking, employees understand this more easily than a mission. Keep it short and simple, so that everyone in the office can memorize it. One powerful sentence that everyone puts into practice every day will do more for your business than a long-winded statement dropped into some obscure filing cabinet.

An excellent example is Harry Rosen Men's Wear, a high-end clothing chain. Here's their statement: To Exceed Our Customer's Expectations. This is printed on the back of every salesperson's business card, and everyone who works there knows it. Each employee also has the authority to turn this statement into action. For example, if you bought a pair of pants that needed altering, and you had to have them tomorrow but couldn't pick them up, the salesperson would ensure that they were delivered by courier. No problem. That's going the extra mile. We suggest you keep your own personal statement of purpose to one meaningful sentence. Make it generic enough that you can serve your purpose in many everyday situations.

LES:

My purpose statement is: **"To use my God-given talents to positively impact as many people as I can during my lifetime, in a way that significantly improves their lives."** This gives me a multitude of opportunities. I can serve business people through our Power of Focus training programs. I can also share ideas by writing books, blogs and magazine articles as well as recording audio programs and videos. Or I can simply offer a word of encouragement and a smile to someone who needs a boost—for example, a waitress who is feeling pressured because the restaurant is short-staffed. Or a parking lot attendant who rarely has a conversation with any customers because they are in too big a hurry to extend a greeting.

JACK:

My purpose statement is: **"To inspire and empower people to live their highest vision in a context of love and joy, in harmony with the highest good of all concerned."** Similar to what Les stated above, there are many opportunities and many forums for accomplishing this.

I can write books, conduct seminars, give speeches, write articles, appear on radio and television shows, motivate and mentor my staff, consult with other organizations, develop a self-improvement curriculum for at-risk, inner-city high school students, or simply inspire the person sitting next to me on an airplane.

MARK:

My purpose statement is: **"To help kids of all ages to love free enterprise and business profitability, using inventiveness, creativity and innovation."** I can speak to hundreds of teenage entrepreneurs at a conference, or, like Les and Jack, I can also have an audience with one young person for ten minutes. It's amazing how you can touch someone with a few well-chosen words of encouragement and support. Sometimes it only takes a moment to make a positive difference.

We have also developed a statement of purpose for our *Chicken Soup for the Soul* series. It simply reads:

TO CHANGE THE WORLD, ONE STORY AT A TIME.

Dave Albano Is Someone Who Likes to Live Large.

He also lives on purpose by raising money for worthy causes. So when he sets a major personal goal, he creates a secondary charitable target to go along with it.

As an outdoor enthusiast, Dave recently decided to really test his capabilities. At age forty-three, he's currently climbing the Seven Summits, the highest mountains on each of the seven continents on earth—magical peaks that have been climbed by a unique "club" of less than 200 people. They are Kilimanjaro (Africa), Denali (North America), Aconcagua (South America), Carstenz Pyramid (Australasia), Vinson (Antarctica), Everest (Asia) and Elbrus (Europe). This multi-year goal obviously requires tremendous discipline and focus, as well as considerable resources.

Dave recently summited Kilimanjaro—19,340 feet. Here's a brief account of his experience:

"Africa was hot, I mean stupid hot! My buddy Ralph had asked me to coach his twenty-three person team to climb Kili, as the mountain is affectionately known. Most had never been on a mountain, but the purpose was to raise funds for multiple sclerosis (MS) research, a very worthwhile pursuit.

"We trudged up the massive slopes of the mountain for five full days with the summit covered in snow, in full view. Our African guides constantly reminded us of our daily Swahili mantra—'polé, polé' which means—slowly, slowly. The trick to a successful summit is proper acclimatization which could only occur through a painfully slow ascent.

"On the night of day five, our summit bid began. It started at the highest elevation I had ever achieved at that time. We were well prepared, knowing that this was a mental game as much as a physical one. I felt strong and refreshed despite the oxygen-depleted atmosphere. Little did I know how much worse it would get! We travelled in the darkness, single-file, our headlamps lighting the way. Six hours later, we reached a major milestone at Gilman's Point, which sits atop the crater rim at 18,638 feet. The true summit was about another two-hour hike to Uhuru Peak at 19,341 feet, which is the highest point in Africa.

"About 15,000 people attempt to climb Kili every year, but only 30 percent ever make it to the top, and about a dozen actually die annually attempting the climb. More people have died on Kili than Everest because people underestimate it. I intentionally did not take any altitude sickness medication to see where my body would tank, physically. I found out fast! Literally a few steps after Gilman's Point, a vicious headache set in accompanied by horrible nausea. I emptied the contents of my stomach on the crater rim. "Focus Dave....Focus," I kept repeating to myself. I just put one foot in front of the other.

"When despair sets in, you want to quit. I couldn't believe how hard and fast acute mountain sickness walloped me. However, I thought, 'I didn't come all the way to the heart of Africa to turn around now.' Besides, this was bigger than me. I had coached our team the entire trip just for this moment. I promised folks back home I'd fly their flags at the summit. I had people sponsor me for the fundraiser if I reached the top. Focus—onward—upward. For every step, I had to stop and take three breaths before I was able to lift my other leg. Step... Breath...Breath...Breath...Step...Breath...Breath...Breath....It seemed like an eternity. For two full hours I continued in this trance, purely focused on the patch of stone, dirt and ice in front of me where my next footstep would fall. Finally, at long last, I dragged myself to the summit. I was the first of our party to do so, and through The Power of Focus I flew a flag bearing those exact same words that inspired me to the top.

"The joy and the elation I felt is hard to describe. Just the very act of *stopping* rejuvenated me. I spent a good half-hour on the Roof of Africa, soaking in the experience, re-charging, revelling in a dream come true. I wept at the enormity of it all...knowing I was only halfway there, since the top of any climb is simply the half-way point. To be successful, you still have to get down! The incredible effort it took my body to move was mind-numbing, and I knew the only cure to my ills was to get back down as soon as possible.

"Seventy-five percent of our mountain team made it to the top that day *and* we collectively raised over $300,000 for MS. My next ascent of Mt. Aconcagua in Argentina, the highest peak outside the Himalayas, is only a month away. Everest and the other summits are soon to follow. I feel confident as I continue training, knowing a lot more money will be raised for other great causes. And the people I meet along the way during these unique adventures will add greatly to my growth and experience. Live Large!" (See more of Dave's story at www. DaveAlbano.com)

Contribution

You'll know you are making a difference when:

- You take time to listen as a stranger shares a heartache.

- Your child hands you a custom-made card, with a verse that makes your eyes go moist.

- People describe you as a genuine giver.

- Your customers keep coming back year after year.

- Going the extra mile for others is something you do naturally.

- Unexpected opportunities come from "out of the blue". It's called payback.

- You may be physically tired, but your heart feels full at the end of the day.

—*Les Hewitt*

Insights

One of the more common questions we receive is, "What's the difference between living your life on purpose versus setting new goals every year?" That is a meaningful question.

First, some people discover their life's purpose at a very early age, while others go through their journey and never figure it out. That's still a bit of a mystery. Why would a young man like Terry Fox be inspired to run across Canada to help eradicate cancer, whereas a wealthy influential rock star (or businessperson), succumbs to heroin addiction and fritters away their life in a useless fashion? These are two ends of a pretty wide spectrum. Our observation is, for most people, their sense of purpose evolves.

Living on purpose is directly connected to giving. The key phrase is, constantly adding value to others. Some people are cut out to be teachers, counselors, pastors, missionaries and coaches. Some are destined to be doctors, nurses and surgeons. Others are given the gift of making money. And then there's a whole range of occupations in between, all service-oriented. Ask yourself, are you experiencing joy in the value you provide to others, in your current job, career or business?

Purpose is very personal. People of faith would say, "God is guiding you to serve in his image—just follow his promptings." Then there are individuals where a sense of purpose is thrust upon them unexpectedly. The stories of Terry Fox and Anna Jarmics in this chapter are perfect examples. You've hardly started your life, when suddenly—WHAM!—you get hit by a two by four.

Purpose is definitely connected to inspiration. As author Bob Buford says in his book *Half Time*, for some people, it's moving from success to significance. Often, wealthy people are not happy, despite their financial success. The answer to filling this void can arise from the simplest awakenings. Like the multi-millionaire whose friend brought him to a war zone in Europe and demonstrated the need for handicapped children to have functional wheelchairs. The delight in the faces of these grateful children was life changing for the businessman whose own life had become one of boredom instead of fulfillment.

Purpose and goals are also linked. When your purpose is ignited, goals become an essential part of your Action Plan. Your vision expands and along with it, the need for measurable targets to help you live your vision. Gen Y'ers like Aaron Trenouth seem to have an awareness of this already. That's most encouraging!

Review this chapter again carefully, and more than once if you are at a defining moment in your life, where a sense of purpose is calling you to make a major shift in direction.

"WHEN YOU SEE WHAT YOU'RE HERE FOR, THE WORLD BEGINS TO MIRROR YOUR PURPOSE IN A MAGICAL WAY. IT'S ALMOST AS IF YOU SUDDENLY FIND YOURSELF ON A STAGE, IN A PLAY THAT WAS WRITTEN EXPRESSLY FOR YOU."

—Betty Sue Flowers

ACTION STEPS

Discovering and
Living
Your Purpose

The ten questions below were formulated to help you determine if your life is centered around purpose. In combination with the key points in this chapter, they will help you clarify a definition of purpose that works for you. Before responding, think about each question and read the comments. Then simply check "yes"; "don't know/not sure"; or "no."

1. Do you recognize what you are really good at and what energizes you?

❏ yes   ❏ don't know/not sure   ❏ no

Many people never find their niche because they avoid analyzing their career objectives. They fall into jobs and never actually ask themselves, "What do I do well? What type of life do I want to lead? What type of work creates positive energy for me?" It's important for you to know and use your special skills.

2. Do you fully utilize your most-enjoyed skills?

❏ yes   ❏ don't know/not sure   ❏ no

Many people stagnate in their jobs. They are capable of doing so much more, yet they are afraid to challenge themselves. There are four separate categories of job expectations. Unfortunately, most people fall into the first three.

A. "It's just a job. Any job is okay as long as the pay is good and I can do my own thing after work."

B. "Work has to be regular. I need the benefits, vacations and security of a permanent job."

C. "I want substance and content in my profession, trade or vocation. I want to use my talents and be challenged."

D. "Work is not related to money; work is a path to further learning and personal growth. Work focuses me on something that I really believe needs doing in this organization, community, or world."

3. Does your work further some interest or issue that you care deeply about?

❏ yes   ❏ don't know/not sure   ❏ no

Caring is the basis of all purpose. It requires an openness to everything around you. To develop care, you need awareness. You should not be burdened by a sense of duty or obligation. When you care naturally, it's because something has profoundly touched and moved you.

4. Do you see yourself, through work, as making a difference in the world?

❏ yes   ❏ don't know/not sure   ❏ no

The "rust-out syndrome" is prevalent in today's society. Because so many people find work to be meaningless, they lose motivation.

Work must offer more than money and status; it must offer you the chance to make a difference.

5. Do you view most days with a sense of enthusiasm?

❑ yes   ❑ don't know/not sure   ❑ no

When you are serving a purpose larger than yourself, you will feel more committed and become more enthusiastic. Remember, the years fly by quickly, so approach each day and each task with zeal.

6. Have you developed your own philosophy of life and success?

❑ yes   ❑ don't know/not sure   ❑ no

Everyone needs a set of principles to live by. Too many people, however, accept the values of others and never develop their own. They do not reflect enough upon their lives; instead, they worry about getting approval from others. Real power comes from acting out your deep, personal values.

7. Are you taking the necessary risks to live your philosophy?

❑ yes   ❑ don't know/not sure   ❑ no

No one is ever completely sure of the path to follow, but those with the courage to believe in themselves and their ideas, with the potential of some loss involved, are the true individuals. You must take the risk—have the courage to be true to yourself.

8. Do you feel a sense of meaning and purpose for your life?

❑ yes   ❑ don't know/not sure   ❑ no

Terry Fox is a wonderful example of someone who had a deeply felt purpose in life. His memory spurs us to raise our own expectations of what we can be. You can choose to focus your vigor on what gives you the deepest feeling. You can occupy your time and talents with people, commitments, ideas and challenges that feel purposeful.

9. Do you have active goals this year relating to your purpose?

❏ **yes**   ❏ **don't know/not sure**   ❏ **no**

Purpose as a part of our lives serves as inspiration. But it is really our goals that motivate us on a day-to-day basis. Our lives are empty when we do not have something to strive for. Goals, though not always easy to achieve, provide the satisfaction of accomplishment, which in turn enhances our sense of self-worth.

10. Are you living your life to the fullest now instead of hoping that things will work out someday?

❏ **yes**   ❏ **don't know/not sure**   ❏ **no**

Why wait for the lottery? Use your potential now instead of taking it to the grave. It's time to live within your values, and with purpose.

> **Score your results as follows:**
>
> • For each **yes** answer give yourself a **0**.
> • **Not sure** or **don't know** scores a **1**.
> • Each **no** answer scores a **2**.

Now add up your score. As these questions are subjective, there are no right or wrong answers. However, use the scoring analysis as a general guideline. Here's how it works:

If you scored between 0–7, your life is pretty focused, you have a sense of direction, and you are intent on making a difference.

If you scored between 8–15, you have a sense of purpose, but you need to clarify your commitment. Are you really living your values and "walking the talk" every day?

If your score was between 16–20, you run the risk of not using your potential and just wasting your life. Please note: This high score may also mean that you are experiencing some sort of crisis, or major transition.

Now that you have had an opportunity to think about what purpose means to you, construct a one-sentence statement that captures the essence of your life's purpose as you currently see it.

Choose your words carefully, and as always, be specific.

_____

_____

_____

To reinforce your purpose, embrace this statement every day. Print it on a special card that you can keep close to you. Develop the habit of re-affirming your statement of purpose until it becomes totally ingrained in your consciousness. This is the catalyst that will change your behavior and allow you to actually enjoy living your life on purpose.

If you are not able to create a meaningful statement after doing this questionnaire, don't be too concerned. Often it takes months (and sometimes years) to clarify this. What will help is to keep searching and thinking about what you are doing and why. The answers will eventually present themselves to you.

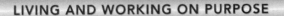

LIVING AND WORKING ON PURPOSE

TAKING DECISIVE ACTION

CONSISTENT PERSISTENCE

ASK FOR WHAT YOU WANT

THE CONFIDENCE FACTOR

BUILDING EXCELLENT RELATIONSHIPS

OVERCOMING SETBACKS

DO YOU SEE THE BIG PICTURE?

IT'S NOT HOCUS-POCUS, IT'S ALL ABOUT FOCUS

YOUR HABITS WILL DETERMINE YOUR FUTURE

Congratulations—you did it!
Now, feast on the ideas in the special bonus chapter.

Ideas to Make You Rich

> "ORDINARY RICHES CAN BE STOLEN, REAL RICHES CANNOT. IN YOUR SOUL ARE INFINITELY PRECIOUS THINGS THAT CANNOT BE TAKEN FROM YOU."
>
> —Oscar Wilde

Despite the negative business connotation with this chapter number, we thought it would be very reassuring and affirming to introduce you to five of our Power of Focus clients, who we've been privileged to work with over the years.

These individuals have successfully sidestepped various setbacks including economic roller coasters and have all become wealthy. We want to emphasize that despite the anxiety, fear and uncertainty that has created financial storm clouds and devastated previously strong nations, there are individuals from a broad spectrum of industries who have found a clear path to riches. In the pages that follow you will learn a little about their background, but more importantly we have asked them this nuts and bolts question:

"What are the five specific strategies that have contributed most to your success?"

You will notice some overlap in their answers. That's very important to digest, because it reinforces the fact that sustainable success only requires focus in a few areas.

So, as a final "hurrah" we are pleased to share with you the twenty-five strategies that have caused these five exceptional Achievers to rise to the top of their game. We encourage you to feast on their wisdom and use what is most relevant to create your own path to riches. One final note before we pull back the curtain. **Let's be clear about the true definition of RICH.**

The dictionary tells us the word rich means "having a great deal of money;" that is, enjoying financial wealth. Other terms are "of great value" and "rich in resources". Our experience is this. When you provide great value in the marketplace, you will attract monetary riches to you. More importantly, being rich in personal resources is the key to enjoying true wealth. When you are rich in spirit, rich in character, rich in relationships, rich in faith, rich in health, rich in giving and rich in wisdom, you will know and appreciate how it feels to enjoy abundance and all its fullness.

There is one other final piece we have added to complete this special 10th Anniversary Edition. It will give you a glimpse into the future. You'll learn about the Gamechangers—exciting cutting-edge companies who are attracting many Gen Y'ers into their unique business culture. These pioneering companies are creating new trends, seriously questioning conventional wisdom and focusing on being socially responsible, as well as profitable.

Now, let's welcome our five exceptional Achievers who are each making a big impact in their own particular niche. We will proudly take just a little bit of the credit for their outstanding success. Beneath each of their five best strategies, we have posed a direct question. Take time to reflect on your answer. You will probably discover some gaps in your business. Remember, the advice from these Achievers was gleaned from many years of trial and error. But today they are all rich! Model their advice and you can have a brighter future, too.

#1

SAM BECKFORD:
THE SMALL BUSINESS MILLIONAIRE

Easy going, humble, generous and a razor sharp marketing genius are all words that describe Sam Beckford. Strong family values are also a big part of his make-up. However, Sam's early experiences as an entrepreneur were less than stellar. Here's the story in his own words:

"After graduating with a business degree I naturally decided to start my own business. I thought I knew everything there was to know about business, so I took the leap. The first business failed within a year. After that I tried four other business ventures that were all mild to massive failures. After losing all of my money and money I had borrowed from family and friends, I decided to get a real job. That job lasted less than six months and I was fired. My wife had taught piano lessons through university and we had toyed with the idea of opening a music teaching studio. I initially dismissed the idea because I never believed that a business like that could make any real money. We decided that even if the business only made a modest amount of money, at least it would be better than having a regular job with rigid schedules.

"We opened the business by making fifty dollars' worth of photocopied flyers and dropping them on the doorsteps of three thousand houses. We didn't have money to lease commercial space so we rented space from a local elementary school in the evenings. A few months later the business started picking up a little and we were up to about eighty students. We tried looking for a permanent commercial space. One landlord of a commercial plaza met us and told us he would not rent space to us because he didn't believe that our business would make it. He told us that we should even get into a different type of business if we wanted to be successful, like maybe opening a restaurant.

"We eventually found a cheap six-hundred-square-foot space on the second floor of a different old plaza. We decided to focus all of our energy on making our little business successful. I started reading at least one book a week to learn everything I could about being successful in small business. Reading *The Millionaire Next Door*, I learned that most millionaires made their money by starting boring, dull, normal businesses. That one discovery gave me the belief that we could be successful, and even become millionaires one day from our little business. The following year we opened a second location and added dance classes to our music lesson programs. We figured that if families were there taking classes anyway, we may as well offer them more classes to take. We kept learning, reading and focusing on making our business successful.

"A few years later we opened up a third location of our business. Instead of renting a space we were able to buy a small commercial warehouse condo. After that initial purchase we saw what the true opportunity of our studio was, commercial real estate ownership. Over the next ten years we were able to acquire over nine million dollars of commercial property by using various creative financing strategies. That was a pretty big leap considering that when we bought our first commercial property we had not even owned a house before.

"Also, instead of franchising our business to expand and add more locations, we started sharing our ideas with other dance and music studios.

"This turned into an even bigger business than the studio business. There are over twenty-two thousand studios across North America. A lot of them were great at teaching but terrible at business. Sharing the ideas that worked well for us helped them—and us.

"In 2006 we bought a piece of waterfront property and built our dream home, including an exclusive coaching center. I call the property Creators Landing and I use it to show people how to expand their business, own real estate and live a semi-retired schedule. Most weeks I average fifteen to twenty hours of work per week, total. The rest of the time I spend with my kids who we home-school so we can take six or seven trips per year.

"I believe that the main reason for my success was deciding to focus on the opportunity that was right in front of me. Success is a lot closer than you think in most cases."

Sam is releasing a book based on his amazing success, titled, *The Small Business Wealth Triangle: The Ultimate Strategy to Semi-Retire Faster, Richer and Happier.*

The three points of the triangle are:

1. Your primary business—how to run it profitably using very little of your own time.

2. Your alternative business—something you do for fun, you love doing and that can also be profitable.

3. Real Estate—own the building(s) that house your primary business.

Sam Beckford is a genuine self-made millionaire who lives life to the fullest, keeps business simple and is humble about his success. His honest down-to-earth approach to business and life is a refreshing change from the greed-driven financial entrepreneurs and politicians who have been creating headlines recently for all the wrong reasons. Way to go Sam!

Sam Beckford's
Top 5 Success Strategies

Reflect on the direct questions below each strategy.

1. Think Big, But Start Small Today

"Having big dreams is good, but if you don't have an opportunity that is small enough to apply your action to now, the dreams remain in the future. My business success, which translated into wealth, started by taking action on a small business that I started with fifty dollars and grew into a three-million-dollar enterprise. I didn't wait until I had everything in place to start big. I know guys who are always chasing rainbows or the "big score" but never start action on something they can easily get started on, control and grow."

Question: Are you taking focused action on your short-term goals, and are they linked to a bigger vision?

2. Decide to Give It Away Before You Get It

"The first year that I made a substantial amount of money from my business was the year I decided to give away 100,000 dollars to church and charity before I even made it. That year money seemed to flow to me naturally. Why? I had no guilt, fear of success or worthiness issues about wanting the money. The money was not just being made to enrich me it was being made to help others. When you commit to a goal that is bigger than yourself, the money flows to your effort."

Question: Are you making a significant contribution to help others in need?

3. Develop Your Goal Magnet

"My favorite success phrase is: "Discipline is remembering what you want". Writing goals down and thinking about them every day brings you closer to them. When I have choices of three activities I could do, I ask myself: "Will this activity get me closer to my goal or not?" If you ask yourself that question daily you will end the year with more goals accomplished than you thought possible."

Question: Do you read your most important goals every day?

4. Learn to Earn

"If you are willing to learn more than your colleagues you will out-earn them too. I can beat any business competitor in my field because I am willing to out-learn them. Education is the one edge a small company can use to beat a bigger company that is well financed. Ten years ago when I started my business and I was competing against a much large, better financed competitor, I decided that my advantage would be to know more. I read 700 books on business, sales, marketing and anything else that would give me more knowledge than they had. Today my company is in the lead and their company is pretty much at the same place they were ten years ago. I didn't have a monopoly on the books I read or the courses and seminars I took, I just made the decision to invest in education. Vince Lombardi, famous coach of the Green Bay Packers, once said: "The will to prepare to win is more important than the will to win". Be willing to put in more training time and you will win more on the business field."

Question: Do you set aside 30 minutes or more every day to read something meaningful or inspirational?

5. Become a "Get Back on Track" Specialist

"Life happens. You will get knocked off course several times, sometimes several times a day. Become an expert at springing back into action when an unexpected event stops your momentum. Never think the day is "shot" when an interruption happens. Get back into action and keep working toward your goals even when it seems like you aren't moving."

Question: How fast do you bounce back when a setback occurs? How could this be improved?

For more information: www.creatorslanding.com.

#2

KAREN STEWART:
CHANGING THE DIVORCE PARADIGM

A defining moment in Karen Stewart's life happened unexpectedly one morning when relaxing in the bathtub with her three-month-old daughter.

Her husband's intrusion suddenly turned a happy family scene into a chilling, unwanted reality. Standing emotionless in front of his wife and daughter, he announced, "I'm not happy, Karen. You just don't do it for me anymore. I'm thinking about moving out." The next five years for Karen were ones of turmoil, self-doubt and roller-coaster emotions as she battled through a traumatic divorce that left her with 500,000 dollars in legal fees and another half million dollars in personal debt.

Married for over seven years with three young children, Karen felt cheated by the legal system that had drained her finances and exhausted her energy. One thought had surfaced however. "There has to be a reason for this pain, angst and hardship." There was. Karen began to imagine what a new divorce paradigm might look like; one that was grounded in a common-sense approach to save people money, time and stress and to protect the children. In 2006, she launched Fairway Divorce Solutions, after developing The Fairway Process™ for couples. This unique system enables couples to make a clean break while protecting their sanity, wealth and children. Her book *Clean Break* is a must-read for anyone contemplating separation or divorce.

Karen is a fighter and a person who sees opportunity even in the worst situations. As a twenty-one-year-old ambitious entrepreneur, she authored a university paper about creating a mission statement. Here's what it said, "My mission is to build a business by identifying an unmet need." She had put herself through college by selling Mary Kay cosmetics. This start-up business required taking out a 2,000 dollar bank loan at 20 percent interest. Her motto was, **Take the risk and be relentless!**

At the age of twenty-eight, Karen opened her first financial services company, going on to specialize in the industry for over two decades, successfully building and selling a number of financial companies. When she first started, she admitted she had no idea how to do it. She built Milestone Asset Management Group to more than 100 million dollars in assets, delivering a highly integrated investment platform for a clientele of high net worth individuals.

From the start, Karen decided to build her company very differently from the traditional industry model. She had two fundamental values that were embedded into her business culture immediately. These were: (1) Everyone on the team had to be 100 percent client focused and (2) Show integrity at all costs!

Her instructions to her team were to stay laser focused on the consumer. One way of doing that was to help them discover their genuine needs. Karen found that customers often didn't know what their needs were. To solidify this business model, Karen was one of the first in the country to introduce a fee for services plan.

This was performance based—if the client's portfolio does well, then we will do well, too. This also guaranteed a high level of accountability for everyone on her team. At the time, the standard business model was commission driven, lacked accountability and was profitable whether the client did well or not.

Karen demonstrated other new initiatives such as not having individual brokers owning a book of business, herself included. Instead, her company was process oriented and team centered. With the valuation now based on the total company's performance, this would ensure a better selling price if the company was taken over or sold. Again, a very different approach compared to traditional methods.

Another unique advantage was Karen's philosophy on hiring people. In the financial services sector, people were often recruited from other companies. Milestone focused their efforts on elite students who had just graduated from university. Being fresh out of school, they had not accumulated any bad industry habits or been steeped in a different type of culture to the one Karen had established. Training young, smart, ambitious people on a specific system built for success was a key driver in creating Milestone's impressive growth.

Under Karen's drive and astute leadership, the company grew rapidly. It's interesting to note that Enterprise Rent-A-Car has a similar model that has also created outstanding growth and profitability. You don't need to create a new mousetrap when building a business. Just figure out who's catching all the mice and pay attention to how they are doing it!

Another important factor in Karen Stewart's success is her ability to look at herself in the mirror and make changes when she knows they need to be made. You might have the right brand and the best client model but if something in your structure isn't as good as it needs to be, take action.

At Fairway Divorce Solutions, Karen has already made several important adjustments to improve the structure. Responding quickly is very rare in many industries where ego and complacency start to dominate the culture and the biggest opportunities are often missed. Women business owners were rare in the industry when Karen started, making her accomplishments even more noteworthy. The extensive experience she gained in business and finance provided a solid foundation for starting Fairway Divorce Solutions. The company has expanded rapidly across Canada and the United States and is filling a huge need in the divorce settlement arena. Karen's own dramatic story has garnered constant media attention nationally and created speaking engagements for her at major conferences. Her mission now, she says is: "I want to change the way divorce happens."

Karen Stewart's
Top 5 Success Strategies

1. Visualize Your Success

"I had the ability to visualize from a very young age what success looked like for me—specifically. The details do matter. The ability to see myself as a leader and entrepreneur while providing maternal direction to those that work for me, and to see the specifics of colors, size, etc., in advance of materialization is, and was, the key. I know if I can see it then I can become it."

Question: Do you visualize your goals already completed and how it feels, for ten minutes each day?

2. Know What You Want

"The relentless commitment to set goals for the long term and short term is vital. I have always set ninety-day goals that are measurable and articulate. I revisit them daily without fail. I remove myself every ninety days from my office and routine environment to evaluate my last ninety days and focus on setting goals for the next quarter."

Question: Do you schedule a Planning and Review Day every quarter to measure your accomplishments, make adjustments and plan the next ninety days?

3. Maintain a Non-Negotiable Value System

"In the fast and demanding world of business and life, our values can be challenged and we may find ourselves having to negotiate. My value system is my internal guide that ensures that those things that matter to me—my family, my integrity, my business, my friends and most importantly my soul—are never compromised. I know what my priorities are and so it is easy for me to say "no" when necessary."

Question: Do you know your five most important values?

4. Create Balance and Be Present in the Moment

"I eat right, I exercise, I am spiritual and study that daily. I have fun (although not enough) and most importantly my heart is filled with love. People look at my life and often comment on how I do it. It's simple—I am present in the moment, I am well organized, I delegate and I try not to take myself too seriously."

Question: What's one thing you could do immediately to have a better balance in your life?

5. Be a Lifetime Learner

"I am a sponge. I read in excess of fifty books per year. I have learned it's not what you know, but what you know you do not know. Knowing the questions to ask is what matters. Intellect is the wisdom to know what you do not know. I have a lot to learn and I love that."

Question: What book would help you right now? Go find it!

For more information: www.fairwaydivorce.com.

© Randy Glasbergen.
www.glasbergen.com

"Dave usually gets the *Salesman Of The Month* award, but this month I got it! Well, actually, he sold it to me."

#3

PHIL CARROLL:
HOUSEBOATS TO BILLION DOLLAR DEALS!

When you first meet Phil Carroll, the positive energy he exudes is like being caught in a magnetic field. You get pulled into his enthusiasm, passion for life and intensity of focus. This charisma is heightened by his six foot plus frame and a tanned complexion gained from living in Phoenix, Arizona, for the last ten years.

Phil was born to be an entrepreneur. Working a 5 AM neighborhood paper route as a young teenager taught him to start early and run fast! Still in his teens, he started a flower delivery business with a specific target market—hospitals. He became the courier of choice for several flower shops and turned a nice profit.

Phil says his three greatest strengths are selling, selling and selling!

"I sold my wife on marrying me which turned out to be one of my best sales jobs. Twenty five years later, it's still working well. I've always been able to sell investors and attract large quantities of capital and manage it properly and I've always been able to sell the banks. Selling is the lifeblood of every business—you must never forget that. Administration and everything else follows *after* the sale."

One of Phil's most famous sales that attracted nationwide media attention was the formation of Three Buoys Houseboats. His brother Randy and best friend

Dave Steele were the co-founders. All in their early twenties, the three boys started inauspiciously with just two boats. Creative marketing and great salesmanship saw their start-up business soar to become the largest houseboat company in the country with investors buying thousands of boats over a nine year period. The company grew to 400 employees and 30 million dollars in revenues and attracted more than 50,000 vacationers.

To attract more business, Phil decided to create a Club Med atmosphere on the lakes by building a hospitality deck where only their own boats could dock. Some nights they turned the deck into a movie theater by having a huge viewing screen on the edge of the lake. Other times it became a dance floor. The competition was stunned because their boats were not permitted to use it. The "buzz" about Three Buoys spread fast—another example of great marketing skills.

The end of this particular venture came when the government changed the tax law for investors and the banks didn't want to finance the debt on the thirteen Marina's the company now owned. Phil's view of this: "I was twenty nine years old. I learned a lot, particularly about finance and especially cash flow." His advice to young entrepreneurs is, never take shortcuts. Take time to really learn your business. For the past twenty years Phil has focused on real estate, becoming an expert on condominium development. Phil's early approach to goal setting was, go big or go home! Now having extensive experience, he always takes time to create a detailed business plan, thinks everything through and puts all the players in place that he will need for the project. He focuses on what he does best and enjoys most—marketing, sales and finance. Phil is well past the "10,000 hour rule", the yardstick for mastering a specific expertise. He's constantly learning and is passionate about his business and his family.

Now in his early fifties, Phil has opened up a great new opportunity for investors. Having survived and learned from previous recessions, the huge home foreclosure market was something he anticipated earlier than most. In 2010, he established The American Residential Income Fund whose mission is to provide affordable housing for American families. Located in Phoenix, the company is expanding into Las Vegas and Southern California. Homes are purchased in great neighborhoods at the foreclosure trustee sales, then renovated and leased to families. Investors also have the opportunity to purchase homes, with a separate Income Trust established for Canadian investors.

As usual, Phil's business model was thought out in complete detail and he is well on the way to achieving his target of 1,000 homes. Away from business, Phil likes action activities, among them, heli-skiing, snowboarding, hockey, hiking and triathlons. He's also an avid car enthusiast.

Phil Carroll's
Top 5 Success Strategies

1. Pick Your Field and Stick With It

"I learned this the hard way. As an entrepreneur I had lots of ideas and I'd jump into things that looked exciting that would ultimately distract me from my main focus. My strength is real estate—particularly buying and selling large condominium properties. It's important that you understand the industry you are in. Learn everything about it, the players, and the environment. Now my focus is in foreclosure properties. I still use the same strategies. You must see the biggest opportunities ahead of time and commit 100 percent when they arrive."

Question: Are you focused on your best niche or are you scattered far and wide?

2. Be Flexible—Adapt Your Business Model When Necessary

"The fact is, markets change, the economy changes, even whole industries can change. You must be prepared for change. My first business ventures were set up as private companies. Then I shifted to creating a public company when the financials made sense. Now I'm back to running a private enterprise with a small team of dedicated people. This suits my lifestyle and allows me to operate with peak efficiency."

Question: Is your current business model super successful? If not, what would make it better?

3. Stick to Your Values

"The number one priority for me is balance. When I'm out of balance, life is more stressful and I lose focus. When my relationship with my wife and children is great and I'm healthy, my business flows better. I make sure I have regular breaks with my family. This is rejuvenating. When I go back to work I can really turn on the adrenaline.

Another important value is to always be fair in your business dealings. Don't shortchange people. It's critical to build long-term relationships. I've had the same key people around me for many years—bankers, strategic partners and even people whom we've had a few struggles with in the past."

Question: How much time off have you scheduled in the next twelve months?

4. Build Momentum in Every Deal

"As the deal progresses, build your energy and keep everything moving. Make sure you monitor your own weekly targets and keep people accountable for what they have promised to do."

Question: Are you in the habit of creating momentum for yourself and your team?

5. Always Celebrate Your Victories

"After all the effort you put in to hit a major goal, it's important that you celebrate your success with the team. I always buy something special for myself, like a new car or throw a big party. You must have fun, and we do!"

Question: Do you have your next celebration planned yet?

For more information: www.americanresidentialhomes.com.

#4

DEBBIE ROTKVICH: The Jewelry Queen

Born and raised on the South side of Chicago, Debbie Rotkvich is the second eldest of six children. Her father was in the insurance business. There wasn't a lot of money but there was a lot of love in the family. At the age of twelve, Debbie's life as a normal young girl suddenly changed. The news that her father had been murdered, rocked the household. Her mother had to work two jobs, getting up at 4 AM every day, leaving Debbie to get the other kids off to school, including making the lunches.

Money was tight and if anyone wanted any extras they had to work for it. Debbie started to waitress. As a teenager, school didn't agree with her and she found no connection with her peers. She could always talk her way into a variety of jobs and quickly became street smart. Already she had visions of creating a better life. A major motivator was to one day live in a house where she had her very own bathroom!

Debbie's first big investment was to open up a flower shop with her sister. They took out a bank loan for 35,000 dollars, a big amount at the time. Debbie's attitude was, "If it's a choice between investing in someone else's venture and betting on myself, **I'll bet on me first**." Debbie really believed this was the ticket that would change her life for the better.

Lessons were learned in the flower business. Their motto was, do everything we can for our customers. This included loaning out decorative displays free of charge and providing bow-tying classes at Christmas. The business rolled along for five years but at the end of the day the only people receiving money was the IRS. The loan was repaid and the shop was closed.

Debbie married Mike, an easy-going guy who was eight and a half years older and had a long-term career in the steel industry. They started a family but Debbie's drive and energy soon led her into the direct selling industry. She started selling Multiples, a direct-to-consumer clothing company whose business model was based on home parties. Her immediate thought on first seeing the business and the opportunity to control how much income she made was, "I can do this, yes, I can do this!" This was the era when home parties became very popular. Interestingly, when Debbie attended some of these evening soirees with her friends, she was known as "the heckler," and would invariably criticize the presenter and the products.

Now she is on the other end at the front of the room, selling. As a beginner, one key factor that created early success in this business for her was to follow her upline's training instructions to the letter. Unfortunately the business changed hands and Debbie found the quality of the product deteriorating rapidly. As well, the clothes were now being sold in outlet malls at cheaper prices. The end was in sight for this venture all too soon, and it was on to the next opportunity.

Debbie's enthusiasm and "I can do this" attitude, plus a genuine passion for helping her sales team succeed, gained the attention of a distributor who sold fashion jewelry. But Debbie was not interested. It was the same party plan model and she was looking elsewhere to achieve her goals.

However, this distributor wasn't about to give up. For months she kept calling, almost every day. "Come and see my jewelry, just look at my jewelry," was her request. One day, just to get this woman off her back, Debbie relented and met with her. At first the jewelry didn't impress her, but she asked two vital questions: (1) "How much commission do you earn?" (2) "How often do you replace your inventory?" The answers were: (1) "40 percent when you build a team" (2) "twice a year."

This was much better than the Multiples where the commissions were smaller and the clothing inventory was turned over every six weeks. Her final question sealed the deal, and it was a good one. "How stable is this company—what's their track record?" When she was shown the brochure of the company's recent annual convention and the awards and recognition showered on the top sales earners, Debbie was in! Under her breath once again she said, "I can do this. I know I can do this!"

Back then, the 250-dollar starter kit was a stretch financially, but that didn't stop Debbie. The company, Lady Remington at the time, now called lia sophia, had no idea what was being unleashed on them! Debbie Rotkvich rocketed to the top, fuelled by her natural enthusiasm and vision of a better life for her and her family, including that bathroom she had always dreamed of.

It was hard work, but Debbie attracted many other inspired women and finally after several years, she hit her own six figure annual income. Momentum creates more business. Further inspired by the company president who set specific targets that would earn her six times her income, Debbie and her team were totally unstoppable!

In 2010, her business had grown to almost 10,000 people strong and had total revenues of over 100 million dollars, producing almost one third of the parent company's revenues!

Like every entrepreneur, Debbie had her ups and downs, sometime losing key people from her team, other time fighting recession. She's also had to confront non-Hodgkin's lymphoma, a serious illness that has attempted to slow her down. Like many other champions you've read about in this book, Debbie is a fighter. It's a common trait if you want to succeed in the big leagues. A few other notable pieces of advice she likes to share with her team are:

- When you get promoted to a leadership level, don't sit back, be diligent and keep doing the things that put you there.

- Be diligent with your money, too. Debbie always saves at least 20 percent of her monthly earnings, a habit learned early when her family was going through some tough struggles.

- Financial freedom is what you get to enjoy later when you strive and thrive. In the interim you may need to sacrifice some of your time with your family. There's no such thing as perfect balance when you are an entrepreneur. Comforting words for those who carry guilt!

Debbie Rotkvich's
Top 5 Success Strategies

1. Have a "Can Do" Attitude

"Throughout each step of my entrepreneurial journey, my mental pep talk was, "I can do this!" It's important to note, this was sometimes said between clenched teeth when my business was slow. For example, in the early part of the lia sophia jewelry business, there were weeks when I had no shows booked. No shows (parties) means, no business. "I can do this!" was a not-so-gentle reminder to ramp up my appointments and sales presentations, something we all need to be reminded about."

Question: When your business slows, do you remind yourself, "I can do this!"

2. Figure Out How to Duplicate Yourself

"When your business expands, you come to a point where you can't do it all. Letting go is challenging, but essential, especially if you have a controller type personality. Focus on finding champions like I have done over the years. Train them well. Many of my leaders now run their own training events and as they continue to grow, so does my business."

Question: Who else can you train to be a champion?

3. Lead by Example

"Strong leaders don't sit back when they reach a higher status level in the business. Your role will shift, but don't let your work ethic become diluted. When times are tough, that message has to be delivered clearly on a daily basis. Remember, you are always being observed by others."

Question: In tough times, do you step up with a clear strategy that will inspire yourself and others to push forward?

4. Reinvest in Your Business

"I've always had the habit of putting a healthy percentage of my revenue back into the business. Don't be greedy! Because of feeding the business, I now can run my own events for training and recognition with more than 1,500 people attending. You don't grow to a 100-million-dollar business without reinvesting—it's impossible."

Question: How much and how often, do you reinvest in yourself and the business?

5. Focus on Helping Your Team Get What They Want

"Even after twenty years in the business, I still get excited watching my team members accept their rewards as their business grows. The joy in their faces and the realization that they can do this, too, is totally fulfilling. You've got to love your people."

Question: Do you genuinely and eagerly help the people who are helping you to grow and succeed?

For more information: www.rotkvichroup.com.

#5

DON R. CAMPBELL:
CREATING REAL ESTATE RICHES

When Don Campbell looks you in the eye to answer your specific question about real estate, you realize two things very quickly. First, there's an authenticity and quiet confidence, about his demeanor; secondly, you have a strong feeling that the answer you are about to receive will be substantial and accurate.

This comes from more than twenty years of learning the business. Does this point sound familiar now, after having read the previous four stories?

There's no substitute for selecting a niche industry that allows you to maximize your natural interests and talent. The key is to master it, and that's where all of these exceptional Achievers, including Don Campbell, have become big winners. They have taken the time to learn, hone and nurture their skills through practical day to day experience. As you have seen already, street smarts beat theories and concepts hands down.

Don lives in Abbotsford, a small town in beautiful British Columbia. In 1985, he bought his first property with a joint venture partner while working a part-time job at Sears, realizing that he could never retire on that income. What spurred his interest in real estate was the fact that a friend's father was doing incredibly well in the market. Don made a decision to simply model what he was doing. He says, "That's a very important lesson for everyone, to find a successful role model."

Don's introduction to the industry, like most new ventures, involved making lots of mistakes. "I got terrible financing and didn't buy in a region that had all the fundamentals. We bought new. In fact we did everything we could to make this a failure and still made money. However, I learned from my mistakes and made sure I didn't repeat them." Sound familiar?

Don realized buying real estate offered great leverage. Even one extra property, in addition to the home you live in, can create a nice, long-term nest egg, if purchased well. Don's three essential keys to becoming successful as a real estate investor are:

1. You need to have good systems to get the banks to say "yes" to your deal.

2. You need excellent relationships, for example, with mortgage brokers, lawyers, etc.

3. You've got to have follow-through to ensure deals are completed.

Another important point Don makes is you must have a clear picture of what you want real estate to do for you—help you have a comfortable retirement or create a business that can make you wealthy. He suggests a three-year "apprenticeship" before you begin to see some good upside.

However, he's quick to counter that real estate is not for everyone. You need to be able to speak to people and build relationships with bankers, vendors and realtors. He says, "You must be able to tolerate people. You don't have to love them all, but you must tolerate them. The number one way is to surround yourself with like-minded people. Also, you must be able to cut through the hype and the get-rich-quick schemes and obtain unbiased research. You need to know the right questions to ask." Valid points for just about any business in any industry.

Don has consistently grown his real estate portfolio over the years to more than 286 properties, including single family, fourplexes and apartment buildings. During that time he became passionate about sharing his successful system with other people, particularity those struggling to become profitable. His Real Estate Investment Network—R.E.I.N.—is now the most trusted, unbiased educational membership program in the country, with more than 3,000 members.

By his own admission, Don is a research geek and a bit of a perfectionist. He loves poking into the latest government announcements, poring over city developments and has a keen eye for determining the absolute best places to invest. He also takes his investors on an annual bus tour to actually visit the towns and areas where the best opportunities are emerging. It's quite a sight to see dozens of school buses that he's rented for the day, roll into town loaded with ambitious entrepreneurs. He has people from Canada, United Kingdom, United States and Australia enrolled in his program. Don is also focused on running a research and education-based organization. He does not ask his members to invest in his deals nor does he sell property to them. This gives him a unique advantage compared to other groups who typically run investment clubs or have a high-priced "success package" to sell.

Like many authentic business owners, Don is also a philanthropist. His number one contribution is to Habitat for Humanity, who build homes for people who are homeless or struggling to find a place of their own. Don donates all of the profits from his many bestselling books to Habitat. He and his members have contributed more than 800,000 dollars to help those in need. To date, REIN members have collectively purchased well in excess of 29,000 properties valued at more than 3.3 billion dollars, with close to 220 properties being added every month.

Over time, Don has become the go-to person for anything real estate. He is constantly approached by the media to be interviewed for insights into the economy and news about where markets are expanding or shrinking. His monthly membership workshops provide cutting-edge research to keep his students in the driver's seat.

Don's other useful suggestions that are noteworthy and essential for creating a successful, sustainable business include:

- Become the guru in your niche. Court the appropriate media; make them your friends.

- Give up control—focus on what you do best. (again, sound familiar?)

- Your reputation and integrity are two of your most important assets.

- Provide so much genuine value that you will attract people to you.

Don loves to travel, London, England, being one of his favorite destinations. He's also an avid Manchester United soccer fan (same as author Les Hewitt), and also enjoys tennis and hiking. As a big music lover, Don and his wife Connie love attending concerts and listening to great bands such as Irish rockers, U2.

Don Campbell's
Top 5 Success Strategies

1. Choose Your Friends Wisely

"Create a Mastermind of like-minded people who are more successful than you. Surround yourself with positive, forward-looking staff, friends and peers."

Question: Do you have a powerful Mastermind Group? **Note:** If not, send an email to info@thepoweroffocus.ca and we will send you a free audio on how to create your own Mastermind Group.

2. Avoid Plateaus

"Challenge yourself to continual incremental improvement in everything you do. Waiting for major leaps of improvement before you take action will hold you back—continual incremental improvements will get you where you want to be. To use a baseball analogy, keep hitting singles and doubles and you will end up in the Hall of Fame. If you swing for a home-run every time you're at bat, you'll end up being the strike-out king. Choose the better way."

Question: Are you consistently persistent or playing the stop/start game?

3. Never Be a Generalist

"Focus on finding a specific niche you're passionate about. Provide that niche with unique and useable tools so that they can maximize their passions. The wider your target market, the more competition you will have and the more difficult it will be to stand out from the crowd."

Question: Are you a real authority in your chosen market or a minnow in a huge pond?

4. Keep a Long-Term Outlook

"Sadly, many people focus on the dream of "getting rich quick". This is a symptom of our society. However, true wealth is created by focusing on long-term relationships NOT squeezing every last dollar out of every transaction. This is even more important in an uncertain economy."

Question: Are you focused on quick returns all the time, or are you building a sustainable, profitable future?

5. Have Fun and Be Serious

"This sounds like a contradiction in terms, however it is not. Fun, although not often discussed in business textbooks, provides you with a vibrant enthusiasm to continue through the rough spots. This sense of fun will be picked up by your clients and prospects will be drawn to you. Fun does not mean being silly, it means to be relaxed and enjoyable to be around, even while you are being serious. When you can provide serious information to your niche in a fun and entertaining fashion, people will line up to do business with you. It doesn't matter what industry you're in, from industrial sales to software development, the key is the same—be someone people are drawn to."

Question: Are you too intense, unapproachable or even boring at times?

For more information: www.donrcampbell.com.

If you would like to hear free in-depth audio interviews with each of our Five Exceptional Achievers, please email us at info@thepoweroffocus.ca or call 403.295.0500

Gen-Y and Social Entrepreneurism: The Way FORWARD

Andrew Hewitt, age twenty-nine, is a Gen-Y young man who is purpose driven and describes himself as a social entrepreneur. (In case you are wondering, yes, he is related to author Les Hewitt, who happens to be his proud father.)

Andrew's journey started when he was twenty-one years old. He had witnessed hoards of his talented university friends striving for success in high-status careers, only to find themselves numbed by meaningless work routines at heartless corporations. Saddened by this, he spent several years researching why 70 percent of student graduates are dissatisfied with their jobs only five years after graduating. This is an alarming statistic.

He discovered that one reason these young men and women were not happy in their work was because their natural strengths were not being utilized. In fact, many didn't know what their real strengths were. In addition, most had never clarified what their dream career would look like. Instead, the focus had been on getting a degree at all costs. To them, that nice certificate proved you were intelligent and somewhat disciplined.

Andrew himself almost made the same mistake during his four years at university. The first two were all about studying to become qualified. As he puts it, "I was totally degree focused." Then halfway through his studies he began to notice there were lots of extracurricular activities available to him. Various business clubs, regional and national conferences he could attend and scholarships he could apply for, to intern overseas. This was a revelation!

The last two years of his studies became "experience focused," resulting in wonderful opportunities to travel and meet other like-minded students, locally and internationally. He also got to meet many successful CEOs and business owners, broadening his knowledge and experience even further. The result was an acute awareness of what he really wanted to do after his university education was completed. He realized it was definitely not going to be cooped up in a cubicle working for some faceless mega corporation!

Instead, he relocated to Costa Rica, as he enjoyed the tropical climate there and the slower pace of life. His purpose today is crystal clear—to create a paradigm shift in education. An integral component of this is to help young people fix a gap in their awareness, to clarify their greatest strengths and find their dream career. In alignment with this purpose, he is sourcing companies who are using business as a force for good. They are purpose-driven rather than profit-driven, as well as being socially and environmentally conscious.

These companies are called Gamechangers. They are the new breed, creating their own paradigm shift in how we look at business and the world. Compared to many of the autocratic, hierarchical, shareholder-first style corporations, these vibrant new companies have different values and very different missions. They are attracting many young people because of their focus on meaningful work, an enjoyable, flexible working environment and genuinely wanting to give something back to society.

Andrew recently launched a new company to better define and identify these organizations. It's called The Gamechangers 500. If the Fortune 500 was the benchmark for success in the twentieth century, the intention is for the Gamechangers 500* to become the benchmark for the twenty-first century. These are heart-centered organizations that are not only successful at making money, they are also focused on making the world a better place. These companies are redefining the rules of business around fun, fulfillment and fairness to all life.

There are many amazing young people in our world today. Despite the constant negativity we are surrounded with, compounded by politicians and news media, there is a new surging consciousness pioneered by young leaders who are both super-focused and excited about their future. In the process, many aging corporations are being dragged into the same way of thinking; some screaming and kicking for sure, others rejuvenated by a compelling new vision. Not surprisingly, others have already fallen by the wayside, dinosaurs who never noticed the changes occurring. Unfortunately they were content to remain in their old routines and allow complacency to destroy their future.

Do not allow yourself to slumber, the future is now and it's happening fast!

Below, you will find a list of some of the most exciting Gamechanger companies.

Do check their websites to learn about their unique cultures, the people they hire and the vision they are focused on creating. Apple Inc. and The Virgin Group of Companies are two of the Gamechanger giants that have pioneered the way forward with

---

* The Gamechangers 500 is produced by the Gamechangers Institute in Ciudad Colon, Costa Rica. (Gamechangers500.com)

visionaries, Steve Jobs and Richard Branson. There are many more following in their footsteps that may soon be household names, too. Learn from how they operate. If you are not one already, maybe Gamechanger is the title you'd like to be listed under. Onward and upward!

Gamechanger COMPANIES

To know if your organization qualifies as a Gamechanger, or to look inside those listed below, just visit the website www.gamechangers500.com.

- Khan Academy
- Okabashi
- Kiva
- Ideo
- Jamie Oliver
- Elevate Studios
- Lulu Lemon
- Achievers (formerly I Love Rewards)
- Whole Foods Market
- Better World Books
- Tesla Motors
- Zappos
- Mind Valley
- Bloom Energy
- Café Gratitude
- Toms
- Google

Happy exploring!

Note to Parents: If you have high school or college-age children, make them aware of this Gamechanger phenomenon.

How Motivational Speakers Get Motivated.

Great News AHEAD!

Here's an insight to boost the younger generations who may be concerned about finding a good job. **In the next two decades, the majority of the jobs haven't even been invented yet**.

Think about it. The computer revolution only really started forty years ago. Think of all the incredible innovations that have occurred since, and the millions of jobs created as a result. In the 1970s we had no fax machines, cell phones or iPads. The environment wasn't creating headlines and spawning new careers and opportunities, like it is today. Electric cars were limited to the children's toy variety and high speed land and air travel was still a dream for many.

There's one thing about the human mind; it is limitless in its ability to create better and smarter ways of doing things that affect our world. And the human spirit is what creates dreams and the desire to see change happen. The good news is, history proves this has never diminished, despite major tragedies and numerous setbacks.

So take heart, young leaders of tomorrow—your future is bright. Just follow the signs.

"THE VISION THAT YOU GLORIFY IN YOUR MIND, THE IDEAL THAT YOU ENTHRONE IN YOUR HEART, THIS YOU WILL BUILD YOUR LIFE BY, AND THIS YOU WILL BECOME."

—James Allen

Insights

As authors, we have all been privileged to have been surrounded by great teachers, role models and mentors. Undoubtedly, the wisdom of these people has had a profound influence on our awareness, our success in life and our ability to overcome difficult challenges.

The five exceptional Achievers you have read about in this chapter all started with humble beginnings. Through their own vision, enthusiasm and persistence, they not only are enjoying the fruits of their labor today, they have all made a significant difference in people's lives and continue to do so. You will discover true joy in mastering your talents and the ability to offer valuable products and services to a world that is full of companies and individuals who need your help.

The beauty of this is, you eventually rise up to be the mentor and graduate from being the one who was mentored. It's "pay it forward" at its best! So enjoy the journey. Use the most relevant ideas from these five Power of Focus superstars, plus any of our own, to help you reach your next major objective.

In the next few pages, we have some Final Words to launch you on your way.

ACTION STEPS

Twenty-five Wealth Building Strategies

Carefully review the twenty five strategies from our five exceptional Achievers. Answer the accompanying questions to help you unlock their best ideas.

Choose three from the list of twenty-five and write them below.

1. _____

2. _____

3. _____

My best next action for implementing each of these strategies for my own business or career are:

1. _____

2. _____

3. _____

Now focus and follow through!

FINAL WORDS

It's Your Life . . .
Accept The Challenge!

"HAPPY ARE THOSE WHO DREAM DREAMS
AND ARE READY TO PAY THE PRICE
TO MAKE THEM COME TRUE."

—Leon J. Suenes

It's been a privilege to share our latest ideas and new stories with you in this Special Revised Edition of *The Power of Focus*. We hope it's confirmed the fact that there are limitless opportunities available to you. Understand, there are no shortcuts to building a life of substance. It's an ongoing process. It takes time, real effort and a desire to become more than you already are. It's a worthy challenge. However, your biggest challenge starts tomorrow. How will you apply what you have learned between the covers of this book? All the strategies we have shared with you really work. They can dramatically change your life for the better. But only if you choose to use them.

We are all faced with tough decisions. It's part of the human dilemma. Which path do you take, this one or that one? Certainly, there are no absolute guarantees when it comes to charting your personal course for a better future. However, the fundamental habits we have shared with you throughout this book will go a long way to ensuring that your business and personal life will be blessed beyond measure. They have worked for us and for thousands of others. So take up the challenge. Make a decision now to refocus and become the best you can be, one day at a time.

Now is the time to step up and be counted. The alternative is to say, "That was interesting information," and then put this book on a shelf and carry on with your old habits. That would be sad, because nothing much in your life will change. And if you took the time to read this book, you obviously want to improve some things.

Because of what you have read, you are now more aware of how life works. So you have no more excuses for future failure, unless you don't push yourself to make the necessary changes. There are thousands of people, just like you, who have turned their lives into wonderful success stories simply because they decided to change.

You can do the same. You really can. Believe in yourself. Soak up the knowledge you have gleaned from these pages and focus on taking the first step, whatever that may be. Make that a priority. Then take another, and pretty soon your life will change. We guarantee it. With a little practice and persistence, new habits will become a part of you. A year from now you'll say, "Look how much I've changed, and look at the results—I can hardly believe it."

Refer back to these strategies often. Use them as an ongoing guide to help you. And remember, you can really make a difference in this world. It's your responsibility to do so, and also your destiny. Go forward now with courage and new hope. Your future awaits you—seize it boldly!

Sincerely, Jack, Mark, and Les

P.S. We'd love to know how *The Power of Focus* has helped you. Send us your success story.

Email: les.h@thepoweroffocus.ca

Phone: 403.295.0500

ACCELERATE YOUR PROGRESS WITH EXPERT COACHING

If you are facing any of the challenges below, then let us help you refocus, rejuvenate and reignite your momentum.

- ❏ Time Pressure
- ❏ Financial Pressure
- ❏ Unclear Goals
- ❏ Work / Family Balance
- ❏ New Technology
- ❏ Cash Flow Concerns
- ❏ Lack of Confidence
- ❏ Hiring Good People

Our only focus is to help you *exceed* the results you want. Choose from:

- **Speaking Engagements:** Keynotes, Half Day and Full Day Workshops: Ideal for Conferences, Sales Rallies and Customer Appreciation Events.

- **Leadership Training:** Customized programs to help your leaders excel by improving their communication, accountability, decision making and goal setting ability.

- **Stay Focused! Membership Program:** Ongoing weekly support to keep your organization on track, on purpose and on fire!

- **Exclusive One-on-One Executive Coaching with "The Focus Coach", Les Hewitt: (limited availability)**

  For full details contact:
  P: 403.295.0500
  E: info@thepoweroffocus.ca
  W: www.thepoweroffocus.com

> **Ask about our volume discount pricing on books and FREE half-day workshop offer.**

Transform Your Business and Your Life
at an Exclusive 3-day Retreat with
The Power of Focus Authors,
Jack Canfield, Mark Victor Hansen & Les Hewitt

Imagine spending 3 life-changing days sequestered with a small group of ambitious, like-minded leaders and business owners in a majestic Rocky Mountain retreat setting.

The sole purpose of this unique experience is to help you create a crystal clear "Dream Picture" of what you *really* want in your life—in business, personally and financially. And to have you leave with a complete customized system that will ensure you actually LIVE your dream.

This is a rare opportunity to tap into the business and marketing genius of Jack, Mark and Les, who collectively have generated well over one billion dollars in revenue.

Participation at this private retreat is by invitation only and is limited to 24 people.

**For more information and qualification details,
please email:
info@thepoweroffocus.ca
or call: 403.295.0500**

RESOURCE GUIDE

The following is a great list of recommended resources that will further expand your knowledge and ability to harness *The Power of Focus*.

RECOMMENDED READING

Built to Sell by John Warrilow. New York, New York: Portfolio Hardcover, 2011.

Business Stripped Bare by Richard Branson. London, England: Virgin Publishing Ltd, 2010.

Chicken Soup for the Entrepreneur's Soul by Jack Canfield, Mark Victor Hansen, Dahlynn McKowen, John and Elizabeth Gardner, Tom Hill and Kyle Wilson. Deerfield Beach, Florida: Health Communication, Inc. 2006.

Chicken Soup for the Soul by Jack Canfield and Mark Victor Hansen. Deerfield Beach, Florida: Health Communications, Inc., 1993.

Chicken Soup for the Soul: Living Your Dreams by Jack Canfield and Mark Victor Hansen. Deerfield Beach, Florida: Health Communication, Inc., 2003.

Chicken Soup for the Soul: Think Positive by Jack Canfield, Mark Victor Hansen and Amy Newmark. Cos Cob, CT: Chicken Soup for the Soul Publishing, LLC, 2010.

Clean Break by Karen Stewart. Mississauga, Ontario: John Wiley and Sons Canada Ltd., 2008.

Crush It! by Gary Vaynerchuk. New York, New York: Harper Collins, 2009.

Don't Sweat the Small Stuff . . . and it's all small stuff by Richard Carlson. Bolton, Ontario: H.B. Fenn & Co., 1997.

Everything Counts! by Gary Ryan Blair. Hoboken, NJ: John Wiley & Sons, 2010.

Exceeding Customer Expectations by Kirk Kazanjian. New York, New York: Currency Doubleday, 2007.

Focal Point by Brian Tracy. New York, New York: AMACOM, 2004.

Future Diary by Mark Victor Hansen. Costa Mesa, California: Mark Victor Hansen and Associates, 1985.

Get Rich Click! by Marc Ostrofsky. Houston, Texas: Razor Media Group LLC, 2011.

Getting Things Done by David Allen. New York, New York: Penguin, 2003.

How to Handle a Major Crisis by Peter J. Daniels. Ann Arbor, Michigan: Tabor House Publishing, 1987.

How to Reach Your Life Goals by Peter J. Daniels. Ann Arbor, Michigan: Tabor House Publishing, 1985.

In Search of the Invisible Forces by George Addair. Phoenix, Arizona: Vector Publications, 1995.

It's Not What Happens to You, It's What You Do About It by W. Mitchell. San Francisco, California: Phoenix Press, 1999.

Jack Canfield's Key to Living the Law of Attraction by Jack Canfield and D.D. Watkins. Deerfield Beach, Florida: Health Communications Inc., 2007.

Leading an Inspired Life by Jim Rohn. Niles, Illinois: Nightingale-Conant Corporation, 1997.

Man's Search for Meaning by Viktor Frankl. New York, New York: Pocket Books, 1984.

Rich Dad, Poor Dad by Robert Kiyosaki with Sharon L. Lechter. Paradise Valley, Arizona: Tech Press Inc., 1997.

Smarter, Faster, Cheaper by David Siteman. Garland, Hoboken, New Jersey: John Wiley and Sons Inc. 2011

Swim with the Sharks Without Being Eaten Alive by Harvey Mackay. New York, New York: Ballantine Books, 1996.

Switch: How to Change Things When Change Is Hard, by Chip Heath and Dan Heath. New York, New York: Broadway Business, 2010.

The Aladdin Factor by Jack Canfield and Mark Victor Hansen. New York, New York: Berkeley Books, Division of Penguin Putnam, 1995.

The Bible.

The Compound Effect by Darren Hardy. New York, New York: Vanguard Press, 2011.

The Eagle's Secret by David McNally. New York, New York: Delacorte Press, 1998.

The Ego and the Spirit by Fran Hewitt. Calgary, Alberta: Power of Focus Publishing, 2010.

The Greatest Salesman in the World by Og Mandino. New York, New York: Bantam Books, 1974.

The Greatest Secret in the World by Og Mandino. New York, New York: Bantam Books, 1972.

The 7 Habits of Highly Effective People by Stephen R. Covey. New York, New York: Simon & Schuster, 1989.

The On-Purpose Person by Kevin W. McCarthy. Colorado Springs, Colorado: Navpress, 1992.

The One Minute Millionaire by Mark Victor Hansen and Robert G. Allen. New York, New York: Three Rivers Press, 2002.

The Power of Faithful Focus by Les Hewitt and Dr. Charlie Self. Deerfield Beach, Florida: Health Communications, Inc., 2004.

The Power of Focus for College Students by Les Hewitt, Andrew Hewitt and Luc d'Abadie. Deerfield Beach, Florida. Health Communications, Inc., 2006.

The Power of Focus for Women by Fran Hewitt and Les Hewitt. Deerfield Beach, Florida: Health Communications, Inc., 2004.

The Power of Quotes by Les Hewitt. Calgary, Alberta: Power of Focus Publishing, 2008.

The Richest Man in Babylon by George S. Clason. New York, New York: Penguin Books, 1989.

The Secret by Rhonda Byrne. New York, New York: Atria Books, 2006.

The Success Principles for Teens by Jack Canfield and Kent Healy. Deerfield Beach, Florida: Health Communications, Inc., 2008.

The Success Principles: How to Get from Where You Are to Where You Want to Be by Jack Canfield and Janet Switzer. New York, New York: Harper Collins, 2005.

The Tipping Point by Malcolm Gladwell. New York, New York: Back Bay Books, 2001.

The Wealthy Barber Returns by David Chilton. Kitchener, Ontario: Financial Awareness Corp; 2011.

The Richest Kids in America by Mark Victor Hansen. Miami, Florida, Hansen House, 2009.

The Seasons of Life by Jim Rohn. Austin, Texas: Discovery Publications, 1981.

Think & Grow Rich by Napoleon Hill. New York, New York: Fawcett Crest Books/ CBS Inc., Division of Ballantine Books, 1960.

Why Aren't You More Like Me? by Ken Keis. Abbotsford, British Columbia: CRG International, 2011.

Unfair Advantage by Robert T. Kiyosaki. Scottsdale, Arizona: Plata Publishing, LLC, 2011.

1001 Ways to Reward Employees by Bob Nelson. New York, New York: Workman Publishing Co., 1994.

AUTOBIOGRAPHY/BIOGRAPHY

Achieving the Impossible by Lewis Gordon Pugh. New York, New York: Simon & Schuster, 2010.

Buffet: The Making of an American Capitalist by Roger Lowenstein. New York, New York: Random House, 1995.

Business Stripped Bare by Richard Branson. London, England: Virgin Publishing Ltd, 2010.

Long Walk to Freedom by Nelson Mandela. New York, New York: Back Bay Books, 1994.

Made in America by Sam Walton. New York, New York: Bantam Books, 1993.

Muhammad Ali: His Life and Times by Thomas Hauser. New York, New York: Simon & Schuster, 1991.

Steve Jobs by Walter Isaacson. New York, New York: Simon & Schuster, 2011.

The Golden Motorcycle Gang: A Story of Transformation by Jack Canfield. Carlsbad, CA: Hay House, 2011.

Walt Disney by Neal Gabler. New York, New York: Vintage Books, 2007.

AUDIO PROGRAMS

Happy, Healthy and Terrific by Ed Foreman. Dallas, Texas: Executive Development Systems. 800-955-7353.

Magic Words That Grow Your Business by Ted Nicholas. Niles, Illinois: Nightingale-Conant Corp. 800-323-5552.

Maximum Confidence: Ten Steps to Extreme Self-Esteem by Jack Canfield. Niles, Illinois: Nightingale-Conant Corp., 1989. 800-323-3938.

Relationship Strategies by Jim Cathcart and Tony Alessandra. Niles Illinois: Nightingale-Conant Corp. 800-323-5552.

Self-Esteem and Peak Performance by Jack Canfield. Boulder, Colorado: Career Track Publications and Fred Pryor Seminars, 1995. 800-255-6278.

The Aladdin Factor: How to Ask for and Get What You Want in Every Area of Your Life by Jack Canfield and Mark Victor Hansen. Niles, Illinois: Nightingale-Conant Corp., 1999. 800-323-5552.

The 4 Fundamentals by Les Hewitt. Calgary, Alberta: The Power of Focus Inc. 403-295-0500 info@thepoweroffocus.ca.

The Success Principles: Your 30-Day Journey From Where You Are to Where You Want To Be by Jack Canfield and Janet Switzer. Santa Barbara, California: Jack Canfield Companies, 2003.

Your Life by Jack Canfield and Mark Victor Hansen. Niles, Illinois: Nightingale-Conant Corp., 1999. 800-323-5552.

The Challenge to Succeed by Jim Rohn. Dallas, Texas: Jim Rohn International. 800-929-0434.

The Power of Focus Audio Club: Monthly Feature Interviews with Top Achievers and More 403-295-0500 or www.thepoweroffocus.com.

Unlimited Power: The New Science of Personal Achievement by Anthony Robbins. San Diego, California: Robbins Research International, 1986. 800-898-8669.

VIDEOS

How to Have Your Best Year Ever by Jim Rohn. Dallas, Texas: Jim Rohn International. 800-929-0434.

The Man Who Would Not Be Defeated by W. Mitchell. Santa Barbara, California: W. Mitchell. 800-421-4840.

The Power of Purpose (the story of Terry Fox) by David McNally. Eden Prairie, Minnesota: Wilson Learning Corp. 612-944-2880.

DVDS

Have You Gone Missing? Keynote for Women by Fran Hewitt. The Power of Focus, Inc. 403-295-0500.

Inside Job, Oscar winning documentary by Charles H. Ferguson, 2010.

Jack Canfield: Discover Your Soul Purpose. Produced by GAIAM. Available from www.jackcanfield.com.

Tapping the Source. Produced by Waterside Productions. Available from www. beyondword.com.

The Secret. Produced by TS Productions. Available at www.jackcanfield.com.

The Success Principles by Jack Canfield. Better Life Media. Available at www. jackcanfield.com.

Too Big To Fail, TV drama by Curtis Hanson, HBO, 2011.

COURSES

Business Coaching

Canfield Coaching. Salt Lake City, Utah. www.canfieldcoaching.com.

Executive One-on-One Coaching with "The Focus Coach", Les Hewitt, 403-295-0500 les.h@thepoweroffocus.ca.

The Power of Focus Coaching Program, Contact: Les Hewitt, 403-295-0500 www.thepoweroffocus.com.

Personal Development

Jack Canfield's Breakthrough to Success. Santa Barbara, California. 805-563-2936, www.jackcanfield.com.

Jack Canfield's Train the Trainer Program. Santa Barbara, California. 805-563-2935, www.canfieldtrainthetrainer.com.

Insight Training Seminars. Santa Monica, California. 310-829-7402.

OMEGA Vector. Contact: George Addair, Phoenix, Arizona. 602-943-7799.

STAR/Success Through Action & Responsibility. Santa Barbara, California. 805-563-2935.

The Dale Carnegie Course. Garden City, New York. 516-248-5100.

The Hoffman Quadrinity Process. Cambridge, Ontario. 800-741-3449.

The Successful Life Course. Contact: Ed Foreman. Dallas, Texas. 800-955-7353 or 214-351-0055.

Personality Profiles

Consulting Resource Group International, Abbotsford, British Columbia, 604-852-0566.

Kolbe Concepts Inc. Phoenix, Arizona. 602-840-9770.

Personality Plus. St. Paul, Minnesota. 651-483-3597.

Public/Professional Speaking

Patricia Fripp, San Francisco, California; fripp.com.

The National Speakers Association. Tempe, Arizona. 602-968-2552.

Toastmasters International. Rancho Santa Margarita, California 949-858-8255.

Helpful Business Apps

Project management—Flow—getflow.com or OmniFocus

Note taking—Evernote

Mindmapping—iMindMap, Mindjet, Xmind

Expense tracking—iXpensit

Presentation software—prezi.com

Simple slideshow/video creation—animoto.com

GEN-Y RESOURCES

Books

The Power of Focus for College Students by Les Hewitt, Andrew Hewitt and Luc d' Abadie

Crush It by Gary Vaynerchuk

Adventures of Johnny Bunko by Daniel H. Pink

Unfair Advantage by Robert T. Kiyosaki

Chicken Soup for the Extraordinary Teen Soul by Jack Canfield, Mark Victor Hansen and Kent Healy

My Reality Check Bounced by Jason R. Dorsey

The Teens Guide to World Domination by Josh Shipp

Major in Success by Patrick Combs and Jack Canfield

The Richest Kids in America by Mark Victor Hansen

e-Resources

www.Gamechangers500.com

National Society of Leadership and Success—www.societyleadership.org

Discover a career you are passionate about—www.PassionPuzzle.com

Dream Career Internships—www.summerinternships.com

www.TheRichestKidsAcademy.com

Warren Buffet's Secret Millionaire's Club

www.centre.upeace.org

www.kahnacademy.com

www.ted.com

www.therisetothetop.com

Charitable Organizations

Free The Children Organization
Contact: Craig Kielburger
1750 Steeles Avenue West, Suite 218
Concord, Ontario, Canada L4K 2L7
phone: (905) 760-9382 fax: (905) 760-9157
e-mail: freechild@clo.com website: www.freethechildren.org

The Terry Fox Foundation for Cancer Research
Contact: Darrell Fox
60 Sinclair Avenue East, Suite 605
Toronto, Ontario, Canada M4T 1N5
phone: (416) 924-8252 fax: (416) 962-5677
e-mail: national@terryfoxrun.org website: www.terryfoxrun.org

PERMISSIONS

We would like to acknowledge the following publishers and individuals for permission to reprint the following material. (Note: The stories that were penned anonymously, that are public domain or were written by Jack Canfield, Mark Victor Hansen or Les Hewitt are not included in this listing.)

Maria Sosa story. Reprinted by permission of Maria Sosa. ©2011 Maria Sosa.

Gord Wiebe story. Reprinted by permission of Gord Wiebe. ©2011 Gord Wiebe.

Dave Albano story. Reprinted by permission of Dave Albano. ©2011 Dave Albano.

Lisa Petrilli story. Reprinted by permission of Lisa Petrilli. ©2011 Lisa Petrilli.

Sam Beckford story. Reprinted by permission of Sam Beckford. ©2011 Sam Beckford.

Ashley Meszaros story. Reprinted by permission of Ashley Meszaros. ©2011 Ashley Meszaros.

Aaron Trenouth story. Reprinted by permission of Aaron Trenouth. ©2011 Aaron Trenouth.

Andrew Hewitt story. Reprinted by permission of Andrew Hewitt. ©2011 Andrew Hewitt.

Anna Jarmics story. Reprinted by permission of Anna Jarmics. ©2011 Anna Jarmics.

Annette Stanwick story. Reprinted by permission of Annette Stanwick. ©2011 Annette Stanwick.

Chris Keating story. Reprinted by permission of Chris Keating. ©2011 Chris Keating.

Cameron Johnson story. Reprinted by permission of Cameron Johnson. ©2011 Cameron Johnson.

Chauncey Holloman story. Reprinted by permission of Chauncey Holloman. ©2011 Chauncey Holloman.

W. Mitchell story. Reprinted by permission of W. Mitchell. ©2011 W. Mitchell.

Exceeding Customer Expectations excerpt. Reprinted by permission of Kirk Kazanjian ©2007 Literary Productions, Doubleday.

About the Authors

You probably know **Jack Canfield** as the co-creator of the *New York Times* #1 bestselling *Chicken Soup for the Soul*® book series which currently has 225 titles and more than 500 million copies in print in 47 languages. He is also the co-author of *The Success Principles, Dare to Win, The Power of Focus, The Aladdin Factor,* and *You've Got to Read This Book.*

He is also the Founder and CEO of the Canfield Training Group, which trains entrepreneurs, corporate leaders, managers and sales professionals in how to accelerate the achievement of their personal, professional and financial goals.

Jack Canfield has shared *The Power of Focus* strategies in twenty countries at his *Power of Focus* Keynotes and his Breakthrough to Success Seminars. His clients include Campbell Soup Company, Clairol, Coldwell Banker, General Electric, ITT, Hartford Insurance, Federal Express, Johnson & Johnson, NCR, Sony Pictures, TRW and Virgin Records, plus other organizations such as The Million Dollar Round Table, The Young Presidents Organization, CEO and the World Business Council.

Jack has appeared on CNN, PBS, *Inside Edition*, Larry King Live, 20/20, Eye to Eye, *The Today Show, Fox & Friends, Montel,* and *Oprah.*

Jack has personally helped hundreds of thousands of people on six different continents become multi-millionaires, business leaders, bestselling authors, leading sales professionals, successful entrepreneurs, and world-class athletes while at the same time creating balanced, fulfilling and healthy lives. Jack is a dynamic speaker and was recently inducted into the

National Speakers Association's Speakers Hall of Fame. He is a featured teacher in the recent hit movies, The Secret, The Meta Secret, The Opus, Discover the Gift, Beyond Belief, The Tapping Solution and Tapping the Source.

Jack has been presenting these powerful principles and breakthrough strategies for 38 years to corporations, governments and universities in more than 30 countries.

Jack is the Founder of The Transformational Leadership Council and has also been awarded three honorary doctorates.

For further information about all of Jack's resources and training programs, or to book him for a keynote presentation, please contact:

Phone: 800.237.8336

Website: www.jackcanfield.com

Mark Victor Hansen is one of the most dynamic and compelling teachers and speakers of our time.

Chicken Soup for the Soul® is just one of many ideas that has propelled Mark into a worldwide spotlight as a sought-after keynote speaker, bestselling author and marketing maven. His credentials include a lifetime of entrepreneurial success, in addition to an extensive academic background. He is also a prolific writer with many popular books such as *The One Minute Millionaire, The Aladdin Factor, Dare to Win* and others. Mark focuses on thinking big, sales achievement, publishing success as well as personal and professional development.

Mark is the founder of MEGA Book Marketing University and Building Your MEGA Speaking Empire. Both are annual conferences where Mark coaches and teaches new and aspiring authors, speakers and experts on building lucrative publishing and speaking careers.

He is also known as a passionate philanthropist and humanitarian, working tirelessly for organizations such as Habitat for Humanity, American Red Cross, March of Dimes and Childhelp USA, among others. In the year 2000, The Horatio Alger Association of Distinguished Americans honored Mark with the prestigious Horatio Alger Award. Each year, this association honors American leaders who personify the virtues and principles inherent in the success stories written by 19th century American author Horatio Alger Jr. As an award winner, Mark's extraordinary life achievements stand as a powerful example that the free enterprise system still offers opportunity to all. In 2000, Northwood University honored him as the Outstanding Business Leader of the Year and established the Mark Victor Hansen Entrepreneurial Excellence Fund that will help shape the minds of future business leaders and assist in the development of the faculty who will teach them.

For more information about Mark Victor Hansen's products, programs and speaking schedule, contact:

Phone: 949.764.2640
Website: markvictorhansen.com

Known by his peers and clients as "The Focus Coach", **Les Hewitt** understands the real world of business and the struggle to stay focused.

During the last 30 years his organization has created and delivered more than 900 workshops and training programs that have been utilized by thousands of executives, managers and sales leaders. Les is also the founder of The Power of Focus

Coaching Program, a unique focusing system for business people who want greater profits, less stress and more time off.

The Power of Focus has worked with more than 300 companies in Canada, United States, Australia, the United Kingdom and the Republic of Ireland.

Les is an international bestselling author. His first book, *The Power of Focus*, co-authored with Jack Canfield and Mark Victor Hansen (creators of *Chicken Soup for the Soul®*), has sold more than half a million copies in North America and is available in 20 languages. There are currently seven books in the series.

Les has created audio business seminars for Trump University, the home-study business school created by billionaire Donald Trump. Other top tier clients he has spoken for include Wells Fargo, The Million Dollar Round Table, Investors Group, Cameron Inc and Halliburton.

As a professional coach, Les prompts, challenges and supports his clients to make the changes required for consistent success (especially the changes they are resisting!). He has personally coached hundreds of business leaders to achieve exceptional profits and productivity.

His motto is, **focus and follow through!**

For more information on The Power of Focus products or hiring Les Hewitt for a speaking engagement, leadership training program, management retreat or customized individual coaching, please contact our office:

Phone: 403.295.0500
Email: info@thepoweroffocus.ca
Website: ThePowerOfFocus.com

Enhance your Personal Development Library with these great titles

The Power of Focus for Women

This book will stay with you long after you have put it down. The insights you gain will not only enrich your mind, they will open your heart and speak to your soul.

To schedule Fran Hewitt for a speaking engagement or workshop:

P: 403.295.0500

E: info@thepoweroffocus.ca

The Power of Focus for College Students

How do you pick the best major, discover a career you will love and end up with a really cool job? Find the answers in this groundbreaking book.

To schedule Andrew Hewitt for a speaking engagement:

P: 403.295.0500

E: a.hewitt@me.com

The Power of Faithful Focus

The tools you need to actually live your purpose are here. You'll find it exhilarating to focus and follow through every day, with God on your side.

To schedule Dr. Charlie Self for a speaking engagement:

P: 408.307.1339

E: drcharlieself@yahoo.com

Find Your Focus and Tap Your True Talents

ISBN-13: 9780757306983
ISBN-10: 0757306985
$14.95

The Vigorous Mind

Author Ingrid Cummings reveals that the way to health, happiness, and increased performance is to "cross-train your brain" by diversifying your activities instead of specializing in just one pursuit. Using historical as well as contemporary "Renaissance people" as inspiration, the book argues that a return to a generalist gestalt as opposed to an ever-narrowing career specialty will help anyone rediscover what it means to be "well rounded," and how that will yield large rewards in business and in life.

ISBN-13: 9780757315626
ISBN-10: 0757315623
$15.95

Extreme Focus

For many, there is a predominant belief that true success stems from hard work, perseverance, and a little bit of luck. Authors Pat Williams and Jim Denney explain that there is a fourth element, which they have coined Extreme Focus. In this thought-provoking read, the authors reveal how the lack of true success, for many, simply boils down to scattered energy that is focused on trivial pursuits. By learning how to harness this energy into Extreme Focus, you will achieve your goals faster and with more enjoyment.